Rewriting Television

Rewriting Television

ALISON PEIRSE

RUTGERS UNIVERSITY PRESS

NEW BRUNSWICK, CAMDEN, AND NEWARK, NEW JERSEY

LONDON AND OXFORD

Rutgers University Press is a department of Rutgers, The State University of New Jersey, one of the leading public research universities in the nation. By publishing worldwide, it furthers the University's mission of dedication to excellence in teaching, scholarship, research, and clinical care.

Library of Congress Cataloging-in-Publication Data

Names: Peirse, Alison, author.
Title: Rewriting television / Alison Peirse.
Description: New Brunswick : Rutgers University Press, 2025. | Includes bibliographical references and index.
Identifiers: LCCN 2024029521 | ISBN 9781978839618 (paperback) | ISBN 9781978839625 (hardcover) | ISBN 9781978839632 (epub) | ISBN 9781978839649 (pdf)
Subjects: LCSH: Television criticism—Research.
Classification: LCC PN1992.8.C7 P45 2025 | DDC 791.45015—dc23/eng/20240716
LC record available at https://lccn.loc.gov/2024029521

A British Cataloging-in-Publication record for this book is available from the British Library.

rutgersuniversitypress.org

This book is dedicated to my parents. I grew up on the sofa with my dad, John Peirse, laughing at classic Coronation Street, *and crying over* Where the Heart Is. *This book is also for my mum, Helen Peirse, who doesn't love telly* quite *as much as my dad but is willing to become his partner in crime whenever* Vera *or* New Tricks *is on.*

Contents

Rewriting Television

The One-Long-Slow-Idea Book

In 2009, I interviewed for my first permanent, full-time academic post as a lecturer in film and television studies at Northumbria University, United Kingdom. I had written my dissertation on 1930s horror film, and I was at that point employed as a fixed-term lecturer in film studies at the University of Hull, where I taught film theory and analysis, horror film, and modules on Alfred Hitchcock. As such, film studies was a strength; television studies was, assuredly, not. The Northumbria teaching interview panel explained that the successful candidate would teach the "Cultural Identities and British Television" module. James Leggott, leading the panel, asked what I could contribute. I shifted in my chair, somewhat at a loss. I had published a few chapters on television, but they had all been close formal analyses of American cult and fantasy series. My mind went completely blank, and I struggled to even name a British television series. In the end, I wrinkled my nose and shrugged a response: "I could *probably* do a lecture on *The Mighty Boosh*?"

Despite referencing only an early 2000s surreal British comedy featuring Noel Fielding as a fashion-obsessed zookeeper, I still got the job (more for my film knowledge than my television, I suspect). My preparation for teaching the British television module was thus the first time I really dug into television studies as a discipline. For John Corner, "television studies" is "strongly plural," a "straightforwardly descriptive phrase" for the "studies of television," as opposed to "a specialist sub-area possessed of its distinctive approaches and methods." However, he then points out that there has been "a project with more aspiration to coherence and distinctiveness of identity," a "Television Studies struggling to develop within television studies, an aspiration towards capital Letters as it were."[1] Charlotte Brunsdon has long been a leading scholar in television studies and has provided useful definitions of how the field has transformed from "studies of television" to "Television Studies." In "Problems with Quality," published in *Screen* in 1990, and in "Is Television Studies History?," published in *Cinema Journal* in 2008, Brunsdon demarcates three distinct phases of the discipline. The first, emergent phase is the "long 1970s, from 1967 to the early 1980s," characterized by "ontological concerns (what is television?), epistemological debates (what are the appropriate tools and disciplines through which it should be approached, how can we know television?), and a generalized thrust in the argument to legitimize the study, if not the output, of television."[2] The second phase has three overlapping aspects: a focus on feminized serial drama, a concentration on the audience, and a spate of new textbooks "able to draw on the expanding field of television scholarship" for the first time.[3] Television studies' third phase arguably occurred in the early twenty-first century, a period understood by Brunsdon as "a discernible clustering" in research on "widely exported US 'quality' fictional programming" and on reality television.[4]

I lectured at Northumbria University throughout the late 2000s and early 2010s and taught into or led the British television module just as television studies was beginning to move beyond Brunsdon's third phase. There were stimulating developments occurring in aesthetics, emotion, feminism, intermediality, and performance; at the same time, television studies found new directions through transmedia platforms and branding.[5] While I delighted in this work, my delight remained at one remove. I was happy to engage with what others said, to teach and deliver their ideas, rather than, for the most part, to take on the subject myself. But I am now at the point where regular reading, teaching updates, and meticulous citations are not good enough when it comes to television studies. We are now more than a decade on from the early 2010s, and I am not seeing a new wave of evolutionary iterations that I would expect by now. I think we have failed to continue to push at and to diversify our methods and our thinking. I think we have failed to give adequate time and space to reflect upon, first, precisely *what* it is we are doing and, second, *why* we are doing it. A rethinking of television studies is now required.

Television studies may have developed through Brunsdon's three distinct phases, but now, in the second decade of the new millennium, we are in conceptual stasis. This is where *Rewriting Television* comes in. It emerges from my belief that we have failed to sustain intellectual, radical momentum in television studies, a failure that can be located squarely within how we choose and how we use methodology. This book asks, what different kinds of approaches are available to us in studying television? What might new approaches look like? How might we theorize them?

In *Reinventing Film Studies*, Christine Gledhill and Linda Williams asked their contributors to approach "reinvention" in two ways. First, they asked them to consider, "What do we need to know now? What theories, concepts, and methodologies will help us to know?" Their contributors were then expected to either "reframe" or "depart from" the concerns of 1970s scholarship and the inauguration of film studies. A key aim of *Reinventing Film Studies* was an exploration of "the field in light of these reorientations," which involves "not so much discarding the old questions and knowledge, but *rethinking, refiguring, and restructuring* what is most useful from this past," that is, a "self-fashioning of new identities out of old."[6] While I am not attempting to reinvent a discipline (more ask a series of awkward questions to prompt self-reflection about what we do), the concepts of rethinking (and concomitantly, refiguring and restructuring) past critical work are central to this project. To work through my questions, I return to the work of television scholars in the 1990s and early 2000s—that is, at the end of television studies' second phase, a period that can be understood as a particularly rich time of intellectual questioning and contemplation. It is here, I believe, that we can pick up important ideas and perceptive questions with which to underpin the intellectual thesis of this project.

In the 1990s, Brunsdon recognized that after twenty years of development television studies in Britain was solidifying as a discipline. During this period, she contemplated what television studies was, what it was trying to do, and how it might develop further. She reflected upon teaching film classes in the 1970s and how the collaboration between teacher and student was exciting, that it felt like they were making something new. She said that this excitement didn't last long as film studies was swiftly institutionalized, but what she enjoyed was that "sense of *the edge* of the academic—the negotiation of what it is proper to address, and in what terms" and how this "accompanied the development of television studies, cultural studies, and feminist intellectual work."[7] I want to ask, what might the "edge of the academic" look like in television studies today? How might we situate this study in relation to broader debates in film and media studies?

Two years after Brunsdon's essay was published, Christine Geraghty and David Lusted argued that a student of television "has to consider not only *what* is to be studied but also *how* and, indeed, needs to pay attention to the relationships between the two."[8] So, following this train of thought, how might we get to the edge of the academic? What tools do we need?

Around the same time, Corner suggested that there was a "knowledge problem" in media studies. For Corner, knowledge problems concern what "academic enquiries seek to find out, and the kinds and quality of data and of explanatory relations which particular ideas and methods might be expected to produce." Corner then argues that by considering and responding to knowledge problems, "disciplines not only engage more closely and innovatively with questions of conceptualisation and technique, but also develop a reflexive, sceptical sense of their own knowledge production and vulnerabilities."[9] I contend that we are now at the point of a knowledge problem for television studies. Across the course of this book, I ask, what is it that we seek to find out when we study television? What kinds of data can we produce? What techniques might we use for analysis?

Finally, I want to deconstruct how we might do this thinking within our writing. How might we productively play with expectations around academic form? How can we be more reflexive about the original contributions to knowledge that we produce? What might our research look like on the page?

Having Fun

Jonathan Bignell and Faye Woods describe approaches to television studies as "not a set of tools, but more like a group of different languages," that they "do not translate neatly one into another" and "each defines its world in rather different ways." For Bignell and Woods, the four most significant approaches to television are studies of the television as text, television industries (including "production practices and organisation"), television in culture (including representation and "the sociological study of audiences"), and television history (including "broadcast policy").[10] This book does not subscribe to a single approach as outlined above; rather, it cherry-picks elements from each and every category. In addition, it focuses on television drama, within which there are two established routes for study. The first is what Bignell describes as "textual-historicism": an analysis of "texts in their historical context, tying meaning to the period in which the programme was made." The second approach is "immanent reading," an analysis of "the texts and the potential meanings that they carry, reinterpreting them through a modern optic."[11] For Bignell, immanent meaning derives from literary and film studies, in which "the construction of meaning and the aesthetic resources of the channels of communication in image and sound produce dominant pedagogical questions and expectations of what the study of television drama will include."[12] Television takes these principles from history, literature, and film and opens them out in new, medium-specific ways: immanent reading is related to generic expectations and authorial principles, while textual historicism is expanded in relation to wider archival, technological, and industrial connections, or to audience and reception contexts. You will find some minor textual historicism and an occasional nod toward immanent reading in later chapters, but on the whole this book is unconcerned with either analytical mode.

While this book is about television drama, it is not what you think. To work through new methods for writing about television, I offer you a case study of a single television series, but not necessarily through the traditional engagement with "textuality," that is, the "questions of aesthetics, ideology, discourse, narrative, genre, representation, camera work, music, casting, editing, the script, authorship and so on of sound-image relations."[13] In fact, in this book I do not analyze the broadcast television text at all. Furthermore, for my case study you might be expecting an examination of an innovative television program, the kind considered "truly extraordinary" and thus "genuinely worthy of close scrutiny."[14]

But my chosen drama has never had that kind of public or critical recognition. In addition, it is not universally well known (I would be very surprised if you have even heard of the program I focus on, and don't worry about that *at all*—textual knowledge is not the point of this project).

So if it isn't about the text, if I reject immanent reading and textual historicism (for the most part), if it isn't a program you know, then where on earth might we begin?

When I started the research for this book in 2018, I was reading a lot of Joan Didion (a pastime I heartily recommend) and was enthralled by her accounts of working as a screenwriter in Hollywood. In 1973 she published "Hollywood: Having Fun" in the *New York Review of Books*, where she discussed taking a meeting with a film producer and director on location in Tucson, Arizona. Even as their film is in production, she explains, the producer and director "are setting up other deals, other action. By the time this picture is released and reviewed they will be on location in other cities. A picture in release is gone." She explains, "The picture itself is in many ways only the action's by-product. 'We can have some fun with this one' the producer says as we leave Tucson. 'Having some fun' is also what the action itself is called." Didion recognizes that the picture is a "by-product of the action" and that "to understand whose picture it is one needs to look not particularly at the script but at the deal memo."[15]

Didion's concept of the action really resonated with my desire to rewrite television. In this book I prioritize the "action," that is, the talk, the human experiences, the whys and wherefores of the "deal," and I do this through practitioner interview, through accessing and articulating memories. As Kristyn Gorton and Joanne Garde-Hansen suggest, practitioner memories can be used as "a way of explaining the past and valuing television's role within both tangible and intangible cultural heritage, place heritage, personal identity and life story."[16] I consider how the people involved positioned themselves as contributors and then how these positionings affected the kinds of stories they told me about the story of getting from pitch to production. Given this, one strand of this book becomes about not television texts that reconceptualize what we think of as drama but instead the drama of making and writing about television. To ground this idea, I work through the potential intersections between production studies, screenwriting studies, and "writing otherwise."

PRODUCTION STUDIES

In 2013, while I was on maternity leave from Northumbria with Edith, my younger daughter, I taught myself script editing and scriptwriting. I then transitioned my academic work away from film and television studies and into creative practice. I took up a lectureship in playwriting and screenwriting at the University of York and discovered a significant divide between my academic work to date in film and television studies and the creative work and industrial engagement I had begun. I was overwhelmed by the "historical and institutionalised division between theory and practice" that still exists in the academy; I didn't know how to articulate (or transcend) the division "between those creative, cultural and material practices which are knowledge producing (and thus constitute research) and those which are not."[17] I seemed to be running two careers in parallel—academic, and screenwriter and script editor—with no apparent way to directly transfer my expertise in one area to the other.

But then I read a call for papers for a special issue of *Film Studies* on "institutions and agency." I instinctively responded to the editor's positioning question, "Wouldn't it be productive to connect finely tuned microanalyses with broad-based big pictures, professional choices with organisational constraints?"[18] My heart leapt; this was a way to make connections, even if my own "practice" as a creative writer was not involved. I pitched an article on development practices in British cinema and spent a year interviewing participants and writing and revising the article for publication. Through the process I discovered just how useful production studies was for building the kind of conceptual bridge I wanted to cross with my own research. And here I make a case for how production studies might be useful for starting to answer some of the propositions I have outlined so far.

Production studies (or media industries or media production research, depending on how you feel and what part of the world you work in) investigates "how the organizations and individuals who create our media content operate" and explores "the everyday conditions and processes of how media texts come into being and aims to understand how and why media texts take their particular forms."[19] Production studies solidified as a disciplinary approach in the first decade of the 2000s, primarily in the United States and under the auspices of eminent scholars such as Miranda Banks, John T. Caldwell, Vicki Mayer, Jennifer Holt, and Alisa Perren.[20] However, since the 2010s there has been a substantial increase in the explorations of creative practice in British, Irish, and European film and television industries as well.[21] In *Remembering British Television*, Gorton and Garde-Hansen explain that "the underlying economies of infrastructure, networks and production cultures" are "hidden beneath discussions of transcultural texts and audiences."[22] Inspired by the growing body of work in this area, I want to jettison text and audience and bring hidden production contexts to light for television studies. Too often production studies emerge from academics or publications in media and communication studies; there seems an almost invisible barrier—in the United Kingdom at least—between "traditional" television studies work, of the type published in journals such as *Screen*, *Journal of Popular Television*, and *Journal of British Cinema and Television*, and the media production work that takes place in adjacent (but distinct) disciplines.

This isn't to declare that television studies / production studies never cross over—see, for example, the work of Stacey Abbott, Ruth McElroy and Caitriona Noonan, and Susan Berridge—but the kinds of questions asked in production studies (or, relatedly, the "cultural industries" scholarship undertaken by scholars David Hesmondhalgh, Sarah Baker, Anamik Saha, and Kate Oakley) do not seem to trouble a lot of the television studies that I read. I find this disciplinary siloization so frustrating. So when I say I want to rewrite television studies, I am gesturing toward a larger set of questions to ask television studies at large (and particularly those who choose to work on television drama): What happens when we reject the traditional text, audience, and reception studies? What happens when we consider the experience of television for the people who make it? What happens when we ground their experiences within the interpersonal infrastructures and networks that emerge from the nationally and regionally specific production cultures? This shift in focus is ideally suited to draw upon production studies, where media production is understood as "neither a rigid monolith nor a completely idiosyncratic, individualistic practice, but rather a *soft* system bound by interrelated action, whose component parts are often individual human beings with continually shifting frames of reference, continually co-constructing as they go."[23]

To be clear though, this book is not just a verbose justification for a production studies assessment of television; I don't get to title my book "rewriting" on this basis alone. In addition, I recognize Brunsdon's perceptive comment, published over thirty years ago, that there are "always more and less fashionable and attractive areas for research," and I am aware that production studies is (currently) very fashionable indeed.[24] Rather, my decision to explore production is indicative of the wider contemporary "cultural turn in the social sciences and the ethnographic turn in the humanities," reflective of a period of growing interest in interdisciplinary research on television working practices.[25] Production studies has in fact long been recommended as a way of furthering television studies from within the discipline itself. In 2004, Corner suggested that more production research would be helpful as a "greater engagement with the world both of fictional and factual television *making*, a matter partly of explaining constraints but also of exploring means and the application of creative criteria, will usefully complicate our engagement with programmes themselves and with what they mean for viewers."[26]

In *Advancing Media Production Research*, Chris Paterson, David Lee, Anamik Saha, and Anna Zoellner write that "rather than seeking to reveal the substantially hidden world of cultural production," their book "explores many of the contemporary challenges to understanding the nature of cultural production—considering the research process, rather than the research findings."[27] Process is central to this book. Think back to Brunsdon's desire for "the edge of the academic," Geraghty and Lusted's "not only what is to be studied but how," and

Corner's "reflexive, sceptical sense" of "knowledge production and vulnerabilities." Production studies is rigorously attuned to methodology (Geraghty and Lusted's call to ask "how"); and it is far more reflexive (Corner's knowledge production) than most humanities analyses of television drama. Here we have an opportunity to utilize the methods and machinations of production studies within television studies itself, to turn the spotlight away from the text and audience and onto the creators of those texts.

SCREENWRITING STUDIES

If production studies is my first approach for thinking through ideas around television, then screenwriting studies is my second. Screenwriting is an even newer area of scholarship than production studies, formalizing as an area of academic study in the late 2000s. In the 2007 edited collection *The New Film History*, Andrew Spicer studied the figure of the British screenwriter, and in the following year he coedited a special issue of the *Journal of British Cinema and Television* on this very topic.[28] In the introduction, John R. Cook and Spicer write that the issue demonstrates "the rich potential that a focus on screenwriting offers to the understanding not only of a particular form of creative writing but also to the complex ways in which the film and television industries operate at various historical moment," thus "providing the hitherto 'Cinderella' study of screenwriting in British cinema and television with a new impetus and focus."[29] Craig Batty demarcated 2009 as the beginning of the "'screenwriting turn' in screen and cultural studies," and in 2010 the *Journal of Screenwriting* was launched by the publisher Intellect.[30] In 2013, the publisher Palgrave then launched the Studies in Screenwriting series with monographs by Ian W. Macdonald and Eva Novrup Redvall.[31]

You would think that in academia screenwriting would be one facet of production studies, perhaps positioned as one of the earliest stages of media production. Yet it has developed its own, distinctive disciplinary subset that has almost nothing to do with cultural industries researchers nor the (predominantly) American-based production studies scholars. Most of the work done to date on screenwriting has come out of British, European, and Australian contexts, with an unspoken agreement on a methodological approach that hews closely to arts and humanities studies of literature, film, and television. This has resulted in a preponderance of studies predicated upon textual analysis and theories of authorship. In screenwriting studies, the screenplay text has remained the primary object of analysis, creating what Steven Maras describes as a "screenplay-centrism" where the screenplay "is considered to be the only kind of script."[32] Jill Nelmes has edited a book on how to analyze the screenplay, Macdonald dedicates a whole chapter to the "text object" of screenwriting, including a lengthy discussion of multiple forms of synopses and script stages (e.g., shooting script, rehearsal script), and Steven Price offers a chapter considering the "ontology" of the screenplay itself.[33] I'm not necessarily interested in the script itself, when it comes to my case study though (and I *know* I haven't told you what it is yet). The script, ultimately, still has parallels with the televisual text: it is a tangible document, a product, from which you can arguably glean and interpret material, but that is always going to be an act based on supposition, at once removed from the subjective experience of the creative process.

Instead, my method focuses on the commissioning and development stage of making television drama. Development is the transformation of a project from "creative genesis to an industrial activity," encompassing "all aspects of that process from the 'white heat' of conceiving a new idea, to the satisfaction of casting it, into financial deals that will see it realized."[34] Script development, in and of itself, has only recently begun to be studied in academia. If the scholarly study of screenwriting began to develop in the late 2000s, it took nearly a decade before script development, specifically, was examined in any depth. As Stayci Taylor and Batty put it, it is the "hidden practice" of screenwriting.[35] The *Journal of Screenwriting* published the first special issue on script development in 2017, and the first academic book dedicated to script development appeared in 2021.[36] In the *Journal of Screenwriting* special issue, Price suggests that academic research and script development are "inextricably entwined in engaging with a process that requires both an understanding of screenwriting practice and a historically informed understanding of the institutional and industrial contexts within which it is usually performed."[37] By focusing on practitioners' experiences of writing rather than on the screenplays themselves, my analysis offers an opportunity to explore my case study in its specific "institutional and industrial contexts," thus bridging television studies, production studies, and screenwriting studies.

WRITING OTHERWISE

The final strand of this book is a reflexive and experimental approach to academic writing. In *Writing otherwise*, Jackie Stacey and Janet Wolff write of their shared desire to "push against conventional academic modes of writing" and move into "more exploratory areas." Writing otherwise is not about combining fictional and academic writing, nor writing memoirs or autobiographical essays. Rather, it is about "how to write otherwise *as* academics." This can mean combining "academic style with a more poetic or personal one," reflecting on "collaborative possibilities," creative nonfiction, and "mixing visual and textual elements."[38] To write otherwise is to write in a more formally experimental mode, which offers "some kind of cultural criticism" but also often "leaves us somewhere slightly unexpected."[39] Stacey and Wolff point out that writing otherwise can reveal "something of the elusive character" of some of the topics studied, revealing, as it is, "the difficulty of finding a language," particularly an academic language that captures those things "that may drive our intellectual appetites"; at times these projects "write in search of something that may seem to escape discourse."[40]

When I first read *Writing otherwise* I couldn't help but smile, breathe out, slowly, *at last*. In writing otherwise, we find a model (or, if I am honest, a form of permission) to write in a more personal fashion, while, at the same time, retaining a fierce belief that intimate and vulnerable modes of writing are also intellectual scholarship. Stacey and Wolff's suggestion that such writing may leave the reader "somewhere unexpected" also appeals to my more playful qualities: I totally want you to think, where is she going to take us next? But at the same time I always want to earn it, to do the due diligence of reading around, of citation, of understanding, so that we can travel to this unexpected place. Furthermore, their mention of conveying that which might "seem to escape discourse" speaks directly to the material I am attempting to uncover. I reject the television text, I reject the screenplay itself; I am trying to fashion a narrative out of air, from the voices of those experienced in making television. As such, I draw on the spirit of Stacey and Wolff's propositions to consider how "writing otherwise" might look when we write about television drama. I do this through three chapters in particular: chapter 5 on "form," chapter 8 on "story," and chapter 10 on "voice."

It isn't just these three chapters though. I am trying to write otherwise throughout the whole book, specifically in relation to how we introduce and work through intellectual ideas. In her memoir of the AIDS years in New York, Sarah Schulman writes that her ideas are "expressed cumulatively," not just "laid out, or told, or recounted, but rather are revealed by the reader's taking in . . . interviews, dispersed anecdotes, profound shifts in place—by letting it all sink in and add up."[41] Schulman also acknowledges that her novels are formally inventive, using "associative thinking, collage, wordplay, juxtaposition of materials, and other long-recognised methods of art practice" to convey ideas, arguing that "some ideas have to be formally replicated instead of being described. They have to be evoked."[42] I'm fascinated by the way in which Schulman positions the reader as active, expectant, perhaps even angry. As a reader, Schulman has "always most enjoyed books that I can be interactive with. I like to fiercely agree with one idea—and fiercely disagree with the next." This is a dynamic approach to reading that "requires a lot of ideas coming at once, from which the reader can pick and choose. Nothing bores me more than the one-long-slow-idea book, and I promise never to write one."[43]

I am with Schulman on this. I have no desire to write a one-long-slow-idea book either. I've attempted to write the prose chapters in a more conversational and reflective manner than is commonly found in television studies (and certainly in the arts and humanities in general). While Stacey and Wolff gave me permission and Schulman showed me a way it could be done, I am also indebted here to Virginia Woolf's "dialogical mode" of criticism, in which "we, as readers, are entering into a continuous argument rather than passively receiving a polished set-piece."[44] There is no single thesis right at the beginning of this book, then proven over and over in case study chapter after case study chapter, in *marginally* different ways. I find that kind of thing entirely tedious. Don't you? Cumulation and evocation are central to my "writing otherwise." This book is not designed to be dipped in and out of, discrete chapters read, as and when needed (as we often read academic texts). Rather, I am really hoping you will read, as a minimum, several chapters one after another, ideally at a single sitting. After all, as Jane Kilby and Graeme Gilloch point out in their essay on academic form in sociology, "The challenge of writing differently anticipates that of reading differently."[45] I know I am asking a lot here, but I really do think that it is in the sustained, extended contact with the ideas, approaches, and ensuing analysis that the value of this book (might) become apparent.

Conclusion

Earlier, I discussed Didion's theory of "the action" in Hollywood filmmaking. Arguably, the "action" is a useful shorthand for thinking through how television drama is developed and commissioned. However, she also has more to offer us in this essay. She draws on F. Scott Fitzgerald's notes on working in Hollywood, where he suggests that "pictures have a private grammar, like politics or automobile production" and that when revealing this to people, he watches "the blank look come into their faces."[46] There remains a significant gap between academic accounts of television storytelling and the realities of practitioner creative process. This book then materialized out of my frustration that much scholarly work on television drama *is* a blank look at the realities of the process of writing television (Ruth McElroy, Caitriona Noonan, Kristyn Gorton, and Beth Johnson are all exempted, of course).

Didion has similar feelings about film criticism. She explains, "Much of what is written about pictures and about picture people approaches reality only occasionally and accidentally"; she casually destroys critics Pauline Kael and Stanley Kauffman by noting that "some people who write about film seem so temperamentally at odds with what both Fellini and Truffaut have called the 'circus' aspect of making film that there is flatly no question of their ever apprehending the social or emotional reality of the process."[47] She concludes, "The difficulty of knowing who made which choices in a picture . . . eventually infects any writer who makes a career of reviewing; perhaps the initial error is making a career of it."[48] Didion's point cannot help but recall Susan Sontag's assertion in "Against Interpretation," published a mere nine years earlier, that interpretation is not simply "the compliment that mediocrity pays to genius," but in fact "the revenge of the intellect upon the world. To interpret is to impoverish, to deplete the world—in order to set up a shadow world of 'meanings.'"[49]

My hope here, then, is that this book "approaches reality" in terms of what the process of television development and commissioning feels like for those people who make their career in it (that is, the "social and emotional reality"), that it actively avoids making interpretive "meanings" of a text based on formal analysis, and that it demonstrates just how useful it can be to actually talk to the people who commission, write, and develop television drama. To do this, I create several strands of ideas, interwoven throughout the book. My first set of ideas explores how stories are imagined, commissioned, and written for television. The second strand considers how we might use form, story, and voice to write academically. The third strand asks how we can make explicit the development of creative process—in terms of both the construction of television drama and writing a book on the subject. Then, I consider, how might the illumination of both sets of processes be useful? Ultimately, I hope that the findings I make about this project, this process, this way of thinking and rewriting do not "impoverish" or "deplete" my chosen case study or discipline in any way but instead elucidate the generative power in rethinking (how we study) our chosen subject.

CHAPTER 2

Methods

We don't tend to get methods chapters in books on television drama. Methods are prioritized in social sciences and often in media and communication, but arts and humanities are rather averse to this kind of thing. In this chapter I am going to convince you why methods matter. The first half of this chapter is an account of my case study for the book, the how, why, and when it was chosen, and how this process intersected with my interest in production and screenwriting studies and writing otherwise. The second half of this chapter then focuses on interviewing as a qualitative research method, and ethics, power, and transcription. Methods are a creative approach entirely suited to my subject matter, given that method is "something we do in order to understand, create, encounter, connect, disrupt or engage the world," and that research methods, in particular, are distinguished by "the practice of reflection on and transparency about choices of practice."[1] As such, this chapter is an attempt to evidence precisely *why* we need to take methods seriously in television studies (no skipping ahead now; behave, methods *are* interesting).

NARRATIVE

My methodology, at its broadest, can be understood as a mode of qualitative research designed to explore narrative. In the social sciences, phenomenology as a method dominates approaches to narrative research. Phenomenology explores "how people experience their lifeworlds, including their sensory and emotional experience of phenomena and events; their thoughts, perceptions, and imaginings; their desires, intentions, and actions," which is achieved through "in-depth understanding, and clear, often detailed, description of experience-in-context."[2] As I am particularly interested in television screenwriting and how this works within the production of a series, I am keen to speak to those people involved in the imagining, commissioning, and development of the television case study. I want to understand not only the context for their decisions but their experiences of making those decisions and how they impacted upon the stories being told. I will talk more about phenomenology in chapter 5, but for now I want to signal the priority that the experience of practitioners will take in my work.

Then, I have chosen to examine a single case study: one television text with which to work through my ideas. In qualitative research, case studies are recognized as "intensive," predicated upon "detail, richness, completeness and variance" with a focus on "developmental factors," which means the case study evolves over time. In addition, case studies are also framed in "relation to environment."[3] Understanding the case study as a method—the unit of study, the depth of detail, the refinement of the case study across an extended duration, a refinement impacted by external factors—is ideal for studying television, given that series transform in response to industrial, commercial, and interpersonal factors, and decisions around the progression and commissioning of future series emerge directly from the temporally specific industrial environment.

However, the origins of my chosen case study and my decisions around my approach can be traced back to 2015 and to some of my rather less methodically rigorous decisions. By 2015, I had left Northumbria and was working as a lecturer at the University of York, where I attended the Northern Television Research Group (NTVRG) symposium "Revisiting Melodrama in Contemporary Television." This symposium was organized by television studies scholars Kristyn Gorton, Hannah Andrews, and Amy Holdsworth. The melodrama symposium was exciting, and while I didn't have any inclination to study melodrama itself (horror remains my one true genre), I was riveted by the discussions taking place. As we were leaving the symposium to go for dinner, Faye Woods mentioned to me that Christopher Meir was putting together a special issue on the British production company RED Productions for the *Journal of British Cinema and Television*. I have long admired RED, from being a teenager transfixed by *Queer as Folk* (Channel 4, 1999–2000) in my little bedroom in Leeds, through to being a mum of two in Newcastle, my heart aching for my much-missed Yorkshire landscapes as I devoured *Last Tango in Halifax* (BBC One, 2012–). As soon as I got home from the symposium, I combed RED's production history to find a program that would spark my interest for a project to pitch to Meir.

Given I have built my career on my expertise in horror, I was delighted to find *Bedlam* (Living TV / Sky Living, 2011–2012) hidden in RED's production history. This is my chosen case study for this book (it's okay—I wouldn't have heard of it either unless I had been combing the RED production histories, and I'm going to tell you all about it, so don't fret). *Bedlam* is a supernatural horror series that ran for six episodes on Living TV in 2011 and six episodes on Sky Living in

2012. The genre was what first drew me in. RED is known for edgy, realist northern drama, for *Happy Valley* (BBC One, 2014–), *Clocking Off* (BBC One, 2000–2003), and *Scott & Bailey* (ITV, 2011–2016); what were they doing making supernatural horror? I soon discovered *Bedlam* is the first (indeed, to date, only) horror series made by RED. This gave me my initial research question for my pitch for the journal special issue: why did RED make *Bedlam*?

Then, *Bedlam* was made in the 2000s. This was an unusual time to make original British horror television. At this point, there were only a handful of recent British precedents. These included anthologies and mini-series: *Ghosts* (1995) and *Crooked House* (2008) for the BBC; *Chiller* (1995) and *Oktober* (1998) for ITV; and *Ultraviolet* (1998) and *Dead Set* (2008) for Channel 4 / E4, plus a few series with very limited runs: Sky One's *Hex* (2004–2005) and Channel 5's *Urban Gothic* (2000–2001). BBC Three's *Being Human* (2008–2013) was the only real outlier for this period: an original British horror drama with sustained critical and commercial success. Given this context, I found RED's decision to make *Bedlam* all the more intriguing. This created my second question: who chose to write a horror series, at a time when the genre was decidedly unpopular? In addition, *Bedlam* was the first original drama for Living TV and was commissioned at a time when almost no U.K. commercial broadcasters created original content. So I asked myself, why did Living TV commission this series?

Choosing *Bedlam* as a case study also came out of my reaction to the York melodrama symposium. The advert for the symposium included the following statement: "In the clamor to critique and interpret particular forms of 'complex television' (Mittell, 2012, 2015), a focus on narrative structure and aesthetic style has tended to leave less room for considerations of reception, affect, and emotion. Moreover, certain kinds of television dominate in these discussions, leaving a gap in the debate around contemporary dramatic forms outside 'quality' or 'cinematic' television. . . . We want to reopen conversations about the value and meaning of melodrama in the current context, and consider its potential to offer a different form of engagement with television than that which presently dominates."[4] This is a pointed statement about television studies in the mid-2010s, with allusions to the limitations of an all-encompassing scholarly love affair with narrative and aesthetic analyses of "complex" American television series. It specifically gestures toward Jason Mittell's influential and highly regarded *Complex TV: The Poetics of Contemporary Television*, published in 2015. In this book, Mittell argues that (American) television (drama) storytelling has changed. For Mittell, in the past two decades "a new model of storytelling has emerged as an alternative to the conventional episodic and serial forms that have typified most American television since its inception." He defines this as "narrative complexity," which "redefines episodic forms under the influence of serial narration—not necessarily a complete merger of episodic and serial forms but a shifting balance."[5] Three years after *Complex TV*, Trisha Dunleavy published

Complex Serial Drama and Multiplatform Television, defining programs such as *Stranger Things* (Netflix, 2015–present) as "complex serials" and noting (in an explicit territorial strike) that this is "a label I first applied to American television in 2009," thus, by insinuation, predating Mittell's theorization of "complex tv."[6] By the mid-2010s, the study of American "complex" television—and it's longer-running precursor, "quality" television—had become a standard area of television studies, with a plethora of publications devoted to *Lost* (ABC, 2004–2010), *The Sopranos* (HBO, 1999–2007), and *Breaking Bad* (AMC, 2008–2013), among others.

However, there was a significant critical backlash against the Mittell era of American television criticism in the United Kingdom. In her introduction to the *Screen* special issue "Situating Television Studies," published a year after the York symposium, Karen Lury discusses the position of scholars who opposed this focus on American "quality" television. For Lury, they argue that the focus on a "narrow range of texts" privileges "a particular mode of programming and a specific audience demographic," and such analyses ignore "important issues of taste and gender as well as the (local) economies of television production and consumption."[7] Helen Piper elucidates these problems further in her contribution to the special issue, noting that a couple of "rather questionable aphorisms are presently enjoying covert recirculation in the discourses that surround television." The first is "that nothing resonates as 'universally' as the existential crisis of a white, male American" and that "television is never more 'valuable' than when it most resembles a pre-existing art form." Piper suggests that television as a medium "has lately redeemed itself through association with a succession of internationally available 'cinematic' and complex texts, chief amongst them *The Sopranos*, *Mad Men* and, of course, *Breaking Bad*, each of which has been celebrated by various parties as the 'best television ever.'"[8]

There is much to unpick here: the valorization of "complex" American television drama over the television output of other cultures and countries, the dominance of the straight white male in these television dramas, and the lack of reflective thinking on not only what valorizing these *kinds* of characters and texts might mean but also just why "good" television might be considered "cinematic."

On the latter point, and I know this should be a footnote, but I can't help myself: there is nothing more likely to cause television studies scholars to lose their minds than to approvingly describe television drama as "cinematic," thus denying the medium its aesthetic, narrative, and broadcast specificities. As Deborah L. Jaramillo argues, cinematic "should be a contentious word in television studies . . . in the new conversation about the good looking series, television is positioned as its own limiter, and cinema can somehow liberate television from itself"; developing this further, Helen Wheatley "rejects the idea" that "spectacular television is inherently cinematic."[9] Indeed, when Angelo Restivo's *Break-*

ing Bad *and Cinematic Television*—a title surely designed to invoke eye-popping apoplexy within the community—was reviewed by Hannah Andrews for *Critical Studies in Television*, she opened her review by noting, "The expression 'cinematic television' is likely to raise the eyebrow of many readers of *Critical Studies in Television*. Associated with discourses of 'Peak TV,' television's third (or fourth) 'Golden Age,' or that ubiquitous phantom 'quality' television drama, so-called cinematic values in television have been dissected in both academic and popular criticism for at least two decades."[10]

So, in choosing *Bedlam* to pitch to the *JBCTV* special issue, I wanted to really dig into the thinking about what kinds of programs get chosen as case studies and why they get chosen (hence why I am spending time reflecting on my choices here). My decision to choose *Bedlam* connects directly with Lury's introduction to "Situating Television Studies," about the importance of not only considering the local economies of television production but also loosening the shackles of what constitutes the kind of "good" television that scholars analyze. This isn't to say *Bedlam* wasn't a success: crucially, it's success can be measured commercially, not critically. In its two seasons in the United Kingdom, *Bedlam* had a high audience approval rating and generated millions of viewers. It sold internationally, across the United States, East Asia, and Europe. In the States, it was considered to be one of the two high-profile horror television launches for American television in 2011—the other being *American Horror Story* (FX, 2011–)—and it screened on BBC America, in a "supernatural Saturday" night slot directly after *Doctor Who* (BBC One, 1963–), receiving widespread national attention.

Yet scholars have not written on *Bedlam*, and I know why. *Bedlam* squarely fits within Brett Mills's concept of "invisible television"; that is, "there is television that gets watched and there is television that gets discussed: the two do not necessarily coincide." For Mills, invisible television programs are ones that "despite being long-running and consistently garnering high audience ratings, are repeatedly ignored by the vast majority of academic work."[11] Since the late 2000s there has been an increasing scholarly interest in the figure of the television showrunner and on writers' rooms. These accounts often demonstrate interest in "the divisions of labor in the US television context and in how to understand the contributions of individuals in a context where one professional role [the showrunner] is now identified as the most important for the process as a whole."[12] My study of *Bedlam* is an opportunity to contribute to an increasing body of work on the development contexts for television industries outside North America.[13] *Bedlam* also appealed to me as the three writers and cocreators (more on them shortly) do not yet command that distinctive authorial vision accorded to a privileged few (predominantly male) showrunners working in the television industry. Then, because they made a horror series on a satellite channel, their work falls within Mills's demarcation as a program that exists but seems "not to be seen," a program "simply overlooked or looked through as though it were not there."[14]

Mills's point has direct parallels with the central precepts of narrative research in the social sciences, in which "the everyday takes center stage." In narrative research, "although the great societal events are not ignored, narrative work pivots on the ordinary, the stories and events that tend to go unnoticed because they are run-of-the-mill, rather than remarkable."[15] The choice of *Bedlam* exemplifies a stance directly against the typical canonization of texts in television studies; as Bignell writes, it is significant that it is "examples of BBC programs and not ITV ones that are most readily used as examples of the achievements of British television drama (and British television in general)."[16] We can extrapolate from this to point out that programming of (British) digital terrestrial channels is the preferred object of analysis when compared to subscription-based direct broadcast satellite channels Sky and Freesat.

And yet the point of this book is not to illuminate some overlooked British television drama. That would be a bit niche, even for me. In their overview of case study research, Thomas A. Schwandt and Emily F. Gates write, "A critical question for all researchers employing cases as the basis for their research is, 'what is this a case of?'" This is designed to focus the researcher and the reader's attention "on distinguishing the phenomenon of interest from the studied unit or instance."[17] When I study *Bedlam* in this book, what am I really studying? How does analyzing one program (and a relatively unknown, low-budget British horror series at that) teach us anything about rewriting television—whether this is the study of television writing or television studies more broadly? More bluntly, as one reviewer of the manuscript for this book put it, why should we care?

This is a fair question: who cares about *Bedlam*? And if you don't care about it, why would you keep reading? My case for keeping you comes down to value, that is, the value of case study as method. Bent Flyvbjerg writes that a common "misunderstanding" of case studies is that it is "difficult to summarize and develop general propositions and theories on the basis of specific case studies."[18] To offer a solution to this misunderstanding, Flyvbjerg turns to narrative. He suggests that examining a case study is not about generating data to then unpick and summarize key facts (in short, an approach that completes and closes down the topic). Rather, he proposes that we embrace the openness of the case study. Authors may "demur from the role of omniscient narrator and summarizer" and instead "choose to tell the story in its diversity, allowing the story to unfold from the many-sided, complex and sometimes-conflicting stories that the actors in the case have told researchers." Then, authors can avoid grounding their study in "the theories of any one academic specialization," choosing instead to "relate the case to broader philosophical positions that cut across specializations."[19]

I follow these excellent suggestions in this book. First, I reject omniscience as a narrator. I'm talking you through my story, as it happens. Then, I also reject a dry, unbiased, objective analysis of my case study, choosing instead to ground the reading of my participants' everyday experiences in my everyday experience of living in the world (there's the phenomenology for you). I offer a clear, detachable framework for doing this kind of work in chapter 10. Then, while my ideas are grounded in the history of television studies, I also draw upon film, media and cultural studies, social anthropology, ethnography, literary studies, and social sciences. As the book progresses, you will see a further drawing upon narrative nonfiction, New Journalism, oral histories of music, modernism, and personal essay collections. I also structure significant aspects of this book using screen-writing and playwriting technique and reflect upon this in chapter 8.

In short, this book is not about *Bedlam*. It is not even about British television. It is a book that uses a case study to ask big questions about methodologies in television studies. Attempting to ask bigger questions of a discipline through one small case study may look dubious, but it is from the particular and the specific that useful and universal precepts *can* emerge. This is an opportunity to question what we take for granted in what we study and how and when we study it. Really, this book asks, what are the challenges involved in writing television drama, both as a practitioner and as a scholar studying the subject? How do we *do* writing (for or about) television?

These questions, to me, are a good enough reason to keep reading.

Access, Power, Anonymity, Ethics

Having settled on *Bedlam* as my case study, and having written three research questions (Why did RED make *Bedlam*? Why horror? Why did Living TV commission this series?), I pitched my idea to Meier and his coeditor, Andrew Spicer, and began researching the writers of *Bedlam*. When doing production studies research, I've learned to reach out to the writers first. They are usually more interested and more available than anyone else involved in the production, they are usually ignored in the show's publicity, and they usually have stories to tell. I found *Bedlam*'s writer-creators David Allison, Chris Parker, and Neil Jones on Twitter and discovered that Allison lived nearby. I messaged him with a pitch, he responded, I sent him a DM with more details, and he agreed to the interview. In March 2018, we met up for lunch at the Nation of Shopkeepers pub in Leeds.

I interviewed Allison in the same way that I interviewed everyone for this book, with each person allocated a single, one-to-one, unstructured interview. Unstructured interviewing is a qualitative "data-gathering technique" designed to explore "people's views of reality and allows the researcher to generate theory," as opposed to quantitively orientated accounts designed to test hypotheses.[20] The generation of theory through *doing* the interviews is an important distinction to make; this project is predicated upon an inductive approach to data analysis. Rather than using the interviews to test a hypothesis, I utilized them to map out a model of the *Bedlam* development process. I allowed interview questions to materialize in response to the interviewees' experiences of going through the development and commissioning of the television series. With this approach, you can "obtain a kind of undeniability of results provided the findings come with detailed accounts of the phenomena that allow readers to see the stories unfold and to relate to the experiences of the people involved."[21]

We can conceptualize this data through "personal narrative evidence," that is, "retrospective first-person accounts of individual lives," motivated by a desire to "examine varieties of selfhood and agency 'from below' and in practice, as constructed in people's articulated self-understandings."[22] This is why unstructured interviews are so useful for this approach, not least my desire to explore issues around story (chapter 8) and voice (chapter 10) as they offer "researchers access to people's ideas, thoughts, and memories in their own words rather than in the word of the researcher."[23] Memory is the operative word here. There is a strong tradition of excellent, rigorous scholarship on memory and film and television studies, through the work of Amy Holdsworth, Annette Kuhn, and Susannah Radstone, among others. However, where I wanted to situate the concept of memory was simpler and more ordinary.[24] I knew I would not and could not gather irrefutable facts; this method did not allow for generating indisputable data. I follow here instead the principle of essayist Durga Chew-Bose, who, when writing on film, suggests that "memory fans out from imagination, and vice versa, and why not. Memory isn't a well but an offshoot. It goes secretly. Comes apart. Deceives." She suggests that "memory is trust open to doubt."[25] Through the interviewing process, I used practitioner memories to generate new stories, a principle I explore in much greater depth in chapter 8.

Another key principle was a commitment to listening. Andrea Fontana and Anastasia H. Prokos argue that "the goal of unstructured interviewing is *understanding*," and as such "the researcher must be able to take the role of the respondents and attempt to see the situation from their viewpoint, rather than superimpose his or her world of academia and preconceptions upon them."[26] I did not go into the interviews with the aim of testing a thesis or eliciting a quote to prove a point that I wanted to make. Every interview was undertaken with a commitment to listening and thinking about what was being said. In turn, I was then able to respond to the material that emerged from the interviews: Allison discussed *Bedlam*'s original gestation at the BBC (which I had no prior knowledge of); this gave me a new line of inquiry that resulted in an interview with television drama executive Anne Mensah. Mensah is now vice president, original series at Netflix, but in the early 2000s she was head of independent drama for the BBC and head of drama for BBC Scotland and responsible for commissioning *Bedlam* in the first place.

After interviewing Allison, I put into practice snowball sampling, a recruitment method that "uses interpersonal relations and connections between people" to "access specific populations."[27] I asked Allison to contact his fellow cowriters and cocreators, Jones and Parker, and find out if they would be willing to be interviewed for the project. They concurred, and I interviewed Jones and Parker separately, via video calls on Skype, between March and April 2018 (yes this was pre-pandemic so people video called on Skype; a fact that already makes this work historical). Then, having established a good "origin" story for the development and commissioning of *Bedlam*, from the perspective of the writers, I realized that I couldn't get everything I needed from the perspective of the three writer-creators alone and that I needed the perspective of RED as the production company. This was, in hindsight, a major indicator that the project was much bigger than could be managed in a single journal article, but I didn't heed the signs at this point (more on this error of judgment to come).

I contacted Allison again, asking if he would consider passing on an email to RED's Richard Fee, who in 2018 was a senior executive at RED but had been the script editor for *Bedlam* in 2011. However, Allison suggested I speak to his wife, Caroline Hollick, who was the more senior staff member on the project. I interviewed Hollick in Seven Café, in Chapel Allerton, Leeds, over coffee, in early May 2018. I then approached Fee directly, emailing him and listing the names of the people I had interviewed so far on the project, and then we had lunch later that month at the Pine Marten pub in Harrogate.

The interviews with Fee and Hollick filled in a lot of gaps in terms of institutional procedure, and by the end of May 2018 I breathed a sigh of relief. I was sure, at this point, that my interviewing was done. I transcribed the first few interviews myself, then quickly decided to pay Harriet Mathie, a local professional transcriber, instead. I sent notes to Harriet, providing context (whom I interviewed, what their job was, the key names discussed in the article, the television programs and companies discussed) and directions for content (following social science data preparation principles, I advised that the recording was to be "transcribed in its entirety and provide a verbatim account of the interview" and "ensure that all transcripts are generated systematically," including "elisions, mispronunciations, slang, grammatical errors, nonverbal sounds (e.g., laughs, sighs), and background noises").[28]

When the professional transcriptions were returned, I then went back through them while listening to the audio and made any necessary amendments for clarity. I then sent the transcripts to the practitioners with an explanation of how they had been transcribed and gave them two or three weeks to read through the transcription and respond. I allowed them to redact any or all of the transcript and to amend any sections they felt were misunderstood in the transcription process or they themselves had not explained properly during the interview. It was also an opportunity to redact any information that, on second thought, they didn't want making public. This was my acknowledgment that "the openness and intimacy of the interview may be seductive and can lead subjects to disclose information they may later regret revealing."[29] If they didn't get back to me, I sent a follow-up email, after the deadline, checking in and giving them a further opportunity to have input into their words as transcribed.

Such procedural care is a matter of ethics. As Irit Mero-Jaffe states, "An interview by its very nature is based on a power relationship and where there is power, there lies a potential for the infraction of human rights."[30] However, this idea of power is complicated by the kind of power relations that emerge in this kind of research. For example, as I was using snowball sampling, I was particularly mindful of how I interviewed people such as Hollick and Fee, who (at the time) worked side by side at RED. Interviewing someone's peer, and doing a good job, is crucial: if you are strange, unusual, or rude, you will not get the recommendation you require to further your research. I presumed that if I had really annoyed Hollick, Fee would not have been prepared to meet with me. I was aware of the need to make the experience (relatively) enjoyable, for each interviewee to be happy to spend time with me and actively enjoy (or at least not dislike) the process. I was thoughtful about how I framed questions and in what I order I posed them; reading the room (or Skype screen) and responding in terms of the interviewees' comfort were crucial to the project.

This power dynamic can be contextualized through the principle of "studying up." In her 1974 essay "Up the Anthropologist: Perspectives Gained from Studying Up," Laura Nader argues that anthropology is power. She explains that it is about "those who shape attitudes and actually control institutional structures" and "we need simply to realize when it is useful or crucial in terms of the problem to extend the domain of study up, down or sideways."[31] Studying down is the traditional purview of the anthropologist, of "observing people rather less powerful and privileged than themselves."[32] Studying up, in contrast, is scholars engaging "in research upon men, upper-class people, and institutions with considerable power," a form of elite interviewing where we define elites as "those in powerful positions . . . or those who hold positions of professional prestige," that is, as "individuals who occupy institutional and social power."[33]

Historically, issues of power in ethnographic research have focused on studying down, on "the protection and empowerment of vulnerable interview subjects, rather than interviews with privileged elites."[34] Nader's model, by contrast, suggests that "studying up" might be a better way to consider how elite interviewing affects the data generated. There are many challenges in interviewing elites, ranging from "difficulties with gaining access, to the suggestion that elite participants may seek to exert too much control over research and manipulate dissemination processes."[35] While I did not feel controlled or manipulated by any of my interviewees, either during the interview or in the course of sharing the transcription material, I am aware that my behavior and the questions I asked were tempered by the fact that I was attempting to gain access to an industry run on a network of informal social relations and my access to these individuals could be withdrawn at any moment, purely by word of mouth (and I reflect upon this further in chapter 11).

In a 2009 essay, anthropologist Sherry B. Ortner proposed that when academics study the media industries they are not "studying up," as Nader would see it, but are instead "studying sideways," for "people—like scientists, journalist and Hollywood filmmakers" are "in many ways are really not much different from anthropologists and academics generally."[36] We can also see parallels with Ortner's principle of "studying sideways" within the second phase of television studies. In his 1990 book *Television Drama: Agency, Audience and Myth*, John Tulloch suggested that "the male left-wing academic is, like the socialist dramatists he analyses, both in a position of some discursive power and, increasingly, social and intellectual marginality—which perhaps offers some ground for the avoidance of 'otherness' in the research process."[37] While Tulloch's identity labeling and the type of program and practitioner he studies are removed from my own, the principle remains the same.

Oral historian Valerie Raleigh Yow has argued that "ethical and legal issues are often intertwined" in in-depth interviewing practices, and that is the case here.[38] This is another reason why it is important to share the transcription: publishing some of the material could have had legal implications for the interviewees. Living TV executive Amy Barham signed an exit agreement with Sky, and as such she needed to reread the legal document before signing off on our transcript. Similarly, Sky's in-house HR team wanted to sign off on the transcription of Mensah, who was director of drama and Sky Studios at Sky U.K. at the time of our interview. Their need to review the interview material also relates to the lack of interviewee anonymity in my study. For Annukka Vainio, "Anonymity is one of the core principles of research ethics and is usually regarded as the mechanism through which privacy and confidentiality are maintained." She explains that "core elements of ethical practice include informed consent and the avoidance of deception, harm and exploitation" and suggests that "of these elements, anonymity is unique because it involves modifying of the empirical data, so that the research participants cannot be identified."[39] However, for my case study anonymity would not work. The writers and executives involved in *Bedlam* are public figures and easily identifiable online. Here, I followed Julia Bickford and Jeff Nisker's position that in some cases "actions taken to hide or gloss over" participants' names "would impede the ability to demonstrate authenticity, validity and verisimilitude."[40] Before the interview, I informed the writers and executives that their names would be used and reminded them of this during the transcript revision process.

The anonymity issue does raise bigger questions though. It isn't just about being able to identify the individual; it is about the potential ramifications of identifying them with the words they have spoken. Unlike many creative industries oral histories, where interviewees are often very senior in their career, and beyond too much damage, most of the people who worked on *Bedlam* remain active in the industry today. The majority are midcareer and are still moving up the ranks. The transference of the non-anonymized transcript thus follows research ethics, which "avoids treating people as simply automatons."[41] Here, I was attempting to safeguarding the interviewees' well-being (and my integrity) by inviting them into the process of transcribing and revising the interview material.

However, once the transcripts were approved by the interviewees, I did not share any further work with them. The decision around when to stop sharing is a long-standing issue in feminist social sciences. In the early 1980s Joan Acker, Kate Barry, and Joke Esseveld shared their written material with some of the women they wrote about, but "we have to admit to some reluctance to share our interpretations with those who, we expected, would be upset by them. There was a potential conflict between our feminist frame of reference and their interpretations of their own lives." They were aware that "the act of looking at interviews, summarizing another's life, and placing it within a context is an act of objectification."[42] My position was that the interviewees needed to get to a position of being satisfied that the transcription was an accurate reflection and that they were happy with its publication, and that I would use the material only in its relevant and original contexts. Beyond that though, I shared nothing else. The decision to share notes or academic interpretations (of where and when you stop and why) is delicate: sharing drafts "can produce unanticipated results because participants may find it to be overly academic and in this sense to deviate from their own sense of reality," or participants may "disagree with important parts of the draft, especially parts that might have been unrelated to their own contributions."[43]

I was delighted with the material I elicited from Allison, Parker, Jones, Fee, and Hollick, and I found the transcriptions fascinating. I really enjoyed the investigative process of interviewing, of piecing together clues in the ever-increasing detail of *Bedlam*'s story, and I had a million ideas of how to take the research forward. I wrote a very embryonic paper, reflecting upon the research questions and potential parameters of the project, that I presented at the SCMS conference in Toronto in 2018. The paper went well, and I returned home to the United Kingdom to write a first draft of the article for the special issue. I had four months to meet the July 2018 deadline.

It seemed completely reasonable. But then, then, the project fell apart.

The Rashomon Effect

I planned to write an article of around seven thousand words for the special issue. But when I started to write the first draft, I encountered three major problems. The first was the writers. I am an experienced interviewer, having worked as a freelance arts journalist in my twenties, and I have also interviewed many practitioners in my academic research. But there was something particularly compelling about the *Bedlam* story told by three different writer-creators. Allison, Parker, and Jones were all happy to talk at length about *Bedlam* and reflect upon their own creative process. Interviewed separately though, each unknowingly gave *their* version of the story, with different emphases in moments of importance—one filling in the blanks on the part another had skipped over, another opening a new area for inquiry in their recollection, a third talking freely about an aspect of development that the first would not discuss. As you would expect, they were all fantastic raconteurs, and their interviews created an almost overwhelming deluge of material. My discovery of this echoes Miranda J. Banks's own research on media industries, in which she notes that writers "are not just aware of their position and role within the industry—as many [practitioners] are—they are also uniquely articulate in their analysis of that role" and that "their facility with words ensures that the clarity of language and their choices of terms withstands exploration and analysis as scholarly data."[44] Or, as Todd Gitlin observes in *Inside Prime Time*, after interviewing over two hundred people, "Getting people to talk was not the problem I anticipated; the problem was to evaluate millions of words." He comments that Hollywood is "a place where many of the practitioners are brighter and more engaging than their products, and the story of the making of the show more revealing than the show itself."[45]

It isn't just the first half of Gitlin's comment that is true; the second half is as well. This was my second problem. I had inadvertently stumbled onto a fascinating moment in the making of a television drama. The story of the making of *Bedlam* was stuffed with enough protagonists and antagonists, ABC storylines, and five-act turning points to fill an eight-part series. It had, in the sense of a classically structured story, "obstacles, surprises, ups and downs, good times and bad times for the character," or in our case, the three writer-creators.[46]

The problem here then was that I had no sense of how I could satisfactorily fit this into a single journal article without the evidence and analysis becoming shallow and broad. I considered splitting the research into several articles but realized that the story would then be lost: the parts did not work outside the whole. Nonetheless, I pushed forward with a painful, unsatisfying first draft of the article and came in at thirty thousand words (which made me feel quite sick). After writing this draft, it also became apparent that I needed to interview the people at Living TV (for series 1) and Sky Living (for series 2), and the thirty thousand words written did not even include one word from these potential interviewees.

I panicked and emailed Meir, asking for a month's extension, to which he kindly acquiesced, and I plunged into the Living and Sky Living interviewing. My lead into the Living TV staff came via Hollick. In our interview in Chapel

Allerton, she discussed Barham, the executive producer for Living TV. I found Barham on Instagram and messaged her, only to discover that she had left Living and was working as a filmmaker in Los Angeles. Nonetheless, she agreed to talk over Skype, and then she contacted Claudia Rosencrantz (head of Virgin Television when *Bedlam* was made) on my behalf. I interviewed Rosencrantz over the phone and cold-emailed Mensah, the former head of independent drama at the BBC (who first developed *Bedlam*) and then Sky Living drama head (responsible for commissioning series 2). After my phone interview with Mensah, Rosencrantz referred me to Jenny Reeks (former head of ITV Drama and executive producer on both series of *Bedlam*). This process began to make apparent not just how collaborative television development is but also how many people have input into a story. I started to despair over the seemingly runaway scope of the project, each interviewee throwing out the name of someone else central to *Bedlam*'s development.

This limitless sample was also very hard to reconcile with my commitment to reveal the contradictory thoughts, opinions, and feelings of all major individual practitioners involved in the project. I just couldn't see how I could do this adequately in a journal article. I was encountering the downside of what James Andrew Miller has described in his oral history of the Creative Artists Agency as "a bit of a 'Rashomon effect' in the telling (or retelling) of tales, all parties having their own perspectives and agendas." He explains that "in typical Hollywood style" many of those interviewed "have spent years rewriting their scripts; artfully obscuring facts, intentionally fogging the view, others have jumped to conclusions and made assumptions without knowing the full story."[47] Or, as screenwriter Craig Mazin has commented, writers are dangerous people "to try and discern history from, because we are particularly good at lacing together the narrative we want you to hear, and those narratives always flow towards a purpose or a point, the dramatic intent of the narrative."[48] This statement applies just as well to script editors or channel executives; each person I interviewed had a powerful grip on storytelling and narrative construction. There's another important point from Miller though: his acknowledgment of the inability to ever get the "full" story. Each new interview uncovered new angles or aspects of the story not picked up in previous interviews, even offering different readings of the same situation. I became uncomfortably aware of the desire to conduct "just one more" interview, to find just one more story, one more point of view, to just really "complete" the project.

I interviewed Reeks in December 2018 and then collated my transcriptions: 82,000 words to analyze. I brought the interviewing to a halt as new issues then materialized. The first problem was the way I was writing about people. No matter how I tried, I couldn't reconcile my desire to integrate the practitioner interviews with academic form. I went back over television studies articles that incorporated practitioner interviews and was dissatisfied with how the material was used. Many academics treat interview material as truth, a fact spoken by the person who was there, rather than a subjective story told of an experience (which I will discuss at much greater length in chapter 5).

I turned to social sciences research on unstructured interviewing and found support for my position. Fontana and Prokos point out that many unstructured interviews are "not reflexive enough about the *interpreting* process," that neither the researcher nor data is ever really neutral or unbiased; in these weak accounts "improprieties never happen and the main concern seems to be the proper (if unreflexive) filming, analyzing and reporting of events. But anyone who has engaged in fieldwork knows better."[49] Similarly, Vicki Mayer, Miranda J. Banks, and John T. Caldwell argue that part of the reason for writing *Production Studies* is not only to "alert social scientists to the cultural histories of the contemporary media institutions they are analyzing and entering as field researchers" but also so that humanities scholars understand that they "must be mindful that all texts, whether found in an archive or one's own field notes, are *constructions* . . . we suggest a healthy dose of skepticism and reflexivity."[50] This was the way forward, conceptually, but I wasn't sure how to proceed.

How could I incorporate this kind of reflexive thinking into my work? What would it look like? I realized that my difficulties in representing the experiences of people was a question of voice. As bell hooks puts it, in her creative writing class she was taught "a notion of 'voice' as embodying the distinct expression of an individual writer."[51] In screenwriting, voice is "a distinctive tone. It is physically unique, individual, unlike any other."[52] I wanted to connect these ideas around voice to story: How can I express the voices of the interviewees in an engaging and intimate manner that reveals them as distinctive, unique human beings? How do I express their voices in a way that tells their stories? I also began to wonder (a little more quietly, to myself), can we do more with voice in our academic writing?

I had a problem not only with the voice of my interviewees, namely how to get *them* as individual people, down on the page, telling their story, but also with form. The academic model for incorporating interviews into your television analysis is to introduce the interviewee and/or the context, quote the interview extract, analyze the quote in your own words, and then relate the analysis to the article or chapter's larger thesis. This model not only fails to adequately capture the nuanced, individual, emotional lives of those practitioners but also is limited in its ability to adequately set the practitioner's stories amid the voices of other contributors—something that seemed central to what I was trying to do.

At this point, I had to make peace with the fact that this project was not going to materialize at any point soon and certainly not as a coherent journal article. Although I was loath to admit it, I knew at this point that this project was a book (despite the fact I didn't want another book to fight with, given I was already under contract to write one on horror film, which was the actual subject I had based my career on). I emailed Meir and confessed I couldn't submit to the special issue. I received a disappointed but polite response, and I sat back, feeling a little relieved and more than a little guilty.

Conclusion

In withdrawing from the special issue, I reached several conclusions. The main one was that this book would be as much a story about the difficulties in writing about making television as a story about how television gets made. Given this, I then asked myself, what would happen if I tried to create a genuine dialogue, *on the page*, between the makers of television drama? How might these stories and voices coalesce to create a more experimental approach to academic form? To what extent is that form capable of emulating the very subject that it explores?

Then, if I do work out how to do this, how do I situate this multiplicity of perspectives, this "Rashomon" experience of television making, within and through the scholarship in production studies, screenwriting studies, and writing otherwise? On the idea of writing otherwise, what would happen if I wrote an academic monograph that genuinely aimed to be a page-turner, that you keep reading because you wanted to, not because you should? (I'm not sure why this still feels radical, but it does, to me at least.)

These questions became the basis for the rest of this book. So when you turn to the next chapter, think about the questions I ask here, and then ask yourself, what would happen if I just wrote like this instead?

Cast of Characters and Dialogue Key

Cast of Characters

DAVID ALLISON. Cocreator and cowriter, *Bedlam*

AMY BARHAM. Executive producer for Living TV, *Bedlam*, series 1

RICHARD FEE. Script editor, *Bedlam*

CAROLINE HOLLICK. Script executive, *Bedlam*

NEIL JONES. Cocreator and cowriter, *Bedlam*

ANNE MENSAH. Head of independent drama, BBC and head of drama, BBC Scotland; later, executive producer for Sky Living, *Bedlam*, series 2

CHRIS PARKER. Cocreator and cowriter, *Bedlam*

JENNY REEKS. Executive producer for Living TV and Sky Living, *Bedlam*, series 1 and 2

CLAUDIA ROSENCRANTZ. Director of television for Virgin Media

NICOLA SHINDLER. Founder and chief executive of RED, executive producer for RED, *Bedlam*

Dialogue Key

- Punctuation "to suggest delivery rather than conform to rules of grammar"[1]
- An em dash (—) "indicates an interruption of speech or train of thought"[2]
- Ellipses (. . .) indicate truncated speech
- Brackets ([]) indicate a significant pause
- Italic type in speech indicates emphasis

CHAPTER 3

"Edgy Sex . . . Not Just Boring Sex"

DAVID ALLISON: There were originally four of us who have known each other for as long as we've ever had a career. My first ever writing job back in the late 1990s was *Hollyoaks*, and so was Neil Jones, Chris Parker, and James Payne.

CHRIS PARKER: We met doing *Hollyoaks*, but since then I've spent almost a decade writing for *Coronation Street* and *EastEnders*.

NEIL JONES: David was pitching to Anne Mensah at the BBC. So he was pitching an idea of his own and, eh, it didn't go over and Anne said at the end of the meeting—

DAVID ALLISON: Off the back of *Life On Mars*, our mentor said, because that had been written by a team and that was quite unusual for British TV because everything is very authored and very single writer—

NEIL JONES: "What I'm *really* looking for is a show that's team—written by some writers who are already friends."

ANNE MENSAH: So I probably know what he means by "mentor." I don't know if I would use the same terminology. Because, if anything, it gives me too much niceness. It was more that, our tradition to develop for television comes from the fact that we have a really strong theater tradition, which is amazing—but it tends toward writers writing alone. I always thought that there was something interesting about writers choosing who they work with and at that time nobody was pitching for the shows that they came up with together.

DAVID ALLISON: She said, "Is there any group of people you would like to work with?" and I said, "I literally know exactly who that team is and we really, really want to do this."

NEIL JONES: David went, "Oh that's us! We're working on something." And we *weren't* working on anything at all it was just opportunistic, you know!

ANNE MENSAH: It was just being interested in David's writing but thinking, okay, is it interesting to get David and a bunch of people that he would choose to work with together? I thought that that was an interesting way of working.

And I like the idea of challenging conventional norms about how you work. Although lots of people had team-written before. But it was particularly the idea that they all knew each other. That was a fun way to do it.

CHRIS PARKER: We had that original brainstorm session in 2006.

DAVID ALLISON: We went away to a hotel for a weekend and we all had a go at pitching to each other erm a bunch of ideas. *Bedlam* was originally Neil Jones's pitch, my friend Neil.

NEIL JONES: I, I, I spend way too long on ideas. I have them gestating for absolutely ages before I think right "I want to pitch that." Probably too long really. And I had sat on it for a long time. In fact, I really didn't want to pitch it the day we all did our own ideas, so I pitched something else. And then I went, "I got this thing as well, you know, I'm not sure it's working really," and everybody went, "Oh yes, yes, that makes sense, that's good!"

DAVID ALLISON: So, I went to meet Anne and just basically, I said, "We've got four ideas here. Let me pitch them all at you."

NEIL JONES: I had the bones of *Bedlam* but eh, really it was just the bones, it was only putting it into that process with the others that made it into a real pitch.

DAVID ALLISON: And the one that she really liked was *Bedlam*.

ANNE MENSAH: I can't think of another piece that was playing with horror or young people, like a mix, a relationship drama . . . with a genre format. Not only do I think that it was unique then, I think that it is unique now. I love stuff that challenges expectations. That has relationships at the heart of it. Because sometimes relationship shows . . . they can be much of a muchness in as much as: there is the one who fancies that person. . . . How do you make them stand out of the crowd? To do something that was in the horror genre but that was also well written from a relationship standpoint, that was interesting.

NEIL JONES: My lasting memory of it was writing and writing and writing episode 1 over and over again during our BBC time.

DAVID ALLISON: I don't think there was a single person alive who didn't have a go at episode 1 at some point.

NEIL JONES: The show that came out was radically different from the pitched one on that day. It was quite a different beast. It was much more *Buffy*-esque . . . it was a female—Jed was a female protagonist in the original pitch. Jed was going to be a younger female cousin of Kate. It was a girl, a female flat-share. It was a lot frothier really than where it ended up. It was probably wearing its Joss Whedon influence a bit heavily.

DAVID ALLISON: When BBC Three was first sort of, taking off, we were going to be one of those pilots. But it just took forever and what was surprising to us is that it turned out they had another supernatural flat share drama in development called *Being Human*.

ANNE MENSAH: One of the tricky things about the BBC is that there is lots of stuff that's developed, all in one go.

NEIL JONES: At the time we were saying to the BBC, "Are you really going to do *two* flat share horror stories?"

ANNE MENSAH: And so, unlike where I am now, it is not my final say-so on whether something goes or not.

DAVID ALLISON: *Being Human* ended up being piloted and . . . we were a bit high and dry. It sort of staggered on for a little while but, we definitely felt like . . . there is a sense of "one in, one out" on those types of shows and, that we'd missed that window.

ANNE MENSAH: It just didn't quite make it at the last hurdle. And that was quite common. In a way, it's never an indication of the quality of the project because there is so much that's in development at the BBC. You are sort of fighting for space. Particularly at BBC Three at that time—I think that they might have only had one or two dramas a year. It was really tiny.

DAVID ALLISON: If it's in development with a channel, it's in development for "X" period of time but uhm, sometimes actually it can be exhausting and frustrating to get them to make the decision to say no because they'll hang you on, hold you on.

ANNE MENSAH: From my point of view, as soon as I have talked to my bosses at the time and knew that it wasn't . . . going to be one of the ones that are going forward. You put it into turnaround straightaway.

———◆———

DAVID ALLISON: That's, that's how it started uhm . . . was that . . . was that what had happened . . . ? I'm trying to think how did we end up? I mean, obviously, my wife [script executive Caroline Hollick] works at RED.

CAROLINE HOLLICK: I think because Dave and I are married, and I was very nosey about the projects that he was developing with Neil and Chris.

DAVID ALLISON: Uhm, that is obviously a shortcut, at times, because I don't like to work with RED too much but, but it's good.

CAROLINE HOLLICK: So I did go with *Bedlam*, "I really want it, I *really, really* want it!" and whether Neil and Chris err, got slightly bounced into it by me.

DAVID ALLISON: My wife is a real massive fan of the genre, so I know for her it was really exciting because she had been wanting to get her teeth into doing something like this.

NEIL JONES: [RED script editor] Richard [Fee] and [RED executive producer] Nicola [Shindler] and Caroline were all really *actively* involved in it and *all* played a massive part in the show.

RICHARD FEE: The script editor role can really vary from project to project. You know. Working with—Russell [T. Davies] for example—yeah, you're not going to be . . . giving, like heavy script notes, because it's the nature of who he is, how he writes, his relationship is very directly with Nicola. So [script editor in that case] can be a bit more of a . . . not administrative role, a bit . . . yeah . . . less actively creative. Whereas there are other projects, there is a much more active creative role for the script editor. To actually generate the story. And that applies to *Bedlam*.

CAROLINE HOLLICK: The script executive is a role that script editors take on when they have a role in the genesis of a project. Sometimes people have worked really hard to build relationships with writers and they work on a project which, you know, ends up with a green light. Sometimes trooping them through those, early stages. And, if they've been . . . involved very early on it's a way of marking that it's more a decision-making role within the development process.

DAVID ALLISON: I think, actually it was hard for Neil and Chris because essentially our creative person in charge, helping run us, was Caroline.

NEIL JONES: Caroline was a horror fan as well and she brought a lot to the table. She was *very* heavily invested in the show. She was very committed.

CAROLINE HOLLICK: I'm sure they went away and kicked the cat! Complained to their wives although David couldn't complain to his wife. Or sometimes he did. Sometimes he did.

DAVID ALLISON: It was weird, it was the first time we'd worked together and that was . . . you know.

CAROLINE HOLLICK: I know they were really keen to work with RED, and really keen to work with Nicola.

NICOLA SHINDLER: Executive producer? It means that I am over everything. So, from development ideas, giving notes—Caroline and Richard put it into practice and I give those notes, from agreeing the writers, from pitching it to the different broadcasters, overseeing all the auditions, choosing a director, a producer, watching it every single day when we are filming. Editing, marketing, press, selling it. Everything.

CAROLINE HOLLICK: And it was a departure creatively for RED. I don't think we'd done a genre show like that before.

NICOLA SHINDLER: I remember that conversation. But also, I actually *really* like genre so for me it was a natural progression. I really like watching horror. And ghosts. And thrillers. [Although it] doesn't mean that it is something I am good in just because I watch it either.

CHRIS PARKER: It's a real outlier in terms of RED's output because . . . up until and since really, it's always been kind of realism based, your absolute kitchen sink feel to everything, which is also the background we all came from, you know.

CAROLINE HOLLICK: People have got quite fixed ideas about what they think RED do.

CAROLINE HOLLICK: Nicola's—the RED aspect of *Bedlam*—I think that both Nicola and I feel that we brought to the table is—"does this feel real, does this feel credible?"

DAVID ALLISON: All that kind of stuff that could be told in any drama and is not supernatural. Treading that line, what is real, and what feels real to the audience.

RICHARD FEE: We get asked a lot by agents and writers, "What are you looking for?" Uhm. And, we don't know what we're looking for. We don't have . . . a set of criteria in our heads of *what* a RED show is and what we're looking for. If it's a really good story. If we feel really engaged with it. Then it's a RED show.

CAROLINE HOLLICK: Nicola was really excited about doing something differently that wouldn't necessarily come out of . . . the kind of *Clocking Off* . . . you know . . . that sort of tradition. *Bedlam* shows that actually we are really versatile. And not pigeonholed.

NICOLA SHINDLER: It was about testing ourselves and seeing whether we could . . . work in a genre that had such different rules from anything that we had done before.

CAROLINE HOLLICK: There was a very, very smart executive [at Living TV] called Amy Barham. Who is . . . *now* a writer/director working in LA.

AMY BARHAM: I was head of acquisitions for Virgin Media Television. Which meant that I . . . was looking after the budget for . . . all of the channels that we owned, which were Living, Bravo, Travel, Virgin 1, and Challenge. I would be doing the key buying for the big-ticket items, so *The Sarah Connor Chronicles*, *Grey's Anatomy*, and all that stuff. Given that all our channels basically ran on . . . US, Australia, or Canadian acquisitions, there would also be a lot of buying [. . .] of much smaller stuff. So my team would be trying to find those things before anybody else in the UK and license them before anyone else. For as low a price as we could (laughs). Once a year when the pilot screenings came out, we would go to LA with Johnny Webb who was our MD and Claudia Rosencrantz who was the head of television for all the networks. We would go and watch all the pilots at all the different studios and then decide on what we wanted to bid on. The other channels would all be doing the same and so there would be a bidding war.

CAROLINE HOLLICK: And Amy had been out to the LA screenings and she was really unimpressed with the quality of the shows that they were being offered.

AMY BARHAM: The acquisitions market got really insane in terms of the costs of licensing shows and when you're licensing a show you only own it for three years.

CLAUDIA ROSENCRANTZ: You put all your marketing and money into a brand that, you would suddenly be rebidding to keep. So you had no control over that property and the relationship between that property and your channel.

AMY BARHAM: Three years later you find that ITV have come in with a bigger offer on renewing and you've lost one of your key shows. There was at the time a lot of questioning of why we needed to spend so much money.

CLAUDIA ROSENCRANTZ: It did get to the point where it just seemed ridiculous.

AMY BARHAM: You probably heard the stories at the time, Channel 4 paying a million dollars for an episode for *Lost*, like that's not an exaggeration of where things got to.

CAROLINE HOLLICK: The new stuff coming up, Amy just found it really boring and expensive.

DAVID ALLISON: Living decided they wanted to commission their own original drama for the first time.

AMY BARHAM: Claudia Rosencrantz said, "This is insane, why are we not making our own? Then we would own it. And it would never be able to go anywhere else."

CLAUDIA ROSENCRANTZ: My overall strategy when I took Living, and all the other channels . . . there was a big job to be done of rebaking the cake and making it commercially successful. I needed to move away from the things I had inherited without undermining the success that they had delivered: weight-loss programs, soft features, daytime content that people go "Oh, women like that." I don't think women do like that in the evening. I think they like incredibly intelligent programs because, guess what, women are incredibly intelligent. The whole idea that women liked all this nonsense was rubbish. It was time for the channel to reach a new, mature phase in its life.

DAVID ALLISON: This is about the changing landscape, think about that, it's quite early for them to do that—so many channels now want original content, everyone wants original content, to own their own thing.

AMY BARHAM: I think that's all down to Claudia. Claudia came from [from being controller of entertainment at] ITV so she had that . . . confidence of being a major broadcaster in the U.K. and, the rest of us had all come up in cable and satellite, and so we had a cable and satellite kind of "ooh but can we? ooh but." And Claudia just came in and was like (*coolly*) "Of course we can." Not like (*sings*) "Yes we can! We can do it! We're the little engine that could!" She's like "We are not the underdogs. We are Living. Everyone should be wanting to work with us. Why would they not be?"

CLAUDIA ROSENCRANTZ: Scripted is an expensive genre, so I had to feel very confident the channel was ready to do that. It transforms the whole channel. It is a massive piece of branding.

NICOLA SHINDLER: And, you know, it is a really big step. I am actually doing it for the third time now, working for a channel on *their very first* scripted drama. And every time that happens it is really hard for the channel to—because they are paying so much more money than they would for anything else. But they are never paying enough money. Because they are taking a little risk. And . . . you have to reassure them all the way along that you understand what their audience needs while you are going to try and push for something good.

AMY BARHAM: And so because I was the person [as head of acquisitions] who had a focus on scripted content, I got put in charge.

CLAUDIA ROSENCRANTZ: One of the things I enjoy the most is trying to make sure people are doing the right jobs for them and are actually performing at their maximum potential. It has always given me the most pleasure, making sure people grow and change. I thought Amy had a very good eye, and she was flailing around thinking "I don't know if I want to do this. I don't know if I want to do that." It was obvious the things she gravitated toward and was good at—and the ones she wasn't—so. . . .

AMY BARHAM: Claudia, she just really believed that we could make it work and she is like *evangelical*, you just follow her because she's one of those people that you're "Yes alright, sure! If you're saying it then that's the way it's going to be I guess!"

CLAUDIA ROSENCRANTZ: It is part of my personality. I am quite feisty. I thought, well, you build it and they come. It is as simple as that. If you have very low ambitions, then how are you ever going to do anything? All the decisions I ever make really do seem to be slightly nuts at the time but, looking back, a lot of them have worked.

AMY BARHAM: Originally, we started thinking a bit as coproduction opportunity: is there a project in America or Canada that's a cable project that maybe we could put some money into? I started exploring that with agencies and production companies in the States and projects were coming our way and there was just nothing in particular that was like floating our boat. It was real . . . noninspiring stuff. And then Claudia and I sat down a couple of months into this and . . . she said "Maybe we should look at trying to fully commission something from a U.K. production company."

CLAUDIA ROSENCRANTZ: The first thing I did was hire [former ITV head of drama] Jenny Reeks.

JENNY REEKS: We were work chums for years.

CLAUDIA ROSENCRANTZ: Jenny has always been the best at commissioning extraordinary, accessible, compelling drama.

JENNY REEKS: ITV had its strands and I filled its strands. We had done classics. We had done cosy. We had done cop dramas. We had done investigative dramas. We had done factual dramas. But this was the first time I had the opportunity to work for what I thought of as a young, Channel 4–type audience.

CLAUDIA ROSENCRANTZ: I had to beg her to do this and drag her out of retirement.

JENNY REEKS: I had retired because I had been diagnosed with glaucoma . . . I had other health issues . . . boring stuff, I had cancer and things and I felt a bit more vulnerable. I thought "Hey, I had a great time so now I'll stop." But then I stopped and god it was so boring. And I felt an awful lot better, I thought "There is nothing wrong with me now." And so it just happened.

CLAUDIA ROSENCRANTZ: I said to her "I am not going to commission a piece of scripted unless you are overseeing it."

JENNY REEKS: I like Claud. She is a great girl.

CLAUDIA ROSENCRANTZ: Jenny is the person I really trust the most, to this day, on script.

AMY BARHAM: Jenny came on board. She's amazing.

JENNY REEKS: Looking back I suppose I was okay.

CLAUDIA ROSENCRANTZ: I just trusted her.

JENNY REEKS: This was a whole new world for Living and I wanted it to appeal to a younger audience but not to exclude an older audience. I did want it to be eye-catching. I met with Claudia and Amy and I told them all the companies I was thinking of approaching.

AMY BARHAM: She approached people, I don't remember us putting out any kind of a bid for it or anything, because we didn't want to be prescriptive about what people would come back with.

CAROLINE HOLLICK: People suddenly dug up all the scripts they couldn't get going anywhere else.

AMY BARHAM: RED came back with *Bedlam* quickly because they had developed it elsewhere.

JENNY REEKS: There were about sixty scripts and outlines submitted by different companies. Half of them were scripts and the other half were outlines. When I read the scripts, the first thing I did was jot down an aide-mémoire of my responses in this old exercise book. I bought it so I could write in things about my income tax but I never seemed to get around to that. *Bedlam*, I put "with a good look and a sophisticated approach this could a winning show. Needs snazzy central casting for Jed and Kate. I can't see it being as scary as *The Ring*, although it could do with more deaths." I laugh to myself now as I look at that. I was obviously anxious to escape the shackles of ITV. It's quite . . . *more deaths*, more shocking deaths.

I whittled [the sixty submissions] down to nine. I would have done big reports on seven or eight which I sent to Claud and Amy. The shortlist was *Bedlam* for RED. Shed had put in—they wanted to take *Bad Girls* further and call it *Very Bad Girls*. There was *Mammon*, from Jane Hewland's company [Hewland International]. Supernatural . . . about young, badly behaved bankers.

There was *Holmes and Watson* which was Left Bank, which is the one that, you know, Benedict Cumberbatch and all that. That was . . . we could have had. . . . That was quite a goer for us except that it needed a whole lot more money than we. . . . It needed U.S. coproduction. That obviously got made. Very famously so.

CAROLINE HOLLICK: We had a script. That makes a big difference when you're going out to other broadcasters. Rather than going with an outline and then having to sort of twist their arm to try and find enough money to pay for the script and—particularly if you've been working in acquisitions or factual entertainment where the . . . tariffs are so much lower—it can seem quite shocking how much money you have to pay for a pilot script.

CLAUDIA ROSENCRANTZ: The script existed. It was quite far down the road of development. I was very happy about that. It was a shortcut for us to turn it into a quality drama we could just get on with.

JENNY REEKS: No [the shortlist] weren't all scripts. It was very annoying when they weren't. If you are suggesting a series you should give a little bit more than an outline. I think it is very lazy not to have a script. But most of these people can't afford to do scripts on spec, so I don't expect it. But you definitely have an advantage with a script.

CAROLINE HOLLICK: It's a reasonably big investment for a broadcaster to pay for a script. You are talking thousands of pounds. So, you can go to a newer broadcaster like Living, who haven't commissioned any original drama. If they can read a script it's much, much easier for them to take a call on whether or not it's right for them.

JENNY REEKS: Of course. All those things. And, if you've got a script, for a start, you know if it's an absolute minger. And you know what you can contribute to it and where you can prop it up if it needs it. You might still want something, even if it's got a lot of problems, because there are other things about it—the writing may be dazzling, or they may have wonderful casting attached—that sort of thing.

AMY BARHAM: We definitely had an eye toward doing something paranormal because that's what Living is based on, and that's our core audience. I read the *Bedlam* script and I sent an email to Claudia, "We've found it, it's brilliant, it's exactly what we wanted."

JENNY REEKS: On my shortlist, *Bedlam* is top.

CLAUDIA ROSENCRANTZ: I read it and thought, "Yes this is absolutely perfect for Living. Perfect." To do a really quality piece of horror, I don't think that had done before on a pay TV cable channel. That was exciting. I personally can't stand [the genre] but our viewers love horror. It was a very good genre to kick off the first ever scripted series on Living.

DAVID ALLISON: And so, yeah, so RED took it to them and it was ready made.

JENNY REEKS: Well it was top because it felt right for the channel.

AMY BARHAM: And the production company is *amazing*.

CLAUDIA ROSENCRANTZ: RED and Nicola had made a lot of television for Jenny at ITV and she trusted their ability to deliver.

JENNY REEKS: They were a forward company. They were going places. Nicola Shindler, you know her pretty well by now I imagine? Intimidated? Oh no, she's fine. She's just a woman. A person. Come on. She's jolly nice.

AMY BARHAM: For me, a lot of it came from Nicola because I knew who Nicola was, I was very admiring of her as a woman and what she had achieved.

JENNY REEKS: She's one of these very confident women who were a generation on from me. I was kind of confident but not so confident if you know what I mean. She is a different sort of entity to me.

ANNE MENSAH: Nicola is one of the preeminent producers in the whole country. Genuinely, second to none. She is a completely unique individual. You don't get very many of those people that can run an entire company, run that many shows, deliver with quality to a number of different channels and outlets. She has done Netflix. She has done Sky. She has done BBC. She has done ITV. And she has done high-end, factual drama, right through to relationship shows. I mean, it's pretty singular. It is an amazing achievement.

AMY BARHAM: And how great Nicola was at making dramas that I had really liked myself as a viewer, just in my free time, and so for me I was just really like . . . flattered to be able to work with them because . . . I knew that they produced such quality stuff, and they'd won BAFTAs. They were basically the crème de la crème of the people you could work with.

NICOLA SHINDLER: I was very aware of the channel and what they wanted and I like working to a strong brief, I think it enhances your artistic journey not inhibits it.

CAROLINE HOLLICK: Living TV were very, very clear about their demographic, they knew exactly what worked for them.

CLAUDIA ROSENCRANTZ: I wanted Living to be for women. I wanted it to be the destination channel for women in pay TV—most pay TV subscribers were driven by male interests, like sport. I wanted to make Living very valuable so that in a household where there was a discussion about how money was spent, there would be something compelling for women. Perhaps, in a couple, there would be, "Well, you get your sport and I get Living."

JENNY REEKS: Claud was always good—very imaginative. A good brain. So confident too. To know what you think is a wonderful gift.

AMY BARHAM: We wanted it to be able to be something that our audience could sit down with their husband or their boyfriend or whoever they lived with, we didn't want it just to appeal to women we wanted it to appeal to a broad audience, with a slight skew toward female. That was basically what we were looking for: sexy, paranormal, sixteen to thirty-four.

CHRIS PARKER: I'm glad that we were . . . commissioned by Living because it forced us to put that female perspective at the center. And that was driven by the demographics of that channel. I'm glad that that was put in place from the start really. Because I don't think it would have felt like a priority to us . . . as three men at that time, to be honest.

CAROLINE HOLLICK: *Supernatural* was one of their biggest shows. *Ghost Whisperer* was going really well for them.

AMY BARHAM: We were talking about *Supernatural*, we were talking about *Ghost Whisperer*. Those were the two big ones. The longevity of those series was important to us because we needed to be able to think that this show could run for multiple seasons, in the vein of *Supernatural*, in the way that you have your core cast but they keep developing and different storylines keep coming up.

CHRIS PARKER: Living had done a lot of supernatural shows but they were mainly things like, uhm, *Most Haunted*.

NEIL JONES: They had all the *Most Haunted* stuff.

AMY BARHAM: I mean, *Most Haunted* [] for us? Yes, it was definitely a massive part of what we were doing and a massive part of Living and what people knew Living to be. And that audience were definitely a key audience we were trying to appeal to, but I don't remember us talking internally . . . as much about that as we were at just focusing on the drama side. Like what does this need to look like dramatically. It definitely needs to feel glossy. It needs to feel American.

CLAUDIA ROSENCRANTZ: We couldn't have some amazing piece of acquisition drama sitting next to some badly funded, badly made drama. That would look terrible.

AMY BARHAM: Our audience know us for very high production value drama, because it's come from a U.S. network where the budget is like two million an ep or whatever so we can't let them down with something that looks subpar, it has to look amazing. The money has to be on-screen. The stars have to be great stars. It has to feel American in the way that it's written and the pacing.

CLAUDIA ROSENCRANTZ: It had to fit with all the standards I had. I had very, very high standards.

AMY BARHAM: The writing—[the pilot episode] felt American in a way that I mean that as a complete compliment because it was written . . . pace-wise in a way that I felt our audiences would get. It was young people, it was sexy, there was sex in the first episode, and edgy sex as well not just boring sex, and it was a really good female character but also a really cool male character. And I loved the idea that there was this mental hospital and doing it up had woken up these spirits.

DAVID ALLISON: We had a well-developed script and a strong steer for the series. And lots of great ideas, we had more than enough ideas for episodes.

CHRIS PARKER: Nobody was really expecting a show like this. On Living in particular.

NEIL JONES: That's why they bit our hands off for it really.

AMY BARHAM: I could just see infinite episodes. Because of the big building [the series was set in]. But I also loved the arc of Kate, her dad and where we could go with that. Like how far would he go and then how far would she go and how much was the building making their decisions for them, and were they possessed? It got my brain firing so much. And obviously thinking from a budgetary point of view, we did need it to have a precinct. To enable us to build sets and to have one specific location that the majority of the action took place in because it would enable us to put the majority of our money on the screen, to really, really make that budget work. And so as soon as I see it's mostly taking place in this building, I'm like "that's the icing on the cake" [*laughs*].

CLAUDIA ROSENCRANTZ: I remember our finance director saying, "The road to drama is littered with failure. How do we know it is going to be a hit?" And I said

"Well it will be. Because I will make sure it is a hit and I will work with the right people who I believe can deliver a hit. It will work and it will be the right commission for the channel."

Amy Barham: And this was probably about a year into us having made the decision to do it so it just felt like suddenly, wow this is going to happen.

Neil Jones: So it was kind of like, episode 1 took years, and then all of a sudden Living went "Yes we'll do it."

Chris Parker: We were so thrilled that it hadn't *died*.

Nicola Shindler: I actually remember where I was standing when it was green-lit. At home, I remember being outside, convincing them that I could do it. In my back garden. It is weird, I don't remember many things in life but I really remember that. I have no idea why. I think it is because I was speaking to Claudia and that was unusual, because mostly I would speak to drama commissioners.

Claudia Rosencrantz: At this point I said, "As long as Jenny is happy, I'm happy. I will now let her get on." Between Jenny and Amy, they worked on the day to day of it because I was running thirteen channels or something. Sometimes I closed them. Sometimes I launched them.

Neil Jones: And there it was, we needed five more episodes!

Claudia Rosencrantz: Off we went at incredible, breakneck speed.

CHAPTER 4

Commissioning

I know we need to discuss what just happened. I get it. Chapter 3 is not what academic book chapters are supposed to look like. This is not a one-off either: chapters 6 and 9 and the coda continue in this scripted mode. From here on in, this is how things are going to work: we will have a scripted chapter that furthers the story of *Bedlam*, then we get a prose chapter with analysis of scripted content, followed by a companion chapter on what I am trying to do structurally with this book. So, for now, bear with me because rather than going all-in on what *that* was in the last chapter, I first want to think about what chapter 3 might tell us about commissioning practices in television drama.

Channel commissioners and heads of drama in Britain wield a huge amount of power over screen storytelling, yet there is little academic attention paid to what they do and why and how they do it. Commissioning is defined here, in the words of Caitriona Noonan, as the activities of a person or a team "with decision-making powers around commissioning content," where "power is exercised through relative creative autonomy and budgetary control" through "a dedicated commissioning editor who is supported by a team of editorial and production specialists."[1] Commissioning studies are underexplored in television studies, screenwriting studies, and production studies. Laura Mayne's article for *Journal of British Cinema and Television*, Hyun Jung Stephany Noh's essay for *Journal of Japanese and Korean Cinema*, and Florian Krauß's study for *Journal of Popular Television* are the only recent examples published in traditional film and television studies journals.[2] Anna Zoellner leads the study of commissioning and commissioners in media and communication studies (where more production studies work tends to be found), publishing nuanced, thoughtful analyses of the industrial development of ideas, based on firsthand ethnographic fieldwork.[3] In their monograph *Producing British Television Drama: Local Production in a Global Era*, Ruth McElroy and Caitriona Noonan dedicate a subsection of a chapter to the commissioning process and the role of the commissioning editor, understood as "operating as an intermediary between the broadcast organization and the program supplier."[4] They offer several useful definitions of this role, which I will come back to later in this chapter. For the most part however, when production studies explores commissioning, it is usually through a rigorous sociological or business studies underpinning and published in media studies journals.[5]

In contrast in screenwriting studies, attention is often "focused on the very process of how films or television series come into being," which is a more useful starting point for us.[6] Early on in her book on Danish television drama, Eva Novrup Redvall asks, "Where do ideas for television series come from? How do writers, producers and broadcasters settle on the ideas to pursue and what are the stages and challenges in developing ideas into series for the screen?"[7] This focus is paralleled in Ian W. Macdonald's book on screenwriting and the "screen idea," published the same year. Macdonald suggests that the screen idea is a way of thinking through "what lies behind what is on screen—beliefs as well as practice; what individuals or teams are contributing; what institutional structures relate to their activities; how orthodoxies and common norms are (or are not) applied" etc.[8] We can see how this approach has value for reading through the genesis of *Bedlam* at the BBC, but it does not necessarily give us the grounding in commissioning that I am looking for.

Similarly, in *Screenwriting: Creative Labor and Professional Practice*, Bridget Conor defines screenwriting as "an industrial, marginalized, individualized, collaborative and exclusive form of work," an often contradictory set of adjectives that creates an accurate sense of the experience of being a writer within a system of industrial work practices.[9] This resonates with the experiences of *Bedlam*'s writers and cocreators as they were put into turnaround at the BBC, before being picked up by the wife of one of the writers, who worked at RED. But, as before, this position focuses more on the individual writer(s) within the larger system rather than those who have power within the institutional structures of the system itself. As such, while existing screenwriting studies provide a valuable intellectual underpinning for this work, they understandably foreground the experience of the writer. There are exceptions, not least in the work of Marilyn Tofler, Craig Batty, and Stayci Taylor, but they are in the minority.[10]

Given this relative lack of material on television commissioners and commissioning practices, in this chapter I bridge the division between these disciplines. Drawing on the material generated in chapter 3, I explore how television texts are shaped by different types of practitioners (screenwriters, production company staff, broadcasters) and how these practitioners operate in relation to each other within and across different institutions (freelancers, production companies, television channels). I illuminate the multitude of incremental ideas and decisions that led to the commissioning of *Bedlam* and demonstrate

how commissioning is deeply imbricated within existing professional and
personal networks in television production.

THE 2000S: AMERICAN TELEVISION/BRITISH SCREENS

American television drama dominated British satellite and terrestrial channels
in the 1990s and 2000s. Paul Rixon has studied acquisitions staff at broadcasters during this period, arguing that buying and scheduling are "dynamic" roles,
albeit ones "guided, limited and constrained by the wider socio-ideological-
economic-industrial context."[11] Here, I want to extend these principles into a
consideration of the contexts of commissioning original British television drama
in the 2000s. Horror, science fiction, and fantasy series were particularly appealing genres for broadcasters during this period, their decision making led by the
popularity of *The X Files* (1993–2018), first airing on BBC2 in 1994; *Buffy the
Vampire Slayer* (1997–2003), arriving on BBC2 in 1998; and *Angel* (1999–2004),
screening on Channel 4 from 2000.[12] The American acquisitions had aesthetic
and narrative appeal for British audiences. American dramas seemed "much
faster, glossier, and more exciting than their British counterparts," which had
"been steeped for much longer in a naturalist/social realist tradition" and a
"studio *mise-en-scene*."[13]

The U.S. acquisitions also made financial sense: the programs "recovered their
high production costs in the American market, and then were sold to the United
Kingdom at relatively low rates; in turn the U.K. broadcasters were attracted by
these imports as they attracted a fair size audience while costing far less than
commissioning domestic productions."[14] The dominance of American imports
was particularly apparent on smaller television channels such as Five and "youth
skewing satellite channels, such as Sky One and Trouble," which relied upon "US
imports to attract their target demographic."[15] By the mid-2000s, even the major
terrestrial channels recognized the popularity of American television drama.
Large broadcasters such as ITV significantly increased their buying at the annual
Los Angeles pilot showcase. In 2007, Jay Kandola, then director of acquisitions
for ITV, bought a show from every U.S. television network showcasing work that
year. She explained that she wanted the U.S. studios "to understand that ITV
was back in the market for US shows and you have to put your money where
your mouth is."[16]

In the same year that Kandola made a splash in Los Angeles, Claudia Rosencrantz took on the role of director of television for Virgin Media. Prior to her
work at Virgin, Rosencrantz was controller of entertainment at ITV, where she
commissioned many of the channel's most successful television series, including *I'm a Celebrity, Get Me Out of Here* (2002–) and *The X Factor* (2004–).
Rosencrantz's new role involved running Virgin's portfolio of digital entertainment channels, including Living TV, Bravo, and Virgin 1. These channels ran,

in the words of Amy Barham, Virgin's head of acquisitions, primarily on "big-ticket" U.S., Canadian, and Australian acquisitions. As she explained in chapter 3, Barham and her team "would be trying to find [a big drama series] before anybody else in the United Kingdom and license them before anyone else, for as low a price as we could." However, with the entry of ITV and other big channels into pilot season, the market was undergoing radical change. Barham and Rosencrantz discovered that while they were still able to secure U.S. imports, retention of those imports proved to be increasingly difficult. Shows were renewed every three years, and as Barham explains, other channels such as ITV would come in "with a bigger offer on renewing and you've lost one of your key shows." She reveals, "Claudia said, 'This is insane, why are we not making our own [drama]? Then we would own it. And it would never be able to go anywhere else.'"

Due to the high cost of commissioning, developing, and producing original drama, Rosencrantz's decision was a major outlier for commercial British television in the 2000s. Her vision demonstrates an early recognition of original television drama as a "premium" product for a subscription channel, a premium that "enhances the value proposition of subscription services" because "distinctive content helps secure viewers' willingness to subscribe."[17] Rosencrantz also concurs that making original television drama "is a massive piece of branding," a comment that reflects the cultures of television executive work in the 2000s. As John Thornton Caldwell explains in *Production Culture: Industrial Reflexivity and Critical Practice in Film and Television*, published in 2008, "With the current proliferation of programming choices and the expansion of channel competition during the digital era, branding has shifted from its status as an off-screen concern of marketing personnel and ad agency research to a self-conscious form of promotional reflexivity that has also altered the very look and sound of contemporary television."[18]

While Caldwell is writing on American television cultures, many of his ideas are translatable to the specifics of our British case study. Rosencrantz's explanation of her decision making serves as evidence of the changing climate of executive-level television making in the 2000s. In addition, we can also see how she is utilizing the language of branding culture as director of television for Virgin Media. In this role, she oversaw many channels, including Living, and as she notes, Barham and Reeks "worked on the day-to-day of [*Bedlam*] because I was running thirteen channels or something. Sometimes I closed them. Sometimes I launched them." It is specifically her role as director of television that gives her the bird's-eye view of what the channel can be, allowing her to lead on the "branding" of the new version of Living as "valuable" for "women" and what that might look like in terms of audience and content.

In addition, her recognition of branding goes beyond channel identity and filters down to the script. Caldwell argues that "all screenplays are branding opportunities," that a script is "a financial prospectus, a detailed investment opportunity, and a corporate proposal."[19] Rosencrantz recognizes that while she "cannot stand" horror, the paranormal focus plays well to her intended audience for the channel. Her position reflects the undervalued work of scholar Brigid Cherry, who has for decades systematically pointed out the extensive female audience for horror, particularly for women from their mid-twenties and older.[20]

Here, the paranormal subset of horror is also important: as Amy J. Vosper has explained, the supernatural and psychological subgenres of horror have found the most favor with female audiences, while the least popular are exploitation and rape-revenge.[21] This suggests that the intended audience is gendered by genre. Rosencrantz's maneuvering can be read through Julie D'Acci's canonical work on women television audiences in the 1970s and 1980s, where "first, network television sought to amass viewers already defined as women, in and by their social contexts, to watch particular programs" and through publicity, scheduling, and advertisements to "*imply*" and "construct" a "gendered audience."[22] Rosencrantz is aware that there is an existing audience of women for Living that she wants to retain, but then she wants to build upon their loyalty while also attracting new women with her original commission.

Finally, Rosencrantz's foresight to commission original television drama for her newly branded channel is made more prescient if we think about streaming services at the time of writing this book, in the early 2020s. Consider how many contemporary scholarly articles on streaming services start from the position that we have now, in the United Kingdom, shifted away from advertising revenue to "subscriber-based economic models"—a full decade and then some after Rosencrantz's proposition.[23] Given this, the commissioning of *Bedlam* can be read as an early progenitor for not only the streaming of horror for individualized audiences on services such as Netflix but also genre-based subscription on demand streaming services such as Shudder, which curate horror-based content for niche audiences.[24] These findings suggest that chapter 3 is useful not only for telling unknown practitioner stories but also for providing a snapshot of a pre-streaming digital service in the 2000s, of British television culture in transition.

THE 2000S: FEMINISM AND BRITISH TELEVISION STUDIES

In his essay "Television Studies: Plural Contexts, Singular Ambitions?," published in 2004, John Corner writes that "in some cases, a stronger and more precise dialogue with past theory" (and he's thinking here about ideology but I'm reappropriating it for feminism) "might have helped to bring greater benefit to the work of moving on." He explains that "it is clear that some of the frameworks of analysis that have taken the place of the older ones have not immediately contributed much more by way of clarity and cogency" and in the new schemes "the political hardly features at all, or else is dispersed into the cultural and everyday so extensively that, in analytical practice, it is hardly to be discerned."[25]

I take these principles to now move forward with a feminist practice of my own: an illumination of women's work in commissioning television drama.

In 2013, Rachel Moseley, Helen Wheatley, and Helen Wood published their "Television for Women" dossier in *Screen*, working through their "explicitly feminist and historical" AHRC-funded project "A History of Television for Women in Britain, 1947–1989" (2010–2014). They point out that "the notion that we are interested in television *for*, and not necessarily *by* or *about* women has often been difficult to grasp, or has been misunderstood, by those to whom we have explained the research."[26] Nonetheless, they still make a case for the need for "a thorough historical interrogation of gendered address through which the value of women's television culture and its relationship to feminism and social change can be addressed."[27] In the dossier, Julia Hallam argues that most academic work on gender and television in the 2000s tended to "rely heavily on textual analysis and theorisation," and there have been "few attempts to understand the ways in which female creatives, defined here as producers, writers and directors, influence the depiction of female characters and their issues and concerns on the small screen."[28] I acknowledge the importance of the gendered address of television, a concept central to feminist work in television studies, and I also acknowledge the importance of Hallam's point about the limitations of textual analysis for theorizing women producers. However, I take my reading in a different direction than Hallam, rejecting the implied relationship between women producers and women characters. Indeed, as Brunsdon pointed out almost twenty years before the dossier, "There is the issue of the extent to which the gender of the producers *does* determine media output."[29]

So, given that feminist television criticism has historically been carried out across multiple disciplines, "including film studies, communication studies, mass communications, cultural studies, sociology, English, women's studies," where each "disciplinary context" governs "the construction of the object of study and the methodologies explored," what might I want to do here with the women whom I have interviewed, whose voices we hear so clearly in the previous chapter?[30] This book sits at the interstices of production studies, screenwriting studies, and television studies, a useful hybrid not only given the long history of feminist work on British television but also because "production studies *is* a feminist methodology" that resists or complicates "traditional power hierarchies" with "a capacity to highlight cultural inequities."[31] As Vicky Ball and Melanie Bell write in the introduction to their special issue "Working Women, Women's Work: Production, History, Gender," published in the same year as the TV for women dossier, this kind of work is not about prioritizing "issues of representation" but about considering "women's experiences within production cultures" in order to shed new light on "women's industrial participation."[32]

In 2018, the Writers' Guild of Great Britain revealed that "the percentage of television episodes written predominantly by women" was only 28 percent, while in the same year Directors UK disclosed that the number of U.K. television episodes directed by women had fallen to just 24 percent.[33] Nonetheless, women now account for around 45 percent of the workforce of television production in the United Kingdom, so where are the women working? In *Bedlam*'s case, the commissioning and development of series 1 was led at the production company by two women executives (Shindler, and script executive Caroline Hollick) and at the satellite channel by three women executives (Rosencrantz, Barham, and Reeks). This is typical of long-standing industry working practices that reinforce a gendered distinction between working on set and working in the office, a distinction that reinforces a traditional patriarchal understanding of creativity as something that the men do (in the male-dominated on-set spaces of production) while the women "toil" in the office or, increasingly, remotely, undertaking the emotional, legal, and administrative labor required to set up and maintain creative projects. However, as I now make clear, commissioning roles are not simply support roles. They are, in fact, a particularly rich area for feminist analysis.

I am not the first academic to be interested in a production-based account of a RED series. Ruth McElroy and Beth Johnson have both explored the work of Nicola Shindler, founder and former chief executive of RED. Shindler is one of the leading figures in British television drama, a venerated and garlanded television producer. In recent years she has been presented with the BAFTA "Special Award," one of BAFTA's highest honors, and has been awarded an OBE for services to broadcasting. Both McElroy and Johnson draw on original interviews with Shindler and in so doing consider how Shindler's articulation of RED as a production company relates to *Happy Valley* and *Scott & Bailey*. Three important points then come out of their research. McElroy states that "as scholars we need better to understand *what television means for the women who make it* as well as for those who watch it."[34] This gets us closer to one of my areas of interest: Who makes television drama, how is it made, and why is it made in the way that it is? Johnson then reflects upon the importance of undertaking original interviews with the people who write and create television, arguing that "the voices of the Shindler and Wainwright are integral to the shape of this piece."[35] Finally, both McElroy and Johnson write about the relationship between writer, executive, and production company, evidencing a growing interest in this kind of work.

Christopher Meir has also examined RED's drama production, exploring "several important continuities between the pre- and post-acquisition versions of the company," thereby highlighting "the importance of distribution partners in television drama production."[36] While his work is valuable, it attends to the end stage of drama production, and I am focused on a deeper understanding of the beginnings of television drama projects. In addition, Andrew Spicer and Steve Presence have explored RED using an "organization, business and management studies" approach.[37] Their framing shows promise but in the end reveals little about how creativity—and thus the practices of creating and refining storytelling—is supported and developed within the company. They then argue that "production companies are not only invisible to the general public, they are also, it appears, invisible to media scholars who continue to be preoccupied with individual writers and directors such as Paul Abbott or Shane Meadows," claiming that such scholars lack "an understanding of the importance of these companies' production cultures to their creativity."[38] Given that Spicer and Presence cite Johnson's monograph *Paul Abbott* and Melanie Williams and colleagues' edited collection *Shane Meadows: Critical Essays*, they are clearly talking about these publications and writers in particular.[39] This kind of territory marking is depressing to read, and it does not further innovation and experimentation in our discipline. The production culture of an organization *is* central to understanding creative process, but their one-upmanship "organizational cultures" model reduces the collaborative complexity of RED to a factory room floor.

Reading Spicer and Presence's article crystallized my desire to focus on the human side of television making. It reminded me that I am most interested in people, in their thoughts and feelings, and in how these thoughts and feelings affect the decisions that they make in their creative work: Who is working with whom? When and why are they working together? Do they have a history, and is it a good one or a bad one? What dynamics of power are brought to bear upon their contribution through the status of their roles and the roles of those around them? This is the lifeblood of television drama: scores of individual people, experiencing, working, learning, refining their craft in the service of making television drama, in whatever form that might take as writer, script editor, script executive, executive producer, or channel head.

According to McElroy, since the late 1990s the number of women working at senior roles in British broadcasting has significantly increased, which has resulted in women having "direct control of a significant percentage of public service broadcaster's commissioning." This control emerged during what McElroy describes as "a period of major change in the history of television," namely "the development of an increasingly multi-channel, competitive digital market in television production, and one in which an increasing proportion of television was getting made by independent production companies, many of whom had women in senior leadership roles."[40] As RED founder and former CEO Nicola Shindler explains, "There are so many more women in senior . . . commissioning, in decision roles, producing roles" (as compared to those working production), and "with a lot of the development process and commissioning process, it is possible to have a normal life."[41]

Prior to Virgin, Rosencrantz was controller of entertainment at ITV, where she commissioned many of the channel's most successful television series. In contrast, Barham reveals that the rest of the team at Virgin had "come up" in cable and satellite and had an "ooh but can we? ooh but" mentality. But Rosencrantz "just came in and was like 'Of course we can.' . . . 'We are not the underdogs. We are Living. Everyone should be wanting to work with us. Why would they not be?'" Given this context, Rosencrantz's prior experience enabled her to pitch for and secure the funding for an original television drama. Rosencrantz put Barham in charge of the project and then hired Jenny Reeks, former head of drama at ITV, as an executive producer. Reeks had commissioned many dramas for ITV, including *Doc Martin* (2004–), *Cold Feet* (1997–), and *Footballers' Wives* (2002–2006), and it was her job to fill all of ITV's drama strands, including "classics, cosy, cops, investigative, factual."

Reeks was keen to be involved because "this was the first time I had the opportunity to work for . . . a young, Channel 4-type audience." Her recruitment was vital to the success of the project. As a former head of drama for ITV, Reeks had a proven track record in working with independent production companies to seek, commission, and then nurture long-running and much-loved television drama for ITV, the largest commercial channel in the United Kingdom. The depth and breadth of experience that Rosencrantz and Reeks brought to the project then created a culture of confidence that enabled high-risk, first-of-its-kind commissioning practices. This finding parallels with Natalie Wreyford's work on the British film industry, where she found that "where conditions of high risk and uncertainty prevail, individuals use risk reduction strategies in their recruitment processes such as a reliance on the opinions of trusted or powerful individuals." She explains that these individuals "in turn reduce their own perceived risk by working with screenwriters who are known to them either professionally or personally."[42] The decision to create original drama is still a high-stakes activity today, more than a decade after the discussions at Living took place. As Shindler confirms, a broadcaster commissioning their first drama is a major step because they are taking a risk and "paying so much more money than they would for anything else."

At this point, Reeks—while officially credited as an executive producer—began to take on the unofficial role of a commissioning editor. McElroy and Noonan describe this role as a "powerful gatekeeper," predicated upon "expert knowledge" that is based around a "creative instinct which interprets audience tastes, attempts to predict demand and positions content."[43] The commissioning editor typically works with a team of staff who reach out to the production sector, but in Reeks's case she did this work herself, drawing upon her extensive network of contacts in U.K. independent television. Over sixty scripts and outlines were then submitted for her consideration, demonstrating the "pre-existing close relationships" that commissioning editors have with "key production companies, literary and screen agencies" and that although "in theory pitches are accepted from all-comers, in practice the opportunities for pitching are limited," which reinforces "a hierarchical system," "enforces gatekeeping," and "concentrates decision-making (and finance) to a small number of senior staff."[44] As Barham notes, Reeks "approached people," including RED. Rosencrantz explains that this was because "RED and Nicola had made a lot of television for Jenny at ITV and she trusted their ability to deliver." RED then submitted several projects to Reeks, including the pilot script for *Bedlam*. Reeks whittled the sixty submissions down to nine and wrote long reports on "seven or eight" (including several supernatural stories), commenting on the story, casting, and financial viability. Financial viability was paramount though: *Holmes and Watson*, later renamed *Sherlock* (2010–2017), is not at the top of Reeks's list, as it needed more money and to be a "U.S. coproduction," a collaboration that Living had, by this stage, explored and discounted.

We can see how Reeks, in her analysis of series submissions, works through the connections between the script, the intended audience for the channel, branding, and genre. Here Reeks performs an important commissioning role, which interweaves financial limitations with editorial consideration. This position chimes with Caldwell's point that "in feature film and in prime time, at least from the buyer's point of view, a fictional scenario is always tied to and considered alongside an economic one."[45] Reeks then placed *Bedlam* at the top of her shortlist and sent her reports to Barham and Rosencrantz. Barham read the *Bedlam* pilot and emailed Rosencrantz, stating, "We've found it, it's brilliant, it's exactly what we wanted." Rosencrantz concurred, "This is absolutely perfect for Living."

There are many reasons why *Bedlam* was such a strong fit for the channel. First, Living's existing American television acquisitions guided their decision making in several ways. Rosencrantz was keen to move away from the previous incarnation of Living, which focused on "soft" "daytime" content such as weight-loss programs, commenting, "The whole idea that women liked all this nonsense was rubbish. It was time for the channel to reach a new, mature phase in its life." Living served its audience's demand for horror television with *Ghost Whisperer* and *Supernatural*, but *Bedlam* presented an opportunity to create homegrown content. Rosencrantz confirms that horror was a "very good" genre for the "first ever scripted series on Living."

Next, the *Bedlam* pilot was built upon a self-contained story of the week, populated by "returning regular characters," thus appealing to both "a loyal, watch-every-week audience and a floating audience, who only watches sometimes."[46] The pacey and sexy style of the story-of-the-week script "felt American," to quote Barham: it was "young people, it was sexy, there was sex in the first episode, and edgy sex as well not just boring sex," with "a really good female character." We will discuss story more in chapters 6, 7, and 8, but it is worth pointing out here that commissioning a drama that "felt American" in the 2000s was about not just its supernatural content but also how that content could generate story longevity. As Barham explains, Living wanted a "show could run for multiple seasons, in the vein of *Supernatural*, in the way that you have your core cast but they keep developing and different storylines keep coming up."

The third important factor for commissioning was that *Bedlam* was a polished pilot script. *Bedlam* had been honed during years of prior development at the BBC, where it was originally developed for the BBC Three channel launch, before being rejected. If you pitch a script outline to broadcasters, Hollick explains, you must "twist their arm to try and find enough money to pay for the script." And if that broadcaster has worked primarily in "acquisitions or factual entertainment" the tariffs (that is, the price the broadcaster pays to screen a program) "are much lower." It can be shocking to broadcasters "how much money you have to pay for a pilot script. . . . You are talking thousands of pounds." Rosencrantz is more direct: "The script existed. . . . I was very happy about that. It was a shortcut for us to turn it into a quality drama."

This leads to the fourth rationale for commissioning: the cultural cachet of working with RED, and specifically with Shindler, RED's founder. Shindler has won eleven BAFTAs for British television drama and was awarded an OBE for services to broadcasting. As Anne Mensah explains, "Nicola is one of the preeminent producers in the whole country," a rare person who can "run an entire company" and "deliver with lots of quality in high-end, factual drama, right through to relationship shows" to "a number of different channels and outlets" including Netflix, Sky, BBC, and ITV. Barham admits that a lot of *Bedlam*'s appeal originated from Shindler and her company "because I knew who Nicola [Shindler] was and what she had achieved"; that RED "were basically the crème de la crème of the people you could work with." As already noted, RED had established good working relations with Reeks from prior ITV collaborations. Working with RED (and thus Shindler) offered security and significant cultural capital for Living, making *Bedlam* a particularly prestigious first original drama.

Craig Batty and Dallas J. Baker argue that the development of scripts is often guided by "the principle of improvement," which raises questions of quality. They ask, is quality "speaking to the *content* of development (what makes a good drama)" or "the *context* in which is takes place (what is the budget; whose vision is it; under what set of rules is it funded)?"[47] We can reappropriate these questions for the commissioning stage of television drama: Is it the content of the *Bedlam* script that secures it commission, or is it the context in which *Bedlam* emerges as a viable proposition for production? Here, content and context are intertwined. The script content appeals to the broadcaster's intended demographic, but just as much, if not more, the importance of the weighting is on the context (the broadcaster's vision for channel, Living's perceived demographic, and the cachet of working with RED). The quality debate is thus exemplified by Batty and Baker's "conflict verses content" proposition, where the content of the script, essentially the "art" of the writing, makes *Bedlam* initially appealing, but ultimately it is the script's ability to work within Living's business contexts that secures the commission. As Anamik Saha points out, "Commodification is at the core of the work that the cultural industries do, transforming an aesthetic expression of culture into a commodity to be bought and sold."[48] Arguably, in this case study, the commodity is Shindler and RED's career history: this is what secures *Bedlam*'s sale to Living.

CONCLUSION

While working on the second draft of this book, I had lunch with Kate Larking at Senbon Sakura in Leeds. Kate is a television producer who regularly works with RED. I told her about my *Bedlam* project, and the first thing she asked was, "Who produced it?" Despite having then worked on this book for two years, I was at a loss to reply (it was Matthew Bird for series 1 and Peter Gallagher for series 2). There are many reasonable justifications I could have given Kate for my lack of knowledge. First, I could have said that I was most interested in the development process, during which producers played a smaller role, or that I needed to draw a line somewhere under the exploratory fieldwork stage for the book to ever actually materialize. I could have then argued that to explore producers and production properly, the way I would want to do it, would be a whole other book, requiring participant observation right from preproduction, rather than a study after the fact. But I didn't say any of these things. I just shrugged, embarrassed, and dug deeper into my bento box.

Kate's question revealed a more prosaic truth, one that I had not acknowledged before tucking into my chicken katsu. The fact is that if *Bedlam*'s producers had been women, I would have probably reached out to them. During the writing of the second draft, I realized that I had grown more and more interested in the stories of the women executives on the project, a true hidden labor of production almost never recognized beyond the television industry itself. As Lez Cooke wrote nearly twenty years ago, traditional studies of television have "tended to subscribe to the 'great man' theory of history in which individual men (rarely women) are identified as being responsible for historical landmarks which are, apparently, achieved solely through their individual genius," and "this role has been associated primarily with writers."[49] By studying commissioning, we have an opportunity to uncover the creative contributions to story and storytelling made by other people within the industry.

Commissioning also offers an opportunity to respond to Caldwell's suggestion that we need to understand both business and economic decision making within the industry as part of better understanding the television text itself. He advises that academia has "created an odd form of mutual 'othering' where critical theory stands as the marginalized 'other' in industrial analysis, and where business functions as the marginalized 'other' in critical theory."[50] The decision making of Rosencrantz, Reeks, and Barham, as executive-level broadcasters, demonstrates his contention that many industry executives understand the connections between text and industry and "seldom shy away from weighing in on economic *and* aesthetic value."[51] Just how much they understand these connections will become more apparent in chapter 6, as we follow *Bedlam*'s series 1 scripts from pitch to production.

Then, in illuminating the voices of *Bedlam*'s women's executives, I attempt to avoid a common pitfall when academics research women in the film and television industries. This pitfall is composed of a generic series of interview questions: How does being a woman contributor change or shape the content of the script? (And here the inference is, usually and reductively, in relation to the representation of female characters.) Or what is it about being a woman that affects day-to-day work? Or what does it mean to be a woman in the boardroom? This is an unhelpful, homogenous approach to dealing with gender and its intersections, an example of the kind of thinking that relates to the "burden of representation" long explored in Black critical theory, in Kobena Mercer's work on Black art, and in Stuart Hall's politics of representation.[52]

Studying commissioning also offers another trajectory for studying women's work in media production. As Erin Hill notes, "Occupational segregation" of certain types of media production work perpetuates "male domination in fields with the greatest prestige and power, the most creative status, and the highest incomes."[53] These depressing and dire facts are born out in the traditional "creative" roles in *Bedlam*. In series 1 men held all the writing, directing, cinematography, music, editing, and production design positions. However, by studying the commissioning (and, in chapter 7, the script development) of *Bedlam*, we can illuminate the power of commissioning roles for women workers. The *Bedlam* story so far actually reveals the limits of the male writers' powers: writers can be proactive, taking the meetings, creating the pitches, deepening and refining working relationships to secure their own networks of support and development, and, not least, writing scripts. But, ultimately, for the male writer-creators to get *Bedlam* on-screen, a whole team of women—at the executive level—push the project forward.

———◆———

Let's pause for a moment though.

Ask yourself, what do I want, as a reader?

Do you really need me to do this? You don't need my words to wrap around the scripted content.

But here's the problem.

Isn't the analysis *the aspect of the writing that makes it scholarly*? In removing the academic discourse that legitimizes the inclusion of the interview material, in not writing about what the quoted words given might *mean* for interpreting television drama, what are you left with?

If we don't interpret the text (whether that be a television episode or interview content), what happens? In "Against Interpretation," Susan Sontag argues that "whatever it may have been in the past, the idea of content today is mainly a hindrance, a nuisance," that "by reducing the work of art to its content and then interpreting *that*, one tames the work of art. Interpretation makes art manageable, comformable."[54]

What if we don't want to conform? What if we don't want to tame the data with didacticism? Is it only when the material is sufficiently controlled, molded by that dry academic hand, that it becomes worthy of your attention?

In the next chapter, I continue to reflect on chapter 3, but this time I ask, if we're not analyzing the content, what might we talk about instead?

CHAPTER 5

Form

The first draft of this book was partly inspired by Rachel Cusk's novel *Outline*, which I read on holiday with Zosia in Valencia. Zosia picked up *Outline* in the bookshop in Manchester airport, enticed by its stark, minimal cover. It's a short book, and I read the whole thing on the flight on our way home. It suited our holiday vibe, as in *Outline* Faye goes to Greece to teach creative writing. Faye is neutral, almost flat, and *Outline* is built upon people talking at her in long, uninterrupted monologues. In a *New Yorker* interview about *Outline*, Cusk explains, "What I'm trying to show . . . is the thing . . . that everyone has an entitlement to, and an ownership of, is form, a sense of literary form. Or artistic form." She suggests we learn form early in our lives: "It's when you get into an elevator, everyone behaves—it's a form," and crucially, "if someone violates the form, everyone's really embarrassed." She continues, "Everyone uses sentences the way they'd drive down Fifth Avenue—because it's there, because someone decided it should be Fifth Avenue, and you should go down it. The sentence, the literary sentence, came to seem a lot like that for me."[1]

This chapter uses Cusk's position as a starting point for thinking about academic form. There have been numerous studies of televisual form, of how the narrative patterning of programs are developed through industry practices and how these practices and formal expectations change at different points in time.[2] However, I have found little reflection on writing *about* television within television studies. In her analysis of form in narrative fiction, Suzanne Keen explores the tools and techniques that fiction writers use to craft stories, noting that "whether they work in inherited traditions, by habit, deliberately, unconsciously, according to formulas, in imitation of admired precursors, or with the deliberate aims of experimentation and innovation," writers use language as a tool to "build fictional worlds" and to create narrators who "introduce readers to imaginary persons who move, think, feel, and act, in those patterned sequences of events that go by the everyday name of plot."[3] Keen's ideas might help us better understand and deconstruct the "inherited traditions" of academic form—in terms of both integrating interview material and writing about television in general. In this chapter I explore how and why I created the script chapters (the story of *Bedlam* from pitch to cancellation, across chapters 3, 6, and 9 and the coda) and how they might work with the prose chapters. I ask, what do we understand by form in television studies? When we write about television drama, how are we supposed to do it? In other words, what is our discipline's equivalent of driving down Fifth Avenue? And then, the most interesting bit, how and why might we want to break form?

How to Use Interviews in Television Studies

You might remember that back in chapter 2 I told you about my inability to write this project as a traditional article. While I had many problems with this project (not least over eighty thousand words of transcript to parse), my major issue was my refusal to engage with the interview material in what appeared (to me) to be an appropriate, academic manner. In short, I did not want to subsume my practitioner interviews, their words and voices, into traditional academic form. Having bailed, shamefaced, on the journal special issue, I did some hard thinking and realized that the first thing I needed to do was decide *how* I wanted to utilize the interviews. So I turned back the canonical books on television drama for guidance.

I began with George W. Brandt's *British Television Drama in the 1980s*, published over thirty years ago, but which remains an exemplar for how to write about British television. Each chapter analyzes the work of a television writer. It offers a potted production or transmission history, a close narrative and visual analysis of a play or serial that he (and with the exception of Fay Weldon, it is always a "he") has written, supported with reference to relevant "highbrow" criticism (e.g., *Sight and Sound*) and social and cultural context. For example, Andrew Lavender's study of Troy Kennedy Martin's superlative *Edge of Darkness* (1985) covers transmission history, background on Kennedy Martin, genre, a description of key scenes in the narrative that are then placed within the social and cultural context of the Thatcher government, and anxieties about the nuclear threat. It culminates in Lavender concluding that *Edge of Darkness* remains "in any estimation, a uniquely emblematic response to its time."[4] Lavender's article is a classic exemplar of how to organize and present criticism on television drama, and I've used it many times in my own teaching. But in terms of form, there is almost nothing here for me. If you are keen to consider the stories of the practitioners, rather than the stories in the text, then how do you go about it?

I moved on to an examination of how interview material was integrated into more recent studies of television drama and concluded that there are four main ways to work with the words of practitioners. Kristyn Gorton's excellent articles exemplify the first approach, in which she interviews television writers Sally Wainwright and Lisa Holdsworth, and writes up the results as single interview-articles.[5] However, as stand-alone pieces that focus on one person, they do not offer a model to integrate the multitude of voices that I hoped to achieve.

The second approach can be found in the work of Robin Nelson. Discussing television production in the 1990s, he states, "The entertainment value of TV drama has come to be placed above other possible functions of usable stories such as, in Dennis Potter's words, 'discovering something you did not know.'"[6] Here, Potter's words, taken from a *Guardian* interview, are included to substantiate Nelson's own point of view. There is no further reflection on Potter's meaning, nor on the context for the original interview. I'm often frustrated by academic articles that draw upon quotations from practitioners taken from popular press; I can't help but feel that much of the time the quotes may well be taken out of context, either from the original interview or between practitioner and critic. It makes me think of Susan Stewart's comment in *On Longing*, where Stewart suggests that "the quotation appears as a severed head, a voice whose authority is grounded in itself and therein lies its power and its limit."[7]

There's also a lack of acknowledgment of the constructed nature of interviews and how practitioners choose to present themselves to the world. This is something that Julia Hallam picks up in her monograph, *Lynda La Plante*. Hallam reveals that La Plante chose to not give access to herself or to her archives, and as such chapter 1 of her book is a "compilation of the public knowledge she has chosen to reveal about herself rather than an in-depth search through her personal archives." Hallam suggests that "all biographical writing is a form of storytelling," and as such, when she pieces together an account of La Plante's life "based on anecdotes recounted to journalists (usually with the intention of promoting her latest work)," this "is no less an account than one based on personal memory, reflection and recollection. . . . La Plante's fundamental talent is to tell stories that entertain."[8] Hallam's perceptive point here is that there is value in constructing La Plante's biography through interviews with journalists. However, what is more important for us is Hallam's acknowledgment that interviews with journalists are a constructed series of stories to serve a specific purpose. But if you don't want to use interviews from other sources, what do you do?

The third approach is demonstrated in Ian Potter's *The Rise and Rise of the Independents: A Television History*. This book aims to engage scholars and fans and utilizes direct quotes from production staff. But the quotes are utilized uncritically as explanatory discourse in a history of U.K. independent television, and like Gorton and Joanne Garde-Hansen, I am "wary of simply utilizing memories for filling in the gaps of history or to construct a more cohesive history" of television.[9] We can also see how the writer is hidden in Ian W. Macdonald's analysis of *Emmerdale*, which rarely includes the voices of those whom he writes about; they remain subsumed within his explanatory discourse. Ultimately, Macdonald is less concerned with the individual and more interested in talking about, from his point of view, "how the system works to create a particular kind of text, and how it comes to be that way."[10]

Jonathan Bignell and Stephen Lacey's *British Television Drama: Past, Present and Future* also mirrors the model of including quotes from practitioners to deepen academic readings. Their book includes first-person short essays from practitioners reflecting on their work histories (such as Irene Shubik working on *The Wednesday Play*) and academics drawing on first-person material (such as when Madeline MacMurraugh-Kavanagh draws directly on Shubik's *Play for Today* book in her own chapter).[11] In this collection, John Caughie's chapter on acting includes traditional prose analysis, supplemented at the end by a coda. The coda transcribes a statement given by actor Timothy West, then presents an extract from a conversation between Caughie, West, actor Prunella Scales, and screenwriter Alan Plater, presented in much the same form as my chapter 3, but spanning only half a page. The chapter concludes without reflection on this material.[12]

There has not been a huge amount of development in this third mode over the years. In 2019, while I was still wrestling with the first draft of this book, the *Journal of British Cinema and Television* published a special issue on RED productions (this was, of course, the special issue that I had withdrawn from). Meir and Spicer's introduction makes a good case for the importance of studying RED, pointing out that 2019 marks the twentieth anniversary of the first broadcast of *Queer as Folk*. They situate the issue within the "industry turn" but point out that production studies tend to favor large (North American) companies, while most British indies are small. The aim of their special issue, then, is to foreground "how it is the production company itself that mediates and synthesizes these forces, creating the conditions for talented writers . . . to do their work."[13] This position makes sense and speaks directly to some of my own aims and aspirations for this book. They also explain that "this is also the rationale for including interviews with key RED personnel, Shindler and Hollick," that beyond "new insights into RED and its inner workings" the interviews provide "readers with original primary source material for future research into the company."[14] However, the two interviews remain frustratingly stand-alone; extracts are dropped into Spicer's article but are included to buttress the explanatory narrative.[15]

In her study of FX's remake of *The Bridge* (2013–2014), Annette Hill offers an excellent example of the fourth and final technique for integrating practitioner interview. With an enviable team of researchers working across a three-year period, Hill conducts qualitative ethnographic research, including forty production interviews with creatives and executives and participant observations during production. Hill's method and questions come closest to my own; she has precise questions (such as "why was *The Bridge* axed?") that are answerable, she has excellent access to television drama practitioners (and, as a large, externally funded project, on an enviable scale and scope far beyond my own), and she prioritizes their responses and opinions in considering how to answer her questions. Crucially, the practitioners are responding to her direct research questions, a situation that creates high-quality, original research findings.

However, when it comes to form, Hill includes the interviews into a past-tense prose narrative that interweaves critical analysis and thinking, interview extracts, and summary of findings from the ethnographic research. For example, in an interview with showrunner Elwood Reid, she explains that he "was keen to avoid what he saw as the failure of adaptations like *The Killing* (AMC, 2011–2014), where even the jumper worn by the lead actress was the same in the Danish and American versions: '. . . I'm not going to follow the original because our show will die if we keep following what they are doing.'"[16] As with many of the television studies examples I draw upon here, there is nothing wrong with this model (I used elements of it in the last chapter when I examined commissioning). I certainly could have used this method to write up the whole book. It makes a lot of sense, and it would have made writing this book *a lot* quicker (sigh). Hill writes fluently and engagingly and employs original, outstanding qualitative data. Yet she is still working within the conventional paradigm that states that you introduce a practitioner, quote them, then bind their words into your own, relating it to the larger theoretical project, subsuming the practitioner into a seamless, dyadic whole. But ultimately this is not what I am interested in, and it is why this project fell to pieces when I tried to write it up the first time as a journal article for Meir and Spicer: no matter how much research I do in television studies, that form, as the *only* form to play with, no longer appeals.

In working through these books, I grasped that my desire to play with form was born of these frustrations with television studies. I didn't understand how, or why, television studies did not, on the whole, engage with interview material in any depth. Television studies has always loved texts, and it has always loved people: but the people it has historically been interested in are real and intended audiences rather than makers. It is only when we shift focus to production studies (and to the adjacent and overlapping creative labor and cultural industries) that we begin to find the makers, to hear their voices. But even here this body of work isn't *formally* doing what I want either.

So where do we go now?

Transform What Is Taken for Granted

When I hit a dead end with television studies, I went back to Didion (obviously). I began to research her writing as part of New Journalism, a retrospective categorization of a form of narrative nonfiction writing "which revitalized reporting as a form of storytelling while giving shape to many of the cultural changes occurring" in the 1960s and 1970s.[17] While there are different models of reportage, most writers working in this mode "emphasize the world view of the individual or group under study, and show an absorption in the aesthetics of the reporting process in creating texts that read like novels or short stories."[18] This piqued my interest as it prioritized three of my favorite things: researching, people, and stories. I then discovered David Eason's scholarship on New Journalism, which he divides into ethnographic realism and cultural phenomenology. For Eason, Tom Wolfe, Gay Talese, and Truman Capote's reports are "ethnographic realism," while Didion and Norman Mailer's publications are better understood as "cultural phenomenology." Ethnographic realism gives "accounts of 'what it is that's going on here' that suggest 'this is reality,'" however cultural phenomenology describes "what it feels like to live in a world in which there is no consensus about a frame of reference to explain 'what it all means.'"[19] I've already touched upon how phenomenology underpins the thinking in this book, and we can see here how cultural phenomenology as an approach allows us to think deeply about form, story, and voice (that is, chapters 5, 8, and 10). Bound up with concerns of literary style, cultural phenomenology can thus also be read as an epistemological strategy "that constructs as well as reveals reality. In ethnographic realism the dominant function of the narrative is to reveal an interpretation, in cultural phenomenology to show how an interpretation is constructed." In this model, Didion's writing is a "multi-layered interrogation of communication" that focuses on "the experiential contradictions that call consensual versions of reality into question."[20]

This is why I have been so drawn to Didion's work while working on this project. Didion's reportage is focused not on the stories "discovered out there in the world but *the story of the writer's efforts to impose order on those events*."[21] I am uninterested in simply *telling* you about a specific program and how it is made. Instead, I tell a story about the construction of how we approach the study of the subject as well as a story of the subject itself. This model considers the way the world is made through individual and shared experience, that is, a subjective and explicitly *constructed* take on living and experience where there is *no* fundamental real life to reveal. All we have are our interactions, feelings, and experiences. Cultural phenomenology is a framework that enables this project to tell a story about telling stories. It creates opportunities to ask bigger questions that go beyond the remit of the analysis of a single television drama: In what ways might we change the writing and reading of a book on television? If we don't study the television text, what might become the object of interpretation? What might experimentation and innovation of form offer such a study? What might a transformation of what is taken for granted—in terms of academic form—actually look like? In her *New Yorker* interview, Cusk promises violation of form and *Outline* delivers it. What might violation offer us as a way of rethinking the way that we write?

While I was musing over this in 2019, I read Lizzy Goodman's *Meet Me in the Bathroom: Rebirth and Rock and Roll in New York City, 2001–2011*, an oral history of New York's music scene post-9/11 (which has since been made into an excellent documentary). Goodman writes that "we were all—every kid in the crowd and every person on stage—chasing the same thing . . . we were all chasing New York City. And for a few magical years we caught it. This book is an attempt to capture what that felt like."[22] This intimate documenting of feelings really resonated with my creative endeavors for this book: an attempt to locate, secure, and articulate an ephemeral part of creative process. The only problem was that I had already read a great deal of social science methodology on interviewing and had discarded the framing of the *Bedlam* interviews as oral history. In academia, qualitative interviews typically concentrate on a particular experience or phenomenon, while "oral histories deal more broadly with a person's past, [often] ranging over a wide range of topics, perhaps in the person's life from birth to present."[23] Given that I am concerned with one specific period in my interviewees' lives (the period of the commissioning, development, and production of *Bedlam*), oral history didn't feel appropriate. Yet when I read *Meet Me in the Bathroom*, I identified the possibilities of presenting material through the direct point of view of the participants.

In her chapter on the band Yeah Yeah Yeahs, Goodman begins,

> NICK ZINNER: The way we write is essentially waiting for Karen to be inspired by something. Once she enters that world, then you can follow. It's just melody, shape and will. Getting into that world, where you're not hyper-judging everything and overthinking. . . .
>
> KAREN O: How do I know when I've got something? It's totally unintellectual. I feel almost like a little kid. I get, like, butterflies in my stomach or I get a wave of euphoria or I get the chills or I cry. I have very visceral and physical reactions to it. . . . It's a different kind of intelligence, emotional intelligence. Your intellectual mind sucks, you know? I wish I could just put that part of my brain away for good.[24]

The oral history presented directly, in a manufactured conversation, felt like coming home. This was the form I wanted to work with. *Meet Me in the Bathroom* is not the first book to do this of course; its shape and structure acknowledge canonical music oral histories that have gone before, including Legs McNeil and Gillian McCain's seminal *Please Kill Me: The Uncensored Oral History of Punk*, which has its own "Cast of Characters" and organizes its interviews in the same way.[25] Quoting the interviews in this way, one after the other, as conversations on the page, allowed me to fashion the story I wanted to tell.

While music oral histories may seem an unusual reference point, we can draw major parallels with polyphonic interviewing in feminist social sciences. In polyphonic interviewing, "the voices of the respondents are recorded with minimal influence from the researcher and are not collapsed together and reported as one through the interpretation of the researcher. Instead, the multiple perspectives of the various respondents are reported, and differences and problems encountered are discussed, rather than glossed over."[26] Polyphonic interviewing was popularized by Susan Krieger in *The Mirror Dance: Identity in a Women's Community*, an experiment in both language and method. *The Mirror Dance* "describes and explains its community's dilemmas exclusively through the voices of community members." Krieger explains that "the book reads rather like a novel in that it proceeds by association, by ordering the stories of many different individuals to create a sense of a whole. Its analysis emerges through its ordering: in the way it juxtaposes, compares and connects the different viewpoints it represents."[27]

While I do not go as far as Krieger, who reveals "there is no authorial voice in the body of work, except in the first chapter" and that "the voices of the community alone analyze and comment upon one another," I am still influenced by this approach and specifically the recognition that the selection and arrangement of material is in itself a creative *and* analytical act.[28] In addition, Krieger's desire to arrange her material in a novelistic fashion is important; the chapters on *Bedlam*'s production are organized chronologically but are demarcated by key peaks and troughs of television development, emulating the arcs of classical narrative structure (which I will talk about much more in chapter 8, on story).

Using oral history as a mode of exploring film and television production is well established in trade and academic publishing. Becky Aikman's *Off the Cliff: How the Making of* Thelma & Louise *Drove Hollywood to the Edge* draws extensively on cast and crew interviews. However, her quotations are wrapped into a long-form nonfiction narrative, Aikman providing setting and detail and intimacy through narratorial devices, switching tenses to accommodate: "Geena realized she *became* Thelma in Susan's presence, slavishly admiring her maternal competence. And Susan found Geena funny and loopy in a way that only someone intelligent can pull off. 'She was game and brave and smart and certainly more diplomatic than I was,' Susan says. 'That's the basis for a love story really.'"[29] Jonathan Abrams's terrific oral history *All the Pieces Matter: The Inside Story of* The Wire comes far closer to my project, as Abrams directly quotes cast and crew as the main body of the work. However, Abrams recaps the development process himself. The last line of his recap is about Carolyn Strauss, the president of HBO's entertainment division at the time: "Strauss purchased the pilot and asked for the scripts for two additional episodes before finally greenlighting the project."[30] At *this* point, the oral history begins. But it's the intangible, ephemeral, agonizing process of development that fascinates me: where Abrams recaps is precisely where I want my oral history to exist.

Nonetheless, Goodman, Aikman, and Abrams's oral histories provided a way to get the words down on the page in a form that satisfied me. I discovered that I could present the story, in the practitioner's own words, as a very basic, stripped-down, script format, which illuminates personal narratives and makes space for the incoherent and contradictory social and emotional reality of drama creation (something eminently lacking in most academic accounts of television practitioner work). The choice of the noun "script" to describe the form of chapter 3 (and chapters 6 and 9 and the coda) is also important. Dallas Baker explains that "despite the clear scholarly value of a creative and critical artefact at all the stages of its existence, the unproduced script is relegated to the margins of both film scholarship and writing scholarship." He argues that scripts are still considered in both industry and academia, a "textual other" that are "rarely seen as complete creative works but rather as blueprints for a finished product" and as such "are rarely studied, debated or discussed in their own right." Baker uses "script" and "scriptwriting" as opposed to screenwriting as a way to emphasize that his text is the primary artifact "of a writing practice," and "by not signaling the mode of production or reception (stage, television or cinema), the term 'script' hopefully reorients the reader from approaching the text as ancillary to a staged or screened production to understanding it as a finished creative and research work on its own terms."[31] It also speaks to the recent turn in screenwriting studies to value scripts as completed documents: as Levi Dean points out, "Scholars have successfully argued that the screenplay is a literary document within its own right, regardless if it is mediated into a moving image."[32]

The script also mitigates the problem where a single practitioner interview is inserted as a "truth," a fact proven, spoken by the person who was there. I've already been through this, at the start of this chapter, and as I think is probably clear now, I reject the use of interviews (often from other sources that have nothing to do with the research) to verify or support academic readings. Instead, my scripted chapters present a constellation of memories, a collage of fragments stitched together through the story of *Bedlam* from beginning to end. By complementing the prose chapters with scripts, I use screenwriting to put into practice Gorton and Garde-Hansen's theory that "memories in circulation, full of their subjective experience, powerfully shape and inform our understanding" of television's "past, present and future."[33] Arguably, subjective experience doesn't just *shape* television drama's history though. We can retool it, to *make* a new version of it. Please note this "a" caveat: even as I create script chapters, my story of *Bedlam* remains a story, not *the* story. I am not trying to "fill the gaps" of history. The scripts represent interviewees "doing memory work: staging their memories, performing them."[34] They are personal narratives, with a limited temporality that illuminates this one point in these people's lives when they made an original drama series together.[35]

Sadly, my *Meet Me in the Bathroom* revelation about form—the decision to present the interviews as a script—did not make this book any easier to write.

Rather, the scripted format then posed a new set of questions. What precisely do I *do* with the script chapters? How do I organize them? I understood then that to structure the script chapters successfully, I needed a narrator and a reader. I needed character and a plot. I needed arcs, turning points, and cliff-hangers. And I will talk you through how I organized, framed, and directed this narrative in chapter 8.

Conclusion

In *Interpreting Television*, Karen Lury argues that analyzing the formal dimensions of the television text is important, "not just for the way in which they can illustrate how programs 'make meaning,' but how they are, *in themselves*, meaningful."[36] Here, paraphrasing her point, I suggest that my script chapters are, in and of themselves, meaningful, for the form they take, the story they tell, and the voices they illuminate. Here, by "meaningful" I mean scholarly. Although we have covered only the commissioning of *Bedlam* so far in the script chapters, I am still confident that we have answered two of the three research questions I posed about *Bedlam* in chapter 2: Why did RED make *Bedlam*? And why did Living TV commission this series? (The question about why horror will be answered shortly, I promise.) I'm equally confident that you could answer these questions by reading only chapter 3. I don't think you need to read chapter 4, on commissioning, in order to get these answers. Chapter 4 *is* an opportunity to deepen and reflect upon this knowledge; but, if we are honest, for the reader, the knowledge is already there. So, if you concur that the script answered those research questions (which I hope you think were fair and reasonable when you first read them), what does this suggest about traditional academic form? Why is a unified prose chapter, composed of synthesized interview and analysis, better than a stand-alone script of original data that readers can utilize to make their own judgments?

The first chapter suggested that the time has come to reconsider what it is we are doing when we study television drama (just as Brunsdon, Corner, Geraghty, and Corner did in the late 1990s and early 2000s). I suggested that method is the place where we now need to do the most work, but I want to make clear, right now, that I don't believe offering scripted chapters is the answer to the problem I posit. Remember our cultural phenomenology leanings. There is not one answer. There is not one way to rewrite television. The script chapters are a model for thinking about what different kinds of approaches there might be out there and thus furthering the discipline's development into its next phase. By drawing on feminist social sciences and oral history methods for interviewing, and on communication studies approaches to cultural phenomenology for organizing the interview material, this chapter also demonstrates how the ideas of different disciplines may have much to offer us.

I'm aware that my approach is contentious, in fact it probably really annoys you if you are a paid-up member of the television studies community, particularly if you write on television drama (and even more so if you write on British television). But even if you are cross with me, wouldn't you agree that this violation of form really does feel like, in Brunsdon's words, "*the edge* of the academic"? That, for the first time in ages, we are negotiating once more "what is proper to address" in television studies and "in what terms"?

CHAPTER 6

"That's TV, It Isn't Like Writing a Poem"

CHRIS PARKER: It felt like the whole process went on for years but actually the writing, brainstorming it, to writing it once we were commissioned, I think it took six months or something. It was just a very intense six months.

AMY BARHAM: We wanted to write all six before we went into production. We needed to know for, ahm . . . purposes of greenlighting it. Everything. We needed a very solid idea of what every episode was going to look like. And we knew it would be six eps.

CHRIS PARKER: When we'd got an episode finished it was like a *massive* relief and we knew we had to get on with the next one. I know six doesn't sound very much but . . . it felt like an awful lot.

DAVID ALLISON: You all do it together. You hammer it out. We had lots and lots and lots of meetings. Lots of very long meetings. Lots and lots and lots of them. Constantly.

NEIL JONES: Basically, we just went to Leeds all the time. We didn't even have a meeting room we went to Seven.

CHRIS PARKER: It's a sort of art center cafe.

NEIL JONES: In Chapel Allerton.

RICHARD FEE: It was a good space because it was relaxed, quiet, we could have a big table. We'd do, generally two days, have breakfast there, have lunch there, and work into the evening, and finish with a drink. In those early days, a lot of it was about . . . narrowing down on exactly what the DNA of the series was. Because we were trying to match a number of briefs.

DAVID ALLISON: The idea of *Bedlam* was you have the anthology series so it was a different story of the week, it was like a ghost *Play for Today* essentially, and it would allow you to just enjoy all the tropes of that genre and to do ghost stuff and horror stuff . . . but you did it in a world where there is a continuing story because there were characters living there.

RICHARD FEE: The intention was to do this horror supernatural show. That was also a young person's relationship drama. That had story of the week done in one episode that you could tune in and watch without necessarily having to . . . have seen, you know, the past four episodes or whatever. So we had to hit all of those briefs.

NICOLA SHINDLER: Yes, but you know what, that is quite normal. The only thing that is not normal now is the story of the week. We never do story of the week anymore. That has gone out of fashion. I think audiences really like story of the week but broadcasters don't. Now we tell story over a much longer time period.

CAROLINE HOLLICK: I *like* the fact that when we set this up with Living there were like these commercial parameters that we had to make work. That's TV, it isn't like writing a poem. It's a commercial process.

NICOLA SHINDLER: Yes. You need to make sure that you are keeping people as entertained and hooked as possible. And especially on a channel like Living, when there were adverts. Because we had to hook into every advert break as well.

NEIL JONES: We just spent hours and hours in Seven, just talking stories.

DAVID ALLISON: We talked about it a lot and we mapped it out a lot and we changed it a lot and we thought things out a lot.

CAROLINE HOLLICK: What the writers really understood, is how much genre needs a strong mythology. You have to set up your rules and your world.

AMY BARHAM: We'd been pitched paranormal stuff [by other production companies] that like, didn't add up. Our viewers are smart and they knew their paranormal backwards so if you were going to write paranormal for them you'd better have some fricking rules in that world because they were not going to stand for airy fairy, "oh they can come in this portal but they can't come out that way," there had to be rules.

CAROLINE HOLLICK: What we'd normally do is, sit round the table and talk about . . . the serial stuff first, and really, the key is where you're going to end. I learned from *Bedlam*, the importance of having a *number* of voices in the room in that early development stage. And it just allows you to really *bold* with your hooks and back story.

CHRIS PARKER: Caroline and Richard allowed us to kind of come up with crazy ideas and we knew if they said "no" then that's that, we can put that behind us. But we trusted them that they knew exactly what they were doing.

RICHARD FEE: So we would all work together on the world building and the serial arcs of characters—which was a big part for Living, you know.

DAVID ALLISON: It's weird because you can't just write your own thoughts completely. You're almost trying to work out a house style. It's really interesting and so definitely some of the interesting discussion was about, "Well, does that sound *Bedlam* or not?" Even though we're just trying to work out what *Bedlam* is: "Does that sound right?"

CAROLINE HOLLICK: Neil did a brilliant job with . . . often having the really *bold* ideas about . . . where the arc story was going to go and I don't think we could have . . . we couldn't have done it without . . . that very strong sense from him of that shape of the series and the mythology.

RICHARD FEE: Neil . . . is brilliant. You know.

CAROLINE HOLLICK: It was quite unusual, particularly not to have one lead writer so much. It had initially been Neil's idea, and Neil was the real genre expert, so he was the closest that we came to a lead writer.

NEIL JONES: The three of us all had our hands on every story really. I think it's probably . . . the, the background that we came from. It was our collective soap experience that made it really, because we had spent a lot of time sitting around tables, structuring things between us. That was probably what made it what it was I think, what allowed us to do it as a team. And that was probably the big difference . . . in writing *Bedlam* and writing a conventional show, really it was . . . uhm . . . a communal process. Although we would have each come with, "Well I've got an idea for a story." We really put each idea through the collective grinder.

CAROLINE HOLLICK: One of the things I learned from *Bedlam* actually is that when you're story lining, the more people you have in the room the better. We replicate that elsewhere now in other shows, using people from the development team. You sit somewhere and bounce ideas, because then we can work out what stands up and what doesn't.

DAVID ALLISON: One thing I really love about the show is that I feel like it's that, I can see all of us in it and it became this thing that we all owned and we're all part of.

NEIL JONES: Perhaps because we were . . . we were friends. It was like being in a band. It was as close as we ever got to being in a band I think.

CAROLINE HOLLICK: I love that. Long as I wasn't Yoko!

NEIL JONES: Everyone talks now about the American writing room system and how that's becoming more of a thing . . . in Britain. But really that was what we were doing, in an informal way, we were all working on all of those scripts at every stage.

CHRIS PARKER: And that's where Richard Fee comes in really because he was kind of . . . he was there at every stage brainstorming stuff with us.

RICHARD FEE: In those early days, because I was new, I was very much [] I wasn't probably the first person to be jumping in with ideas and thoughts. But equally, because I *hadn't* been there from the very start I was in a unique position in that— fresh eyes—so I could be maybe a bit more . . . objective about things and just having a different take.

NEIL JONES: I don't think Richard was there originally. Emily Feller was our original script editor.

RICHARD FEE: I saw this job come up at RED. Emily Feller rang me up and said, "I'm going on maternity leave do you want to do some cover?" And I said, "Yes, definitely!" Ehm, cos *everything* that Nicola has script edited was all the stuff that made me want to work in drama, really—*Our Friends in the North, Cracker.* So. I jumped at the chance, I moved to Manchester. It was a bit of a strange experience because I hadn't been there at the start. So. That project at that point, I was not only trying to figure out . . . what the project *was*, what the writers were like and who Caroline was, but I was trying to figure out my role as a script editor within RED.

CHRIS PARKER: We were [in Seven] almost every week, we would go there to discuss stuff.

RICHARD FEE: And I was probably . . . doing a lot of listening and trying to work out, how the land lied and, exactly, what the nature of the project was. I've had experiences on other shows where . . . you book a function room or something, for these writers' meetings, and you've got a whiteboard and generally no windows ahm . . . and it can feel a bit oppressive. There's something about being in the buzz of a café with stuff going on.

CHIS PARKER: We'd all come from that sort of half hour soap background. Everything is very much . . . *decided* and worked out in advance before you even put pen to paper. [In soap] we'd got a foundation to work on when you start but with this we were just so up in the air, we were constantly asking [] "Yes that's a great idea but . . . can we actually make that work?"

DAVID ALLISON: Often the ideas that didn't make it *sound* really good and when you take them apart there's not enough there.

CHRIS PARKER: We'd think we'd got a story nailed and then we'd pull a thread of it and it would all fall apart so we'd have to go back and start again.

CAROLINE HOLLICK: Sometimes there were just things that didn't work, so we kept having to come back and try it again, try it again, try it again.

RICHARD FEE: That's hard. But when you get it right, it can be great. Actually . . . in that context, *interruptions* are sometimes useful. Somebody bringing drinks, and loads of teas or whatever. Just breaking your train of thought . . . can . . . trigger something. Or, start you down a new path. Whereas if you're just sitting in a room with four white walls staring at each other, sometimes you can have [*laughs*] long periods of silences where [] you're struggling to . . . break through the problem.

CHRIS PARKER: It was only six episodes [] but each one required so much thought and brainstorming [*smiles*]. Loads of our original ideas got thrown out, they just didn't stand up.

CAROLINE HOLLICK: It did take us a little while to . . . get the format of the stories right. How we were telling . . . ghost stories, that was the biggest challenge.

DAVID ALLISON: It was a lot of fun because we talked a lot about what was scary.

JENNY REEKS: My first note was that it was not scary enough.

AMY BARHAM: It needs to be scary. This was the time when *Paranormal Activity* had just come out. People wanted to be scared and those things were doing well and people liked *Most Haunted* because it scared them.

CHRIS PARKER: Drama doesn't have to have that sort of black-and-white in terms of the reaction but [] really every episode had to have those *scare* moments.

JENNY REEKS: I thought it could "ping" more. More shocks.

AMY BARHAM: And so we were like, "How do we make sure that in each episode there's like one big shit your pants scare?" That comes out of nowhere so you don't want to watch this alone. So it can become an event that you may want to watch with your friends because you're a bit scared that something—is going to happen.

NEIL JONES: [In the 2000s] there was all the Asian horror, J-horror [film]. The desire to do the series and use technology and the familiar objects that we have around us and try to make them scary and unfamiliar.

DAVID ALLISON: If you're dealing with water you're dealing with *Dark Water*; you're dealing with Asian horror.

NEIL JONES: And also del Toro and all the European stuff. *The Orphanage*.

CHRIS PARKER: Have you seen *The Orphanage*? The one I like is *Candyman*.

NEIL JONES: It felt like it was being done in film but it wasn't really being done on . . . telly.

CHRIS PARKER: One show we were watching and we admired a lot was *Being Human*. [] I forgot! I forgot that it was a direct [] competitor.

DAVID ALLISON: Neil was sometimes going, "God I don't want people to feel . . . ," I said, "we're not ripping something off, we're trying to tell these stories," you know, horror tropes are horror tropes.

CAROLINE HOLLICK: Horror always has images that you have to recognize.

DAVID ALLISON: They're really hard to do because, they've got to be *massive* and outlandish and dark as buggery, so you do go "Oh god this could be *so silly* if it's not done properly."

CAROLINE HOLLICK: Horror can just . . . the narrow line between brilliant, and scary and clichéd. It's really hard.

AMY BARHAM: That was always our worry was that it was going to come out looking like a joke or a bit hokey. Again, that was why we were referencing American drama.

DAVID ALLISON: So often the answer was not to show the thing. So often.

JENNY REEKS: Editing makes things scary. Have you ever seen a film when it is cutting from this to that, and you see the tension in somebody's eyes, and then you're seeing a shot: "What is happening? Oh my god! This is terrible. I am hearing a sound. What is that?!" Editors will do that for you. They are underrated, undersung.

DAVID ALLISON: I think the other big challenge in the series was. To believe that a group of people would stay in that building [*laughs*]. You know [the audience has] to suspend their belief because they know they're getting the horror of the week.

RICHARD FEE: I think horror does lend itself well to story of the week. I think it's probably quite hard to do . . . serialized horror on telly. When you're breaking the tension at the end of every episode. In the traditional TV landscape, the broadcaster wants the audience to come back every week. And if you're doing stand-alone stories, you're kind of giving them an excuse not to come back next week. Which is problematic. So it's trying to find that balance.

DAVID ALLISON: The uneasy truce in the storytelling is between story of the week and long-term series relationship. You know, the characters interacting with each other and the things that are happening that are *real*, like a human being is.

CAROLINE HOLLICK: I loved, loved, loved working with the writer's team, we would problem solve *so quickly*. But you had to be quite careful that, ahm, to both listen to everybody's ideas but also not to get bogged down really. Once we had a kind of a broad sense of a shape, we would then . . . literally have a kind of a document with columns in where—sometimes it would be Richard actually making decisions about what could go into each episode that felt like a balance.

RICHARD FEE: And that's a changing document obviously, because—you might get halfway in and realize that something's going to become more important than you thought, or, or less important, so it's an ever-evolving document.

CAROLINE HOLLICK: Sometimes someone just has to make a decision, and go "Right, we'll do that, that, that and that." And then you've got something written down.

CHRIS PARKER: He helped us to road test story, point out weaknesses in the story. He was kind of like story editor and script editor [] and almost like a producer to a certain extent.

CAROLINE HOLLICK: We would bash out kind of where we wanted to get to, and then do a quite general overview.

RICHARD FEE: Then take it Nicola.

CHRIS PARKER: We'd have meetings directly with her. When we felt we had a story that was solid, we would discuss it with her, so nothing would go any further until she'd said "Yes I kind of like that." She had a very instinctive reaction to the story whether they were good or not. Whether they had enough about them. It was very, very . . . helpful.

CAROLINE HOLLICK: Because what we didn't want to do was three days going down a route . . . to give to Nicola and she just goes "This doesn't work."

NICOLA SHINDLER: At each stage, I read and give notes, read and give notes.

RICHARD FEE: We'd need to get her input on the big stuff as quickly as possible. Particularly with the mythology and worldbuilding stuff. *Even* though you could spend a whole day discussing the Bettany family history and . . . abuse and things like that. Actually, *none of that* might be relevant to what you are writing, in terms of the actual story of the episode. But, it underpins a lot of what is in the episode. If you're doing something—that turns out to be radically wrong—you need to be able to fix it quite quickly.

NICOLA SHINDLER: I probably concentrate less on the story of the week, whether it is police or horror or some intricate part of plot, because I rely on the script team to know that inside out and to make sure that it works logically. Well, I do read that and if I have got a comment, if I don't believe a story, if I don't think it is working well enough, I'll say. But as you get along all the drafts, I probably stop looking at that as . . . hard as everyone else is looking at it. I probably concentrate more on character and big, overarching story. And it has to be pacey. I get . . . quite frustrated if things take too long—which isn't to say that you don't have nine-page dialogue scenes because you do when it's telling the story but I don't think just having scenes for the sake of them is ever justified. Everything has to move story on.

CHRIS PARKER: It was a real eye-opener really in terms of how much work it takes to make an hour-long story work.

NICOLA SHINDLER: We will *always* do at least three levels of storytelling. So, you are telling . . . the plot—what I call plot, which isn't the story. The plot is like the, "Ahhh: I found a dead body in the water and I had to report it to the police," and then the police will come out and see it and then, "Oh my god, is that person who's just run away, is that the killer?" End of episode 1. That's the plot. But then the *story* is: The person who found the body's wife has just walked out on him. He is really conflicted because he wants to see his child but doesn't know how to. And then the policewoman who comes along just so happens to be an ex-lover from school. And so that's the story. And then also you have got: What world does he live in? If he is a teacher . . . you go into the school and you tell the story of the school and you set something up there which is going to kick off as well. And all three of those levels have to have hooks. And all three of them have to work through the whole series.

CAROLINE HOLLICK: Having this very clear creative vision in Nicola means that [] it's quite a straightforward development process.

CHRIS PARKER: That was the brilliant thing about working for RED though. They made so much brilliant stuff—they had an instinct about scripts, even though they hadn't worked on horror before—they had such a good instinct about emotional stories . . . is this character strong enough? Do we know enough about this character to care about them? Are we giving too much weight to this character in this story and not enough to . . . our own series characters?

NICOLA SHINDLER: I don't make something that isn't fundamentally entertaining.

CAROLINE HOLLICK: Nicola would go, "Oh okay, this is what really works and this is what doesn't." If you become too democratic then you never move forwards. The way RED works is it is Nicola's company. She created it and so she's always the last creative voice—although we have a lot of creative freedom and we have a lot of say.

RICHARD FEE: You can't get away from the fact that we have . . . our own tastes, individually. And the fact that Nicola is integral to each show, she is—not integral, that's not the right word—she *is* the company, so . . . her taste is every-thing really in terms of our output.

NICOLA SHINDLER: Yes, *but*. My job is not to impose my own voice over things. Sometimes when I don't like something, it doesn't mean it shouldn't happen. But I think it is probably more than they might think I would go with what they want it to be. Fundamentally, they are *inside* the program and they understand it inside out. Often they have come back and said, "Oh you are right." I will keep saying if I don't think something makes sense or I don't think it is good enough. But if they think that there is a really good reason that the story goes in that direction then I totally listen.

CAROLINE HOLLICK: We would make sure we knew exactly what Nicola wanted, work with her, and I would try not to throw . . . a spanner in the works as well . . . you have to try not to stick your neb in for the sake of it. And . . . so it's a *kind* of hierarchy but with a lot of debate between us if you see what I mean, rather than one person saying, "Right this is how it has to be done."

———◆———

RICHARD FEE: Most of what we've done at RED has been serialized. So actually, *Bedlam* is a little bit of an outlier in that respect.

NEIL JONES: It was pretty much conceived of as story of the week originally.

DAVID ALLISON: That was your A story yeah? The A story has to be half the epi-sode for it, you know, to work.

CHRIS PARKER: We've got all these guest characters every week. You have to give *them* plenty of screen time, establish them, give them a back story, work out their story.

DAVID ALLISON: The audience is coming for the ghost of the week stuff, they really need to have that, that sense of "Ooh, what's that?" You want that. You know in a way the ghost mystery can serve itself every episode. And then your B story was probably . . . the stuff going on in the lives of the characters. Although again, although there was probably like, B1 and B2. Like B1 is lives and love stuff, and B2 is serial story as it impacts our characters that might have some supernatural bent. And then the C story is the serial arc.

CHRIS PARKER: There was quite a lot to do in an hour really.

NEIL JONES: We felt nobody was really doing American style genre shows and at that time they were still all story of the week.

CAROLINE HOLLICK: They wanted us to tell, initially, stand-alone stories because they felt people dipped in and out of drama that you might catch one week but not the next. With those American shows that's what happens a lot.

RICHARD FEE: There are some writers that love writing story of the week and it's great. But it can be quite relentless cos it *eats* so much story.

CAROLINE HOLLICK: We realized that . . . in order to hold an audience . . . without the kind of production values and the star power and the America TV guest stars, you needed quite a lot of serious story to keep them coming back, week on week.

RICHARD FEE: And it's *so* hard to come up with story-of-the-week shows. Like, first of all, there are only so many genres, really, that offer the potential for story of the week. Within that, how do you do something original? We get *very few* things pitched to us by writers that are story of the week. It's very rare that a writer says, "What I really wanna do is a story-of-the-week show." Ehm. *Usually*, it's the development team going to people and saying "We're thinking about doing a story-of-the-week thing in this setting," or "We've got an interesting consultant" so we're trying to ... generate it. There's been a trend in recent years for everything going *much* more serialized. Which as a viewer I *love* because I prefer that kind of storytelling. This is a big generalization and it's not true of everybody but naturally, writers ... find themselves more drawn to serialized storytelling. And the broadcaster—the pendulum has swung so far one way and everything is serialized. But those story-of-the-week shows still do *incredibly* well when you think about like *Death in Paradise*, *Call the Midwife*, you know, they are massive ratings winners.

NEIL JONES: But as we were developing it, American drama started to change and everything started to become ... serialized.

DAVID ALLISON: The hardest thing was the series arc.

CHRIS PARKER: The serial arc, it wasn't set in stone from day one, it evolved along the way.

NEIL JONES: I think it had probably uhm ... lost its way in terms of what the plan was as we went into writing it.

RICHARD FEE: The serial element did crescendo quite quickly at the end of the first season. I think naturally with, serial storytelling—in any series—you want it to ... build to a climax at the end of the first series, and, as part of that as well, you want to be recommissioned, so you want there to be a cliff-hanger. But at the same time, because of the brief from the broadcaster in the first series to deliver strong stories of the week that had a beginning, a middle, and an end, and had resolution. We still had to *do that* in the final episode of the first series. You're trying to [] juggle something that is not straightforward. Something like ... *Happy Valley*, the end of the first season, you can dedicate all of your energies into ... rounding off that story that you've invested in for the whole series. Whereas with this we were having to start a new story at the ... beginning of the final episode.

DAVID ALLISON: The first series arc we messed around with it a lot. The ending we were reworking a lot. A lot, a lot, a lot, uhm.

CHRIS PARKER: Normally when you cowrite you know you work out a story together and then one of you actually sits down and writes it but ... we literally. I think it was a speed thing in the end. There was input from *all* of us in terms of what was actually going to happen ... so it was just a case of crashing it down as fast as possible. All the time there was a clock ticking and we felt the *pressure* of trying to get stuff done.

DAVID ALLISON: I remember the last episode basically the three of us just had to write in between us.

CHRIS PARKER: [David and I] literally wrote half each. By the time we were writing it, it was already in production. It was shooting deadlines that we were up against.

DAVID ALLISON: We had to literally write it in about two weeks. It had to be done. Because the schedule was so crazy.

CHRIS PARKER: What we [also] had a problem with was, we were thinking . . . on a bigger scale we didn't want it to end after series 1 [] but there was no guarantee that we'd get any further episodes.

DAVID ALLISON: You always have to have the chat with the channel when you go "Is this a full stop or a comma at the end of the series? Or a semicolon, or . . . ?" And of course the answer is always "If you're successful we'll have some more, but until the viewers have seen it. . . ." So you have these awkward situations.

CHRIS PARKER: We didn't know what would happen after [series 1] so [] when it came to the end of the series we just thought "*Ohhh we want to make it the biggest cliff-hanger known to man,*" put everything into it because we may not be coming back. If you watch [the last episode of] series 1, it was to get people to think "Ooh what's coming next?" But it backfired cos a lot of people thought "I'm being cheated here. These guys don't know what the story is."

———— ◆ ————

NEIL JONES: I think, *I think* David, Chris and I did notes on each other's drafts.

DAVID ALLISON: I think literally one of us wrote the first, one wrote the second, swapped, edited each other's work and swapped back, so on and so forth.

NEIL JONES: So the script was touched by all three of us before RED got to it. So every episode was written by the team really, even though we had we had individual credits.

CAROLINE HOLLICK: As soon as the first draft is scripted in [Nicola is] incredibly involved. Which is great. As an exec she's very involved creatively from the beginning.

NICOLA SHINDER: It depends on the writer. Like, if it's Russell [T. Davies], I would always just talk to him direct. Some writers want to hear from me direct. Often, because I *need* to trust the script department, I send it over to them. With *Bedlam* I definitely worked with Caroline and Richard. They were all very close to the writers, physically close as well.

AMY BARHAM: [For series 1] we would get a script, Claudia and I would both read it that night if we could, or sometimes I would read it, give Claudia my thoughts and then she would read it that weekend and give me her thoughts on Monday and then we would collate.

CLAUDIA ROSENCRANTZ: [For series 1] I did read the scripts as they came through, but you have to delegate to the people who work for you. I left Jenny and Amy to get on with it. I had a great team, so it wasn't my job to second-guess them every five minutes. I do keep a slightly stronger eye over things that I will perhaps let on, but I don't always know what is going on. You have to trust people if they are making things. I have often worked with people who actually haven't had that much experience, but I intrinsically believe that they are good at what they do, and are very bright, and they can think through the problems that are coming up.

AMY BARHAM: Then Jenny and I would get on the phone or email back and forth. . . . Jenny coming very much from an . . . editorial standpoint: the tone, the pace, the characters, the character development, how are the stories sitting alongside each other, is story A and story B so far apart that it feels like they are just existing in two different worlds? Like, how elegantly are those things woven in, and how are they giving us the emotional flashpoints for the characters that we need to further the show? And mine would be a bit of that certainly but also just trying to come from . . . "We need to keep this story front center, at the ad break this needs to be happening in order to get people back." Then Jenny would relay the notes to RED. Or Jenny and I would conference with them.

NICOLA SHINDLER: The [channel] just come to me. They never talk direct to the writers.

JENNY REEKS: It's either on the phone or in person. As long as Nicola is there and or somebody who is in charge of that episode in some way, who was relevant. I don't care who I talk to, if they are the person that the company has chosen to be the person who needs to know.

NICOLA SHINDLER: I will listen and then I will talk with the channel and I will get to the bottom of what they want. With *Bedlam*, Caroline was probably involved in those conversations as well.

JENNY REEKS: I am very kind when I [give notes]. Some people have a great desire to show their power with it. I have a great desire to hide my power if I have any at all. Honestly, this sounds awfully wanky, if you're giving notes you . . . have to be in the gang. They have to know you really care about it. Then it's like any creative meeting with equals. I didn't ever see it as me being "Now look here, here is teacher. You have made a mistake here because. . . ." It is not like that at all. We are so bloody grateful to them for what they are doing, you know how hard it is. You have to protect people from bad behavior. It's their show. They are not daft.

NICOLA SHINDLER: Jenny was quite hands-off but brilliant. Jenny would give me loads of script notes. Everyone else [from series 1] would not give me script notes, they would just tell you what doesn't work. It's always the same. There is always a pull and push and. . . . The skill is to . . . understand what people are *trying* for, even if it doesn't feel right for what you think the program should be. There is always a reason *behind* what they are saying. I am not threatened at all by those notes. And again, I might have been at the beginning. I think I am a better exec now because I do . . . everyone has a really valid opinion. I am not scared.

JENNY REEKS: Nicola is a woman I couldn't have dreamed of when I was growing up. This woman who actually thought she has every right to boss everyone around and certainly did. She has . . . an internal energy. She opens her mouth and starts disagreeing with everybody. She is great fun.

AMY BARHAM: Nicola is a bit like Claudia, she comes into a meeting, she tells you what's happening and you're like "Okay!" [Nicola] was always very respectful when we would have conversations about the editorial and what we wanted as the channel and that sometimes those weren't exactly the way that they saw the show. She was always just great to get into the meat of things, Caroline too, we really . . . got into it and really sort of shored it all up and, made it exactly what we wanted, with them being on board as well. We had a couple of good fiery conversations [*laughs*].

NICOLA SHINDLER: I don't think we argued!

JENNY REEKS: She's one tough cookie. You don't want to tamper with Nicola Shindler.

AMY BARHAM: I remember sitting in [Nicola's] office and us going backwards and forwards on something. I can't remember what it was, I just remember looking up at her BAFTAs on her shelf above her head and thinking, "Who am I to tell you what to do?!"

NICOLA SHINDLER: Yes, they are there for a reason [*laughs*].

AMY BARHAM: But I was also "I know my network and I know what my audience want, that's where I'm coming from. This has to appeal to them. I'm staying my path."

NICOLA SHINDLER: It's really hard but that is the main part of my job. I have got to keep the channel happy. I have to keep the writers happy as well. I have to keep the actors happy. And I have to keep true to what the program is about. My whole job is about balancing that. Amy . . . might not realize that that is true of every production that we do.

CAROLINE HOLLICK: So what we would then always try and do is collate.

NICOLA SHINDLER: I will talk with Caroline and Richard.

DAVID ALLISON: Rich will be getting Caroline's notes, Nicola's notes and the channel's notes. Trying to put [all the notes] together and make sense of them.

DAVID ALLISON: What a good indie will do, like RED will do, is they'll hopefully protect you from the worst of it but they will work with you to make it, they're on your side.

CAROLINE HOLLICK: We would have the debates about what's right and wrong away from the writers so we can work out our coherent take on it. You need to avoid the writer getting conflicting notes, from all sides. Because there are so many people who've got an input into what's going on at different stages. And then we would all pass it round between us—we'd all meet up again and bash it all through.

CLAUDIA ROSENCRANTZ: You don't need too many sets of notes or everybody goes mad.

———◆———

ANNE MENSAH: They cast Will Young in it, which I thought was genius. I have to say that I thought the casting—I can say it because I wasn't involved in it—the casting in series 1 was spectacular. It was a bolder flavor than you might have got at the BBC.

CLAUDIA ROSENCRANTZ: I remember being very, very opinionated about casting.

CHRIS PARKER: Will Young was the sort of bankable star in a way. . . . At that time particularly he was a big star, you know. On TV and, well he still is, isn't he? And. So. He was the household name. Even though his part wasn't very big or really important in it.

CLAUDIA ROSENCRANTZ: I said "First and foremost, I want everybody in it to be very attractive." That is unusual for British drama. They usually look like Quasimodo.

NICOLA SHINDLER: You listen to what kind of actor channels want. And you make sure that those are the kind of people you are seeing but you also listen to clever people like your casting director who might say, "You have got to see this person. They are about to become huge" or whatever it is.

CLAUDIA ROSENCRANTZ: And I said "Even though it's a horror, everyone needs to look fabulous in it." I think they were all slightly speechless. But you know, why not?

JENNY REEKS: If you are going for that market, it's purely practical. That's what the market demands.

CLAUDIA ROSENCRANTZ: RED sent in loads of possible actors for the lead and the boy that I thought was—just literally had megastar quality—was Theo James. And RED didn't want him. They wanted another boy who I thought was about as sexy as a bean. I said "No, I don't want him. I want Theo."

NICOLA SHINDLER: Ahm. And . . . you just have to manage expectations because quite frankly most commissioning editors think they are going to get Brad Pitt. You have got to listen to that for a while before you put very much not Brad Pitt in front of them. And you have to go through a certain number of rejections before they become realistic.

JENNY REEKS: Living was all in agreement about who we wanted. But Claud was the head, the top of the pyramid. It's best for her to say so. That was her job. The pointy end.

NICOLA SHINDLER: I have no recollection of wanting anyone other than Theo so I am not quite sure about that. Most people . . . they are pushing and pulling in certain directions. They want people who an audience is gonna say, "I want to come to that show" so someone who is recognizable but equally they always want to discover someone and they want someone who is right for the part. So it is just a *total* . . . push and pull the whole time. There is compromise. Oh no, not compromise. Well, you do have to compromise a lot but. You need to know when not to compromise. It's all collaborative—that's the word I'm looking for.

Everything is very, very collaborative and it's hard to manage everyone's expectations. The writers had *loads* of strong opinions about cast. I listen to them but they are going to come lower down in that conversation than the people paying the bills. And that is what everyone has to realize. At the end, if you are paying the money to make the show, it is your choice.

It is *my* job to make everyone think that they have got everything that they want and that they are happy. Otherwise people will go into it a bit depressed. . . . Part of my job is PR and making everyone feel like it was their idea and that they are really happy. It is strategic. I think I am much better at it now. I probably did use to panic and be really worried. I mean, I still worry and I still care enormously but I know that we will get there. Now.

———◆———

RICHARD FEE: Often, a director's come onto the project, maybe four weeks before the read-through? If that? For prep.

CHRIS PARKER: They did have different approaches as all directors do. They were all directors who [] you know they come from the same world as us. Do realist stuff but all have this kind of passion for horror. We were all basically doing something we'd never done before, that includes RED, the directors, us as writers, Nicola Shindler as exec. So it was quite exciting because it felt we could just get away with anything. So that was *really* exciting because you felt like they were just like grabbing the scripts and thinking, "Great what can I do with this?"

CAROLINE HOLLICK: The directors were brilliant, but British TV doesn't make a lot of horror, you know, it was new for a lot of the directors to be doing something so clearly "genre."

CHRIS PARKER: For each episode we would meet the directors and talk in depth about . . . how we saw each scene panning out. They would say, "Look I'm worried about this because we're not sure . . . how it's going to look on-screen," or "You haven't made this clear enough," or "What's the emotion you're trying to get across here?"

DAVID ALLISON: With the director, you just want to understand they have an idea what your vision is. Now they might want to deliver it in a slightly different way, but you need to have those conversations. You are treated as the creator. And you have an important voice.

RICHARD FEE: You've suddenly got this, often quite strong voice . . . yes! Strong creative vision! Coming into the project, quite late in the day. And sometimes you might not see eye to eye *at all*. And you might have very different . . . visions of what it is. And sometimes that can be . . . a misunderstanding, or. You know, it can be all sorts of things.

CHRIS PARKER: The directors would say "Actually, that's going to be possible . . . we're going to be shooting in this little cellar and it's a dead end you can't go through."

DAVID ALLISON: There are things you don't think about and they go "Actually it's really, really hard to do." Who knew it was like water was harder than fire for example? Underwater is really difficult! None of us had had a horror series made so you didn't *realize*.

CHRIS PARKER: They explained the logistics of places that we hadn't actually been to. But they'd say, "Well we can't do this but we could do this." Or you have to rewrite something to fit the new location. In those days, there was a very clear difference between doing something for a satellite channel . . . and doing something for terrestrial. The budgets would be a fraction of what you'd expect if you were making something for the BBC . . . or Channel 4.

DAVID ALLISON: "Can you imagine doing the same scene in this space and how will we do it?" And you're going "How can it still feel dramatic or scary if we haven't got the flaming ball of fire coming down from the dragon?" You know.

NEIL JONES: At the end of [one episode] there's a big lightning rod, on the outside of a building? That was *supposed to be* on the roof of the building . . . it was going to be huge . . . a storm all around the building and—that was impossibly expensive—we couldn't do that.

AMY BARHAM: There were definitely . . . times when they were saying, "This is not doable for this," and we were "Okay but, tell us what you can do, let's work with that, let's try and make this happen." And they worked really hard, they made those budgets go far.

DAVID ALLISON: The biggest challenge was making it for the budget we had. Because it was made for less than the average hour budget for drama. Significantly. Uhm. And that was part of the deal, that was part of how we got it made.

CHRIS PARKER: We just thought, well *how* are we actually going to make this? Is it going to look terrible? We were [referencing] horror films that cost millions to make.

DAVID ALLISON: It was definitely a fear when we first started like "God, is this going to look good? Is this going to come off?"

CHRIS PARKER: Is it going to require special effects that we can't afford? Is it going to look really shit on-screen?

DAVID ALLISON: Look at something like *American Horror Story*, look at the budget that they've got. There's not a lot of British TV that does this kind of thing. At all.

AMY BARHAM: I felt like our budgets weren't so—they were competitive for British drama. They weren't as much as some British drama but they definitely weren't crummy budgets. Claudia was "I'm not doing this strategy unless we can make something really good," so she went out and got that money. So that we could deliver a good show.

DAVID ALLISON: Some episodes work loads better than others. Because you were doing things on a tight budget, on a very tight schedule.

NEIL JONES: It's a factor, in every TV show. . . . Usually, without going too crazy, it's a matter of starting off with . . . what you want to do and then working out what you can afford to do.

NICOLA SHINDLER: I think we do that on every job. Every job. Even the supposedly big budget ones, you have never got enough [money]. Everyone's expectation is that it is always at a certain level and you just have to be . . . to do as well as you can with what you have got and make sure all the money ends up on-screen. And that's what we tried to do.

AMY BARHAM: We were definitely put the money on-screen, let's see the value of it there.

NICOLA SHINDLER: [Put the money on-screen] can mean a couple of things. Some companies take a lot of profit before they even started filming. And that takes a lot of money off screen. Sometimes you pay for things that just don't reflect well. You want to pay for design and for costume. You want to pay for actors. And you don't want to pay for stupid amounts of catering or, wasteful amounts of paper or, too many vehicles when that does not show on-screen. So "money on-screen" is just the mantra that everybody has got to operate by. You spend on other things, but it is about being careful to make sure that they get their value.

NEIL JONES: I remember sitting with the producer talking about an episode as we were getting ready to shoot it and he was going "We can't . . . we can't do this ending, we can't afford the ending." And I remember firing about *twenty different ways* of doing this ending, "We'll do this, we'll do that," and every single one was like, "Can't afford that, can't afford that" [*laughs*] "we just cannot afford *an ending* for this episode." But then I think he had to . . . find it in the budget to do *a* version of it in the end which is why we ended up with a compromise.

DAVID ALLISON: But . . . I mean [*sighs*] the real issue with a show like *Bedlam* was "how can we deliver this practically on the shoot of this length?" Is there a way we *cannot* have them paragliding from the sky on fire?

NEIL JONES: You know it often ends up being . . . to your advantage really, saying "We can't afford to do your original idea," it forces you to go back and "Well I've got to think of another good idea," you know, sometimes . . . it's a better one. Uhm. But it is just the nature of the beast really, it's part of the collaborative thing of TV [] there's no point in scripting something that the crew is not going to be able to achieve . . . so it's finding something *good* that they can do.

NICOLA SHINDLER: That is the other big like . . . not dilemma, like the big push and pull in the job. The conflict. Which is it is money versus art the whole time. Like I said, that's true when you have got millions per episode.

CHAPTER 7

Development

In late 2017, before I began interviewing, I sat down to watch *Bedlam* in its entirety. I curled up on my green velvet sofa, fountain pen in hand, notebook on my lap. My beloved black cat Marla was asleep to the left of me, a hot cup of tea awaited me on the side table to my right. I was ready to binge. This isn't as big a deal as it might sound, given the two-season entirety of *Bedlam* consists of twelve 45-minute episodes (yes, I do know how lucky I am to work on British case study, where the dataset is so small in comparison to many North American productions). At the time I still worked at York (and *yes*, there are several institutional moves in this book, don't judge me) where all my teaching and research focused on scriptwriting and script editing. As such, when I became absorbed in *Bedlam*'s world, I automatically made notes on story and storytelling. In this chapter, I want to begin by talking about my experience of watching the series as a way of leading into the questions I went on to ask the writers. Then, I want to think about how the answers of the writers enable us to better understand the development stage of television drama.

Peter Bloore offers a useful definition of development as the "creative and industrial collaborative process" through which a story becomes a script that "is then repeatedly rewritten to reach a stage when it is attractive to a suitable director, actors and relevant film production funders; so that enough money can be raised to get the film made."[1] For *Bedlam*, commissioned by a U.K. satellite channel and made by an independent production company, we can recalibrate Bloore's definition as the same "creative and industrial collaborative process" from story to script, but with several tweaks. The writing of the pilot is to attract development funding from production companies (for example, to pitch a story to a development executive to encourage the production company to pay for a draft script). The script will then be rewritten with the attached production company with the aim of then attracting and attaching a channel commissioner, who will fund the writing of the rest of the episodes and the production of the series. The writers will work with the input of both production company and channel executives to write and rewrite the scripts to prepare for going into production. Unlike the commissioning chapter, this focus on television development offers an opportunity to look at the work of *Bedlam*'s writers in more depth, as "most of a screenwriter's work is done" during this "pre-pre-production phase."[2] In the first half of the chapter I explore the writers and the challenges they faced as they broke the story for series 1 and drafted the episode screenplays. Then, in the second half of the chapter I focus on the "notes" process of development, during which "heads of development, development executives, script editors, and story editors are all employed to work with the screenwriter, developing their script over many drafts to improve it and support the screenwriting process."[3]

Molly's in Thailand

Early on in my binge, I ascertained that *Bedlam* was a story-of-the-week precinct drama, set in "Bedlam Heights," a former psychiatric hospital being redeveloped as flats by Kate Bettany (Charlotte Salt) and her father Warren Bettany (Hugo Speer). In each episode, the guest character of the week moves into a new flat and experiences a haunting. Then Kate's cousin, psychic protagonist Jed Harper (Theo James), who also works Bedlam Heights, discovers that the haunting is taking place. Jed sees the ghost and then, with the help of Ryan McAllistar (Will Young), researches the ghost's backstory. This backstory relates to the history of the psychiatric hospital. Jed and Ryan then discover why the ghost is haunting the specific tenant, which is usually because of an unpunished crime or a shameful secret on the part of the guest character. Armed with this knowledge, they are able to resolve the situation and end the haunting. The dominant episodic model is supported by a minor, serialized set of storylines relating to story arcs for the core characters and complemented by series-long worldbuilding storytelling.

So far, so straightforward: but the final episode of series 1, "Burning Man," was confusing. This episode was a brand-new story of the week, which felt unusual, even for episodic-led drama. It was only in the BC storylines that the series-long arcs played out, which built to a suitably gothic crescendo between Kate and Jed. But—and this was what was really confusing—this series-long arc did not pay off at all. None of the questions planted throughout the series (say, about the haunting of the building, or the truth behind the potentially horrible history of the Bettany family) were answered at all. Jed, our protagonist, was literally abandoned in a cellar in Bedlam Heights.

With one eyebrow raised, I turned to series 2, assuming the questions would be resolved, but series 2 begins with *all* the original cast members gone, bar Kate's dad Warren. Jed and Ryan are . . . not there, Kate pops up to announce that her flat mate Molly is "in Thailand," then departs. Most of the story cliff-hangers from series 1 remain unrecognized and unresolved. Episode 1 of series 2 introduces Ellie Flint (Lacey Turner), a brand-new protagonist with a brand-new story-line. Ellie is assisted by a new cast of supporting characters, including Keira (Gemma Chan), Max (Jack Roth), and Dan (Nikesh Patel). So, after watching both series, in addition to my three main research questions for the writers, I also had a series of more specific questions on *Bedlam*'s writing and development: Who made the decisions about the episodic and serial narrative and character arcs, across individual episodes and across series? Why did series 1 end in the way that it did? Why did series 2 have an entirely new cast?

Make It Glossy

Once Living greenlit *Bedlam*, the writers had to deliver the remaining scripts for series 1. As writer-creator Neil Jones comments, "Episode 1 took years, and then all of a sudden Living went 'Yes, we'll do it' and we needed five more episodes!" The three writer-creators, Jones, Chris Parker, and David Allison, congregated in Leeds, at Seven, a café in Chapel Allerton, with RED script executive Hollick and RED script editor Richard Fee. The five of them sat around a table and talked through the serial storytelling, the world building, and where they wanted the series to end. Parker admits this was tough, noting, "It was only six episodes" in total but "each one required so much thought and brainstorming" and "loads of our original ideas got thrown out, they just didn't stand up." Fee concurs, reflecting that in the early days of development, "a lot of it was about . . . narrowing down on exactly what the DNA of the series was. Because we were trying to match a number of briefs." He explains, "The intention was to do this horror supernatural show. That was also a young person's relationship drama. That had story of the week done in one episode that you could tune in and watch without necessarily having to . . . have seen . . . the past four episodes."

Fee's point is significant for our analysis. Suzanne Keen argues that "the historical, material and cultural conditions surrounding the production of a narrative often have a profound effect on its presentation," and this is certainly true of *Bedlam*.[4] In the 2000s, when *Bedlam* was first developed, episodic story-of-the-week structures, as seen in *Ghost Whisperer* (CBS, 2005–2010), were still at the forefront of how narrative was managed. This storytelling model was how the writing team initially envisaged the series, and *Bedlam* was initially developed using a franchise and precinct model. Here, "precinct" refers to an important facet of long-running drama, in which the series' setting (e.g., hospital, police station, law firm) shares "the capacity to generate a potentially unlimited flow of episode stories."[5] Every episode took place at Bedlam Heights, with little other location shooting. Most scenes took place indoors, with the drama moving between the residential communal spaces, residents' flats, the staff flats, and the unfinished building work. As Living TV executive Amy Barham notes in chapter 3, "We did need it to have a precinct. To enable us to build sets and to have one specific location that the majority of the action took place in" because "it would enable us to put the majority of our money on the screen, to really . . . make that budget work."

The precinct then becomes the foundation for the franchise. The franchise is "the central element of a genre or concept—frequently a vocation or avocation (i.e., a kind of job or hobby)—that generates a number of stories; a kind of story engine," which is vital for "sustaining output over time."[6] Police, medical, legal and private investigator series are the "big four" franchises, and each possesses a case-of-the-week format, which creates a "story-generating problematic."[7] The franchise provides cases, which create individual stories, which can then be built into episodes. The goal of the franchise is to develop a "series that generate many episodes, a hundred, or even hundreds of episodes."[8]

So far, so straightforward. *Bedlam*'s precinct was the residential apartment block Bedlam Heights. The series then translated "cases" to "monsters" for their story-of-the-week format. The A storyline services the franchise, following the "dominant plotline concerning the principal character" and containing "the most scenes (or beats) within the episodes," while also offering "the most possible evolving plotlines (known as story engines) from episode to episode."[9] In each episode of series 1, a new occupant moved into a flat in Bedlam Heights. The new owner's arrival disturbs malcontented spirits of people who died in the building during its former tenure as a psychiatric hospital. The spirits then make their displeasure known. Psychic protagonist Jed Harper, who works at Bedlam Heights, discovers that a haunting is taking place, and then, across the episode, researches and resolves the haunting. The A storyline was the ghost of the week haunting, a model that creates "mini-narratives that could stand on their own" in each episode.[10]

This is where Allison, Parker, and Jones's decision to write ghost stories became really important for the episodic procedural element of the model. As novelist Sophie Hannah has reflected, crime fiction and ghost stories are both built on suspense, that "the overwhelming majority of ghost stories are mysteries" and "the main thing driving [the reader] on through the narrative is the desire to find out and solve the mystery."[11] Each week a new mystery is posed: Who is the ghost? Why are they haunting? Why have they connected with this person in particular? How do we make them stop? Jed must answer these questions to solve the mystery. The episodic model is then supported by a serialized mix of core cast character and plot development across the B and C storylines. This accords with Trisha Dunleavy's analysis of American broadcast television culture from the 1980s onward and the desire to create series for syndication. The syndicated market is "enticing to drama producers and drama-commissioning networks because it can be highly lucrative," which leads to a preference for "episodic drama series" because "they can be played in any order and can accommodate irregular patterns of viewing," and their more "formulaic and conventional nature" offers "episode volume."[12] We can see this in Barham's comments in chapter 3, that when she read the script she loved the premise that converting the hospital had "woken up these spirits" and would generate limitless monsters of the week; she "could just see infinite episodes."

However, this storytelling model would not last. As with chapter 4 on commissioning practices, *Bedlam*'s final narrative form emerges from the changing dynamics of television storytelling in the new millennium. Stacey Abbott suggests that the 1990s onward witnessed "the gradual transformation of the televisual landscape through the growth of a multi-channel market and development of narrow-casting as a means of targeting niche consumers," which led to "a rise in television horror."[13] As part of this shift, during the early 2000s "narrative complexity" began to increase in popularity as storytelling mode: for commissioners, for writers, for audiences. As noted in chapter 2, through the work of Dunleavy and Jason Mittell, narrative complexity is a mode of storytelling that offers "an interplay between the demands of episodic and serialized storytelling, often oscillating between long-term arcs and stand-alone episodes."[14] Outside of academia, craft books on television screenwriting employ similar language to describe this model. Daniel Calvisi suggests that these programs alternate "between a case-of-the-week episode and a 'mythology' episode that advances a long-term narrative arc," with the expectation that the mythology "becomes more dominant as the series goes on."[15] For Pamela Douglas, these hybrids increasingly merge the serial and series format with "some stories that 'close' (resolve) within an episode while other dramatic arcs continue."[16]

In the late 1990s and 2000s, science fiction, horror, and fantasy television (grouped together by Catherine Johnson as "telefantasy") took up the narrative complexity model with gusto. As Johnson notes of *Buffy the Vampire Slayer* (The WB/UPN, 1997–2003), each episode establishes "a format that offers certain repeated narrative and stylistic pleasures," which "grounds the viewers expectations and provides the network with a recognizable product that offers predictable pleasures repeated each week." However, at the same time, it also "develops a continuing narrative. Actions carry over from episode to episode so that the events of one episode have consequences for the series overall."[17]

By the time *Bedlam* was commissioned, toward the end of the 2000s, serial/procedural hybrids descendants of *Buffy*, such as *Fringe* (Fox, 2008–2013), were popular American acquisitions on British screens. *Bedlam* was developed at a point when how to tell televisual stories had begun to shift, and this shift was being unevenly adopted across national television writing traditions. The timing of the development thus resulted in a complex and demanding brief from the broadcaster, Living. They wanted the 1980s American network television model of a series that could potentially syndicate and run for hundreds of episodes, as with their existing successful American acquisitions *Ghost Whisperer* and *Supernatural*. At the same time, they also wanted television that also reflected the new ways that telefantasy was being imagined.

The writing team then discovered that the already-complex set of expectations around serialized storytelling was about to become even more convoluted. The reason for this was their chosen genre. Allison initially understood *Bedlam* as a "ghost story *Play for Today*," that allowed for a stand-alone story each week, where you are able to "just enjoy all the tropes of the genre," but, at the same time, to set that anthology format within "a world where there is continuing story." However, *Bedlam*'s lineage is more Amicus than Alan Clarke, and Living's desire for *Bedlam* to be what Fee calls "a young person's relationship show" required a jettisoning of the anthology premise and a focus on story of the week instead. This shift in direction originating from the broadcaster, speaks to Susan Kerrigan and Craig Batty's point that in screenwriting, "screenplay readers will fix their own meaning to a screenplay, and it is possible, even likely that this may be different to the fixed meaning originally intended by the author of the work." This demonstrates that development is "the site where the exchange between the reader and writer occurs," that is, "the site where creativity occurs."[18] And here, creativity is compelled by a broadcaster brief that demands an alteration of episodic structure and series structure.

The team eventually settled on an ABC storyline structure for each episode. As Allison explains, the ghost story of the week was the A story, "which has to be half the episode for it to work." Parker confirms, "we've got guest characters every week. You have to give them plenty of screen time, establish them, work out their story." Allison continues, the B story is "the lives of the characters. Although it was probably like, B1 and B2. B1 is lives and love, and B2 is serial story as it impacts our characters that might have some supernatural bent. And then the C story is the serial arc." Hollick admits, "It did take us a little while to . . . get the format of the stories right. How we were telling . . . ghost stories, that was the biggest challenge." This relates to the difficulties of creating horror within episodic series drama (the A storyline), because "the characters must continue from week to week, suspense is diluted; the viewer knows the hero is never in mortal danger."[19] Living TV expected *Bedlam* to do it all: a genre story of the week, a franchise model with a precinct setting, and serialized narrative arcs and story worlds that would encourage deep fan engagement and return viewing. As Parker reflects, "There was quite a lot to do in an hour really." The story decisions in *Bedlam*'s first season then become emblematic of the uneasy competition of the episodic with the serialized; they are exemplars of the difficulties of writing genre scripts when the rules of engagement for television narrative were radically, and rapidly, changing.

The writers also had medium-specific issues to grapple with. The writers cite the influence of the J-horror boom of the 2000s and Guillermo del Toro on their work, while Barham looked to *Paranormal Activity* (2007) as proof that "people wanted to be scared" and (importantly for the broadcaster) that "those things were doing well." The team had to think through how to take the visual and narrative qualities that they enjoyed in cinema, and how they could be translated for the completely different medium of television storytelling. Here, writing horror television becomes a "two-handed trick" that is "impossible without a knowledge of genre that surpasses the audience's knowledge."[20] And of the three writers, only Jones was a horror expert.

It was not just the medium but also the budget that posed significant challenges for the writers. Living's desire to commission an original series that replicated their American acquisitions raised budgetary issues for RED and for the writers that directly impacted upon how stories were told. Barham explains that their audience "know us for very high production value drama, because it's come from a U.S. network where the budget is like two million an ep," so their original drama "needs to feel glossy. It needs to feel American." However, press reports suggest that the overall budget for the full six-episode first season totaled thee million pounds.[21] Parker reveals that "in those days" the budget "was a fraction of what you'd expect if you were making something for the BBC or Channel 4." Rosencrantz explains, "I wanted to see if I could have big hits for no money, having come from running ITV for ten years where I had big hits for big money," while Hollick notes that RED made *Bedlam* "for almost no money." Shindler concurs, laughing, "It was really hard." The budget raised serious concerns for the writers. Parker confesses, "We just thought, well *how* are we actually going to make this? . . . Is it going to look really shit on-screen?" Jones remembers talking to a producer about a specific episode and suggesting "about *twenty different ways* of doing this ending" and every single one was, "can't afford that, can't afford that." Jones laughs, remembering the conversation as "we just cannot afford *an ending* for this episode," demonstrating how the economic structures of television impact upon the writers' decision-making process.

In her book on screenwriters, Natalie Wreyford argues that the "continued reliance on the discourse of the identifiable creative individual is to deny the importance of collaboration . . . in creating well-received screenplays."[22] We can see collaboration in the outlining of the *Bedlam* episodes, which were often led by script editor, Fee. As Hollick reveals, once the team had "a broad sense of a shape" for a story, they would "literally have a document with columns in— sometimes it would be Richard actually making decisions about what could go into each episode, that felt balanced." Fee concurs, "And that's a changing document obviously, because—you might get halfway in and realize that something's going to become more important than you thought, or, or less important."

The writers were then assigned individual episodes. Each writer wrote a first draft and did notes for the other writers' drafts. This is collaborative working in action, Jones explaining that each script "was touched by all three of us before RED got to it," that "even though we had individual credits, all the scripts were team written." This offers further evidence for Eva Novrup Redvall's assertion that screenwriting is composed of "complicated interpersonal and intangible aspects," aspects that need to be taken more into consideration in our research.[23]

NOTES

Of the three disciplinary areas that I explore in this book—television studies, production studies, and screenwriting studies—script development has (inevitably) found a home in screenwriting studies. In 2016, Stayci Taylor and Craig Batty argued that "there still exists a significant gap in academic and industry literature about script development as both a phenomenon and a practice, especially from the point of view of those engaging with screenplays according to the roles they play in developing them."[24] However, since the "Script Development: Defining the Field" special issue of the *Journal of Screenwriting*, published in 2017, this situation has begun to change. In *Gender Inequality in Screenwriting Work*, published in 2018, Natalie Wreyford takes time to explore development in some detail, while in 2021 Batty and Taylor published *Script Development: Critical Approaches, Creative Practices, International Perspectives* and *The Palgrave Handbook of Script Development*.[25] As part of this progression of scholarship, the second half of this chapter considers development from an as yet relatively underutilized angle: script feedback, also known as "notes."

When notes are discussed in screenwriting craft books, it is usually as practical advice to the prospective screenwriter on how to behave or on how to write and deliver as a script editor or development executive.[26] In academia, Batty and colleagues observe that what is often missing is a discussion of the "relationships that occur when collaborating with others in/through script development."[27] *The Palgrave Handbook of Script Development* goes some way to addressing this and dedicates the first ten chapters to "Behind the Scenes of Script Development." However, only two of these chapters explore television drama, suggesting there is still considerable scope for development in this area. Taylor and Batty position notes as part of the "hidden practice" of script development, and here we focus on this hidden practice at a senior, institutional level as I consider how notes move between the broadcaster, the production company, and the writers.[28]

As noted above, the team agreed which stories went in which episode, each writer was assigned a draft episode to write, then each writer gave feedback on other episodes. Then, once the Leeds team were happy with a draft, the script was sent to Shindler, as executive producer at RED. For Hollick, Shindler's level of involvement "is great. Because you don't get that problem of working on something for four weeks and then having to go back to the drawing board." As the executive producer, Shindler was making sure that the script was achieving RED's "three levels of storytelling," predicated upon plot, story, and world. Given Shindler's interest in the three levels of storytelling, she concentrated "less on the story of the week" because she relied "on the script team to know that inside out and to make sure that it works logically." Instead, she considered "character and big, overarching story," making sure the required multiple levels of storytelling were "pacey." She acknowledges, "I get . . . quite frustrated if things take too long."

As such, Shindler's preference for pace played into the plotting of the series, which needed to move fast to satisfy the most powerful executive at the production company. As Hollick explains, RED is "Nicola's company. She created it and so she's always the last creative voice—although we have a lot of creative freedom and a lot of say." Shindler agrees with Hollick's perspective, but with some reservations: "Yes, *but*. My job is not to impose my own voice over things. Sometimes when I don't like something, it doesn't mean it shouldn't happen." Meanwhile, Hollick's job was to understand "exactly what Nicola wanted, work with her" and "try not to throw a spanner in the works as well." She reflects that "it's a *kind* of hierarchy but with a lot of debate between us . . . rather than one person saying, 'Right this is how it has to be done.'"

Craig Batty and Dallas J. Baker suggest that the collaborative nature of screenwriting involves writers and "interlocutors," such as script editors, producers, and financiers.[29] "Interlocutors" suggest that these women executives have a dialogic role with the screenwriters, but this work illuminates a complex set of relationships between the women themselves that directly affects the intention and direction of the series before the writers even receive script notes. Shindler's contributions are an integral part of the creative process, despite her claim that it is "not her job" to impose her voice on the scripts. Her point of view is stamped on the script from the first draft onward, and her feedback continues to deepen and refine the draft scripts at every stage of development.

When Shindler signed the script off, it was sent to Living. Rosencrantz and Barham would, in Barham's words, "both read it that night if we could, or sometimes I would read it, give Claudia my thoughts and then she would read it that weekend and give me her thoughts on Monday and then we would collate." Then, Rosencrantz left "Jenny [Reeks] and Amy [Barham] to get on with it." Reeks and Barham then spoke on the phone and by email. They shared and synthesized their feedback, reading the script from different perspectives. Reeks would approach the script from an "editorial" standpoint, which Barham defines as "the tone, the pace, the characters, the character development," and "how elegantly" the ABC storylines are interwoven, and whether they produce the necessary "emotional flashpoints for the characters."

This definition of "editorial" fascinates me. In academia, we associate editorial as the work of the editor (of a book, of a journal issue, etc.). Or, in our access to industry documents, "editorial" often means the guidelines for a television channel's values and standards, for example, Channel 4's Editorial and Compliance Protocol. However, here "editorial" is used in a way that speaks to these existing definitions (not least their underpinning of power and control), but while also offering something quite different. "Editorial" is the work of Reeks as executive producer but also as the de facto commissioning executive and development executive. We can then see how Barham considers the story as well, but from a more economic mindset; her primary focus was serving the story's needs in the context of a commercial channel. However, as experienced makers of television drama, Shindler and Hollick were equally attuned to the commercial imperatives of the script. Shindler explains, "You need to make sure that you are keeping people as entertained and hooked as possible. And especially on a channel like Living, when there were adverts. Because we had to hook into every advert break," while Hollick concurs, "I *like* the fact that when we set this up with Living there were like these commercial parameters that we had to make work. That's TV, it isn't like writing a poem. It's a commercial process."

Once the Living notes were consolidated, the broadcaster and production company would meet up. As Shindler notes, broadcasters go directly to her, "they never talk direct to the writers." Bridget Conor writes that "confidence—for writers and development partners" is often linked to "notions of mutual respect," that notes are "to be given respect and attention, whatever their substance and motivation."[30] Respect is the crucial noun here, and we can see how Conor's reading of respect applies just as much at an interinstitutional level between broadcaster and production company, as between screenwriters and script editors. The performance of equal power dynamics is integral to creating respect between the feedback meetings between broadcaster and production company. Barham attended face-to-face meetings in Manchester with Shindler and Hollick. She reveals, "Nicola [Shindler] is a bit like Claudia [Rosencrantz], she comes into a meeting, tells you what's happening and you're like 'Okay!'" However, Barham confirms that Shindler was "always very respectful" in conversations about the editorial required by the channel, especially when some of that requirement was not "exactly the way that they saw the show."

The power dynamics of these interactions remained complex though. Barham recalls sitting in Shindler's office "and us going backwards and forwards on something . . . I just remember looking up at her BAFTAs on her shelf above her head and thinking, 'Who am I to tell you what to do?!'" Shindler explains, "There is always a pull and push" in these meetings, and the skill of the executive is to "understand what people are *trying* for, even if it doesn't feel right for what you think the program should be." For Shindler, good feedback sessions are about recognizing that "there is always a reason *behind* what they are saying." As

Barham, puts it, "I know my network and I know what my audience want. This has to appeal to them. I'm staying my path." This push and pull, between what Living wants and what RED wants (and what they can deliver with the budget and resources allocated), is a significant part of the creative process of developing scripts. These executive-level discussions then have a major impact on how episodes and series are restructured and revised.

Reeks's experience of giving notes to Shindler was different to Barham's. Reeks wished to create a situation in which equal power dynamics were performed. However, her concern was not powering "up" to meet Shindler, as arguably Barham is doing, but powering "down." Reeks was sufficiently experienced to recognize that she was representing the client, the client's money, and thus had a great deal of control. Reeks describes these sessions as a "creative meeting with equals," and Shindler confirms, "Jenny was quite hands-off but brilliant." This experience has parallels with the discussion of "studying up" and "studying sideways" in relation to interviewing "elites," as discussed in chapter 2 on method. The differing experiences of Barham and Reeks relates to each individual's career history and how her history had impacted upon the tone and format of the notes meetings. Reeks was a former ITV head of drama who had worked with Shindler on several occasions, while Barham was in her very first commissioning role.

Shindler also recognizes this dynamic in relation to casting. She explains that "the process is collaborative" but "it's hard to manage everyone's expectations." For example, "The writers had *loads* of strong opinions about cast," but ultimately "they are going to come lower down in that conversation than the people paying the bills." She concludes, "That is what everyone has to realize . . . if you are paying the money to make the show, it is your choice." Shindler's point demonstrates the layering of power in the relationship between RED and Living. Reeks, as a representative of the channel, wanted to make her interactions with RED as creative and equal as possible, but at the same time Shindler is fully aware that as Living is paying for the show, Reeks's feedback must be taken seriously. Shindler confirms that balancing these competing multiple levels of interpersonal and interinstitutional expectations are "the main part" of her job. She must keep everyone involved happy, while also keeping "true" to the program.

It is only after RED and Living agreed on an overall direction for the *Bedlam* episode that the notes began to slowly filter down toward the writing team. *Bedlam*'s script editor, Fee, was delegated to collate the feedback from the broadcaster, and from Shindler and Hollick at RED. When the feedback was collated, Fee worked with Hollick to create a single set of notes. As Hollick explains, it is important to "have the debates about what's right and wrong away from the writers so we can work out our coherent take on it." Or, as Rosencrantz puts it succinctly, "You don't need too many sets of notes or everybody goes mad." After agreeing the direction for the notes with Hollick, Fee then relayed the notes to the writers, both over the phone or in person. And finally, then, the writers began to redraft their scripts.

In his article on script development in the *Journal of Screenwriting*, Steven Price describes development as a "paper trail" of "textual drafts, notes, revisions, memos and so forth" that create "a record of a larger process of interpersonal networks visible only to those" who work in the industry.[31] While this model makes a great deal of sense for exploring filmmaking and particular older films, it has little relevance for studying the television industry, in which the "paper trail" of documentation is frequently absent. Development "notes" are Reeks and Barham talking on the phone about their first impressions of the episode script; they are Barham in Shindler's office, going backward and forward over what RED offers and what Living wants; they are Hollick and Fee discussing when and how to compile divergent sets of feedback into one coherent form which will *then* be written up for the writers. In fact, the commissioning and development process is predicated, first and foremost, upon talk, and in the case of *Bedlam*, primarily on the interactions and relationships between the women at RED and Living.

Development is in this sense, experiential: praxis as living, breathing interactions. This is why much of television development does not exist on paper (or email or in Word); the lifeblood of television development *is* the talk, which is why it is largely invisible to those outside the industry. This accords with Steven Maras's position that the industry can be considered as a discursive entity, "constituted through ways of talking . . . and constructed in the interaction and interface of different ideas about creativity, narrative, industry and production, theory and practice."[32]

Although, when I made this point to my friend, Joel Burges—a scholar whose current *Television and the Work of Writing* project is rooted in television archives—he contested my position that development is talk, and (really) talk alone. Joel argued that there are many interesting "documents of production" (to use his terminology) in the archives, including "scripts with notes, casting sheets, emails, and correspondence, all of which give "real-time" insight into the making of television."[33] I cannot deny his point. But I would suggest that when we do access archives, we read this engagement through hierarchies of power. As Maryanne Dever comments in her essay "Archives and New Modes of Feminist Research," "The idea of evidence as inert, fully-constituted and ultimately awaiting our juridical gaze has been displaced in favor of acknowledging archiving itself as a mediating process."[34] After Joel's pertinent comments, I do feel somewhat duty bound to recognize that archives of television development probably do exist, for some people and for some shows, but I would ask us then to reflect upon the following questions: Who gets to be archived? Where is the archived housed? Who gets to access the archive?

Dever continues that when it comes to the context of interrogating the nature of the empirical, we can "reconsider the 'stuff' with which we work and what it is we accept as archival evidence."[35] For archives of development, this might be usefully thought through in terms of access to emails, annotated scripts and so on (all of which I imagine Joel is already working with). However, following this line of thought further, perhaps we can also think of the script chapters as another kind of "stuff" that might be, or become, an archive. Batty and Kerrigan argue that "as a site of creative practice itself," development "can easily be misunderstood because the craft and process of writing a screenplay is often conflated with the result of that process: a completed screenplay."[36] The script chapters can be understood as an archive of evidence that disambiguates process from product, talk from (television) text. As such, the script chapters become a way of committing to print (and thus, to history) the process of developing a series, thus creating a home for material that others may choose to read, quote and work with in their own television studies.

CONCLUSION

In this chapter, I have sought to illuminate the collaborative and creative intricacies of script development for television and to demonstrate the multitude of voices that contribute to the script. In chapter 4, I made a case for the value in recognizing the work of the women executives involved in the commissioning of *Bedlam*, and there is a similar case to be made here. Development might be understood as "closely associated with writing, but it is not considered to be actual writing," yet an exploration of the notes process demonstrates the ingenuity and the complexity of the storytelling work from the women working for the production company and channel.[37] Nonetheless, however I spin this, these women's names are not on the script. In addition, these women are performing a form of emotional and creative labor historically allocated to their gender. As Wreyford has pointed out, development roles are "heavily gendered," "frequently regarded as a nurturing role," and as such are often "seen as a natural fit for women."[38]

Erin Hill explains that by the 1970s and 1980s in Hollywood, women were leaving behind "script girl" jobs as clerks in studio story departments and "fighting their way into mid-level jobs as junior story executives, production coordinators, editors, casting directors, and publicists" (offering some interesting parallels here with McElroy's essay on the "feminization" of British television drama and the entry of women into executive level roles in the 1990s). However, Hill reveals that in Hollywood the "script girls" were then "patronizingly nicknamed 'd-girls'" and faced "the same implicit gender-related expectations they had faced in their old jobs, where it was presumed certain tasks came naturally to them as women." She concludes that even when women became development

executives, if they succeeded "it was as part of a team, and credit for their individual contributions was often assigned elsewhere. This was the price of entry
into what had been male-dominated positions, paid in exchange for tolerance
of women's presence in a workplace that men understood (and often still do)
as theirs."[39]

For *Bedlam* we can parse Hill's reading a little: the women *are* the executives,
and—I hope I convincingly argue throughout this book—they are more powerful than their male writers. The experience of Allison, Jones, and Parker chimes
with Conor's research on British screenwriters, where "writers are always in a
position of inferiority in the development process, always working at the
behest of others and are required to smile and 'take it.'"[40] While I do agree with
McElroy that "it is misleading when individual prominent women in managerial
roles are used metonymically to stand for the whole workforce," I hope that this
chapter has illuminated not only the power but the creativity of these managerial roles.[41] The women working on *Bedlam* required not only extensive editorial knowledge of long-form television storytelling (including act structures,
story lining, episodic and serial narratives, and generic mechanisms) but also
the ability to weigh up editorial issues against intended audience, budget, and
timescales. At the same time, they are also collaborating and compromising
both within and across media institutions to secure a unified vision for the
script that will enable the series to be made. Given this, by studying development we can begin to understand the complexity and creativity of collaboration in the television industry and the important creative role that these executive
roles play in the creation of screenplays. In other words, without Hollick and
Shindler, Barham, Rosencrantz, and Reeks, *Bedlam* would not exist.

CHAPTER 8

Story

Television studies loves story. Horace Newcomb argues that it is almost always motivated by three interrelated questions: "How does television tell stories?" ("form and narrative strategy, as well as production studies, genre studies . . ."); "How do the stories found on television relate to (express, control, limit, expand, shape etc.) the societies and cultures in which they appear?" (including "audience, reception, effects, ideology"); and finally "Why television?"[1] Newcomb reveals he is most interested in "why TV," in those questions "that help explain to others why television continues to be so important. That is what I look for when I read new work. That is just about all I care about, and if I do not find those critical questions, I stop reading" (clearly, Newcomb is never going to get as far as this chapter).[2] *Rewriting Television* is one giant, triple-layer of a story: about how *Bedlam* was made, about how television studies has evolved and continues to evolve, and about how (and later why) I wrote this book. And yet I do not ever ask "Why television?" (Quite frankly if I add any more questions my brain might explode.) Yet we can usefully draw upon his designations, we can rewrite and extend them, in order to ask a fourth question. I am ultimately less interested in "how television tells stories" than I am in "how television studies tell stories." Or, if we are being precise, "How might television studies tell its stories differently?"

MOMENTS OF HUMILIATION

I wrote the third draft of *Rewriting Television* in 2020 while unsuccessfully trying to navigate a global pandemic and homeschool two young children. During this strange and unusual period, I read Virginia Woolf's *The Waves* (in retrospect, I now recognize that I must be some kind of masochist). *The Waves* did suit my mindset for *Rewriting Television* though, and I was particularly taken with Bernard's declaration in the final chapter. He states that "to make you understand, to give you my life, I must tell you a story—and there are many, and so many—stories of childhood, stories of school, love, marriage, death, and so on; and none of them are true." He says that we tell each other stories as children do and that we decorate them "these ridiculous, flamboyant, beautiful phrases." However, Bernard is tired of "phrases that come down beautifully with all their feet on the ground!" He longs for "some little language such as lovers use, broken words, inarticulate words, like the shuffling of feet on the pavement," seeking "moments of humiliation and triumph that come now and then undeniably."[3]

Bernard's outburst gets to the heart of the matter. All stories told, no matter when, where, by whom, and to whom, are narrativized. When we talk of things that have happened in the past, we draw on our subjective perceptions of what happened. From that, we then create narratives, which may bear only a passing resemblance to reality. That is, we tell a story. I first broached this idea in chapter 2, when I framed my methodology broadly through social science understandings of narrative research. But in this chapter I want to go deeper into storytelling. I am fascinated not only with the study of people and how they make television, but also with how we, as academics, might frame these experiences on the page. With my script chapters, I wanted to create a mode that expressed emotion, that represented the moments of hesitancy, of inarticulateness and digression—what Bernard aches for, those "broken words, inarticulate words" that work through moments of "humiliation and triumph." This speaks to the "writing otherwise" strand of this book, which addresses "the difficulty of finding a language, particularly an *academic* language that captures those things that may drive our intellectual appetites."[4] At the same time, I didn't want to go completely experimental (and certainly not as far as *The Waves*). Given that so much of this book is a process of deconstruction (of discipline, of method, of approach) I decided to keep the structural aspect of the script chapters simple. The simplest way to convey narrative is through the telling of a linear story. And then the simplest way to begin thinking about a linear story is through plot.

I decided to tell *Bedlam*'s story through a chronological series of causally related events. I arranged *Bedlam*'s story in three episodic script chapters, each dealing with one or more distinct aspects of the process of making television. Chapter 3 is pitch to commissioning, chapter 6 is development, and chapter 9 is preproduction and broadcast. In short, I demarcated each script chapter as a beginning, a middle, or an end—the origins of classical three-act structure (and then the coda explores what happened after series 1 was broadcast). I then looked carefully at the best places to begin and end each of these chapters to encourage the reader to keep going (the equivalent of writing for *Bedlam*'s ad breaks). I don't know anyone who reads academic books from cover to cover, so in all the chapters, scripted and prose alike, I really wanted to see how far I could get you to go in a single read. I demarcated plot points of ebb and flow into every chapter, I opened each chapter with a new hook, I ended each chapter with a cliff-hanger, and I did my best to make sure that new characters emerged and receded as the story progressed to keep you interested.

Once I had the basic narrative shape of the scripts in place, I decided to work on emotion. While reading this book may already generate in you a wide range of emotions (I dream of enthusiasm but it could well be exasperation), the one I am really aiming for is empathy. In the script (and even in the prose chapters if I am honest), I aim to generate empathy, a condition defined by Olivia Laing as "the capacity to enter into the emotional reality of another human being, to recognize their independent existence, their difference; the necessary prelude to any act of intimacy."[5] Empathy is a foundational element of successful storytelling. You don't have to agree with me or with what I have done, but you must be able to understand why I did what I did and, hopefully, care about why I did it. Empathy is the prelude to intimacy, which in turn leads to deeper engagement with the story being told.

The simplest way to create empathy is through characters. In her "Character in Fiction" essay, Woolf argues that "there is something about people that continues to seem to [writers] of overwhelming importance"; that to study people is an "absorbing pursuit"; to impart those characters on the page, "an obsession."[6] But who are the characters in this book? Where have they come from? There is the narratorial "I" (now there's someone we need to discuss), whom I will explore further in chapter 10, on voice. But here I want to focus on how I created characters involved in making *Bedlam*. Production studies has long examined character, with decades of analysis on how television character is constructed through the work of writers, actors, and crew, but has less to say on how the "characters" included in the analysis—that is, the interviewees—are (re)constructed on the page.[7] In "Aesthetics and Audiences," Charlotte Brunsdon points out that "just like television, academics are obsessed with 'real people,'" but here I switch focus from consumer to producer, that is, from audience to maker.[8] In screenwriting studies, Steven Price acknowledges that screenwriting has tended toward the study of character for "creative production, rather than critical consumption," but here I want to now talk about how I used transcriptions to develop characters.[9]

Working with transcripts did give me some initial cause for concern. In screenwriting, we endlessly tell our students that it is what the character *does*, not what they say, that tells us who they are. But as I was working with transcription (in short, with dialogue alone), there was no action on the page. As you read my scripts, you cannot see what my characters are doing. You can only listen to them. As the script chapters are thus destined to remain oral histories, rather than fully realized action-based screenplays, I understood I had to focus on dialogue to create character. This is easier said than done. In his analysis of screenwriting, Craig Batty comments sardonically that "many people think writing dialogue is easy. It's just writing how people talk, right?"[10] But of course it is not just this. Dialogue is complex. Good dialogue reveals "the speaker's three dimensions, telling us what he is, hinting at what he will be"; at the same time dialogue moves "the story forward rather than bring it to a stop."[11] While I was restricted to using the words spoken by my interviewees, these were still important principles for the selection of material. Every pause, every hesitation, every word, every sentence was chosen with "three dimensions" in mind.

As I worked through the material, I was delighted to discover how clearly the characters' personalities emerged on the page. In the transcripts, Allison emerges as serious, mindful of his chosen words, and what (and whom) he is prepared to discuss; Jones is jolly and sanguine, a real horror lover; Parker is self-deprecating, wry, and, of the three, the most openly reflective of the strengths and weaknesses of *Bedlam*. Once I had established these writers as the primary narrators for *Bedlam*'s story, I then turned to my "supporting characters," at RED and Living TV. However, as the project developed, and I interwove the stories of Hollick and Shindler, Reeks, Rosencrantz, and Barham, their own stories came to matter as much as those of the writers. I discovered that I could weave together Rosencrantz's career development of Barham, Barham's growing realization that she was good at her new role, her own emotional investment in the project, and (as the coda will reveal) her dismay at being abruptly ousted from the series (spoiler!). This created additional plot and character arcs throughout the scripted chapters, adding texture and depth.

As I began to refine the order of the dialogue, I recognized I needed to make further amendments to the words on the page. I had requested that the interviews were transcribed verbatim, with all interviewees' "ahms, uhms, you knows, likes" included. I did this because of my love of verbatim theater, in particular the deployment of colloquial language and the translation of the vernacular, where the shape, rhythms, and word choices in individuals' sentences reveal characterization in a useful way. I was not looking for grammatically perfect statements to fold into scholarly prose; I wanted the cadences and messiness of language to be reflected on the page. But this commitment to a very specific kind of form caused problems. As critic Janet Malcolm points out, "When a journalist undertakes to quote a subject he has interviewed on tape, he owes it to the subject, no less than to the reader, to translate his speech into prose." She suggests that "only the most uncharitable (or inept) journalist will hold a subject to his literal utterances and fail to perform the sort of editing and rewriting that, in life, our ear automatically and instantaneously performs."[12]

Her observation was born out in the practitioners' responses to the transcriptions that I sent them. Many of the interviewees expressed horror at how inarticulate they appeared on paper. You could feel their pain in their email replies; these transcripts were shared within the context of an industry that runs on being brilliant with language, and with the beautiful, clean arrangement of words on a page. In addition, when I placed these unedited transcriptions into the scripts, rather than revealing individual character, the "true" transcriptions became banal; they displayed the inarticulacy of everyday speech instead (the note to self here is, of course, Malcolm is right).

Furthermore, the constant repetitions and filler words destroyed the pacing of the story. It became apparent that this commitment to replicating in written form how people speak does not give us access to reality any more than simply quoting people and folding their words into your analysis does. As Stephen Bottoms has pointed out in his work on documentary theater, "realism and reality are not the same thing, and that unmediated access to 'the real' is not something the theatre can ever honestly provide." He argues that verbatim plays "can too easily become disingenuous exercises in the presentation of 'truth,' failing (or refusing?) to acknowledge their own highly selective manipulation of opinion and rhetoric."[13] Similarly, I discovered that with oral histories, no matter whom you speak to or how you present your material, reality is not accessible.

So, instead, to work through the editing process, I turned back to my playwriting books, looking for reflexive writing techniques. I utilized the formal choices of playwrights Alistair McDowall and Brad Birch to represent speech on the page. This culminated in the creation of a dialogue key (see the "Cast of Characters and Dialogue Key" listing prior to chapter 3's script). I then lightly edited the material to reduce (but not remove all) repetitions, fragmented sentences, and ahms and uhms (a relief, I hope, for interviewee and reader alike) while attempting to retain the natural speech rhythms of the speakers.

My aim, throughout, was that as you read you get a strong sense of the characters. The way I tried to embody the characters of my interviewees is not just what they say, but their word choices, rhythms, and stresses of their own dialogue. If we covered over the names of interviewees, could you still, having so far read chapters 3 and 6, work out who was talking? If you thought about not only what they were saying but also how they said it? When one of the writers sighs, exasperated, stating that "the real issue with a show like *Bedlam* was 'how can we deliver this practically on the shoot this length?' Is there a way we *cannot* have them paragliding from the sky on fire?'" David Allison's voice should be apparent. When an executive proclaims that actors on British television "usually look like Quasimodo," I hope you can tell this is Claudia Rosencrantz. Or, when one executive coolly states, "I am not scared," you should know it is Nicola Shindler.

Having established a basic overarching plot for the script chapters—the beginning, middle, and end of the series—and, having then decided to show character through word choice and rhythm, I began to think about the formal qualities of space, that is, about the way I presented words on the page. As noted in the

Dialogue Key, if I include an ellipsis this means I have truncated the speech. That is a simple editorial decision for length and doesn't tend to have any deep meaning. But I am obsessed with gaps of other kinds, and their potential power for delineating for character and story. If I've included an em dash to indicate interrupted train of thought or brackets to demarcate a significant pause, then this means something. To my mind, this interruption or gap is a symbolic representation of something being thought but not necessarily being verbally articulated. What is hidden, invisible, in these gaps is often more interesting than the words we get to read.

I was also keen to think through what happens when you have one person speaking, and then, on the next line, someone else speaking. Remember, I conducted each of these interviews individually, over the space of about eighteen months, some in person, some online, some by phone. Yet the script presents them as speaking within the context of a group, a chorus, reacting to each other, as in real life, when I relayed a past interviewee's comment to the current interviewee, and got them to respond. In presenting these statements, and responses, one after the other, I wanted to ask, what happens when you lay out an individual's account of an experience, straight after another person's memory of the same event? What does the cut from one person to the next create? What does it suggest that might not be explicitly articulated?

I'm following here David Mamet's Eisenstein-influenced storytelling for directors, where he says, "You always want to tell the story in cuts. Which is to say, through a juxtaposition of images that are basically uninflected . . . let the cut tell the story."[14] My decision to script the interviews was a boon in this respect. In the industry, white space is worshipped. Screenplays are presented with as much white space as possible, for multiple reasons, two of which include making them skimmable and capable of achieving the (very rough) rule of thumb that one page equals one minute of screen time. To achieve the valorized white space, screenwriting becomes about cutting, about paring back the words (used to create sluglines, action, character description, and dialogue) to their absolute minimum. When individual words are at a premium, every word is required to perform at multiple levels: it has to have meaning, it has to suggest, it has to be allusive (it is *so* unlike an academic book). In short, script creates opportunity to minimize and to cut words, "in order to create gaps, or spaces within the text so that others might respond imaginatively." This elision "creates the desire to fill in the gap. It activates people to question, to imagine."[15] In my selecting, editing, and organizing of words, and of the space between them, I make space for interpretation, to indicate what isn't being said, but is potentially being thought.

In the end, this is all about subtext, "the true meaning simmering under the words and actions . . . the implicit meaning rather than the explicit meaning."[16] Subtext is the absorbing material that "dwells beneath words" and creates conflict.[17] It is also a primary method for deepening empathetic engagement, as playwright Simon Stephens suggests "an audience deciphers and interprets the behavior of characters in an attempt to empathize with them."[18] I soon discovered that subtext works better for some characters than others. In transcription, Rosencrantz remains pure text. When she states women "like incredibly intelligent programs because, guess what, women are incredibly intelligent. The whole idea that women liked all this [dieting program] nonsense was rubbish," you don't really get any subtext: she lays it all out on the page (which is, admittedly, completely delightful). Some of the more understated characters benefitted from this approach though. When Jenny Reeks says approvingly "I like Claud. She is a great girl," you have a sense of a history of the working relationship between them; or when Barham says Reeks is "amazing" and Reeks reflects "looking back I suppose I was okay," you are given a window into Reeks's character.

Subtext is also productive for understanding relationships between characters as well: in a later chapter, discussing when Anne Mensah took over Sky Living for *Bedlam* series 2, Shindler reveals that "Anne worries. Or, at least, she worried a lot . . . I feel like Anne really was worried, and I really want to help her feel like everything is okay." Mensah concurs, "Nicola is very patient and has known me a long time." There is so much to unpick in this passage alone: like Reeks and Rosencrantz, it suggests a professional relationship with a friendly, personal dimension. At the same time, it reveals respect, compassion, and empathy but is delivered within a mode of discourse appropriate for a professional interview.

In *Story and Discourse*, Seymour Chatman discusses literary stories based on "pure dialogue" between characters. He suggests that the "apparent structural simplicity" of such work "is an illusion." For Chatman, "Stories that are uniquely dialogic or rely heavily on it require the implied reader to do more inferring." The reader here is required to "divine for himself the illocutionary force of the sentences spoke by characters to each other, that is, what they 'mean' as a function of what they *do* in the context of the action, since there are no direct reports of that doing."[19] This is, in my own way, what I tried to do with the dialogue in the script chapters, to push the (implied) reader (you?) to become more active. As I admitted at the beginning of this book, I *know* I am making you work here. Of course, I also acknowledge that all forms of narrative creation and reception require some kind of work. In his essay on reader-orientated criticism, Robert C. Allen explains that "every story entails someone to whom and for whose benefit the story is being told."[20] What is important here is how the narrative organizes and expresses itself, what Newcomb describes as "a process of *rearranging the world* for imaginative purposes." To achieve this rearrangement, two things are required: first, "the one who answers the questions, who selects events and orders them," and second, the "one who listens, who anticipates, who believes or disbelieves, who laughs or fails to laugh, who places herself or himself into the circumstances by thinking something such as 'I wouldn't have done it that way.'"[21]

By letting you in the decision-making processes that underpin the storytelling of this book, I am suggesting that we all could reflect on how we tell our stories of television, and how we might tell them differently. That is, why we do what we do (as scholars), what we study, and how we do it. Reflexivity remains important for the future development of our discipline, not least because "the creation of narratives . . . is never a 'neutral' act."[22]

AMBIVALENCE

I do grasp though that I am working in nonfiction and dealing with real people's lives, and this playful approach to transcription has serious implications. In her extended essay on long-form narrative nonfiction, Malcolm asks, why can't the nonfiction writer "fool around," take liberties, and "conduct their own modernistic experiments? Why should the writer in one genre enjoy more privileges than the writer in another?" The first time I read this, I was nodding furiously, thinking, "Yes, exactly, why can't I?" But then I was sobered by her answer. For Malcolm, the fiction writer is "entitled to more privileges. He is master of his own house and may do what he likes in it," but the nonfiction writer is "only a renter, who must abide by the conditions of his lease, which stipulates he leave the house—and its name is Actuality—as he found it." Malcolm concedes, "He may bring in his own furniture and arrange it as he likes (the so-called New Journalism is about the arrangement of furniture), and he may play his radio quietly."[23] But that is it. We can see this mirrored in the work of sociologists Jane Kilby and Graeme Gilloch and their "sociography" project, on how to write differently within their discipline. Writing on the work of sociologist Ash Watson, they point out that she "reminds us of what is important about academic writing and sociological writing: it is critical writing; and no matter how experimental, it has to do the work of critique. A sociologist writing fiction is not a novelist: the writing is supported by years of research. Evidence is to hand, in the telling."[24]

Malcolm, Kilby, Gilloch, and Watson all have a point. As I am a "renter" of (intellectual?) property rather than "master of the house," all my play with form still needs to have a meaning grounded in the lived realities of the people interviewed. Then, these interviews have to do something, and I have to critique what is happening when they are doing something. I've already discussed in chapter 2 the ethical process in creating the transcripts and engaging the practitioners in transcript revision. I then always used the transcription in an appropriate fashion, quoting passages only in proper context, with the meaning given by the interviewee. However, my ability to abbreviate sentences and to control who speaks when, and about what, is my choice alone. And it is a choice based on the story I want to tell. As such, despite my careful handling and sharing of the transcriptions, I suspect not all my interviewees will be entirely happy with the story I have created, even when I use their words in their original context. As Kim V. L. England points out, "Exploitation and possible betrayal are endemic to fieldwork."[25]

We can also find parallel concerns in this book's writing of academic histories and in the writing of particular academics and their ideas. I am inspired by the late 1990s and early 2000s scholarship of film, television, and media scholars Brunsdon, John Corner, Christine Geraghty, and David Lusted, and Christine Gledhill and Linda Williams. However, I frequently take their arguments outside of their original context, often extensively so. I home in on one or two lines that really speak to me, often at the risk of distorting the original intended meaning of their essays. There is a bigger reason for doing this though, beyond simply cherry-picking words that please, and here I turn to Sara Ahmed, who can explain it much better than me. She explains that her book *Willful Subjects* is grounded in philosophical arguments, but it is not a book of philosophy, and she is not a philosopher. For Ahmed, "not being a philosopher working with philosophy can be understood as generative: the incapacity to return texts to their proper histories allows us to read sideways or across, thus creating a different angle on what is being reproduced."[26] I like the idea of not philosophy. I like the idea of not television studies. As I told you in chapter 1, I am not, first and foremost, a television scholar. My first three books are on horror film (the book after this one, that I should be writing *right* now, will be on horror film too). This lack of historical allegiance to people, to ideas, to methods, to specific modes within the discipline is all genuinely liberating. As I encounter canonical television studies publications, I am now free to read "sideways," to read generatively, with impunity.

We can bring together these questions around how this book deploys the words of practitioners and the ideas of academics by considering an essay that Brunsdon published in 2015. In this essay, she writes about her experience of attending a conference for the Birmingham Centre for Contemporary Cultural Studies, where she was a former student. At the conference she found herself "being made history," which she wasn't necessarily happy about. She explains, "The ambivalence was something to do with the question of who tells whose stories; a resistance to being made history while still, in my own mind living it. If you tell your story to someone else, and they use it to tell another story, what is left? Is your story still your story?"[27] Brunsdon's last two questions are particularly important. From my point of view, the writers and executives on *Bedlam* told me their story, the way they wanted to tell it, and we agreed it in the transcription. However, I then used the agreed material to tell another kind of story, one that they may only partially accept. While all quotes remain in their proper context, and attributed to their original speakers, with original emphases, I have selected, cut down, and judiciously organized the material with an eye to plot, character, dialogue, and subtext, with each narrative component working together to further the overall story of pitch to cancellation.

This is analytical work, but it is analytical work delivered without fully controlled conditions. As H. Porter Abbott notes, stories are "to a certain degree," "at the mercy of the reader and how diligently he or she reads." This would be a dispiriting position, if it were not for Abbott's follow-up sentence, that "most stories, if they succeed that is if they enjoy an audience or readership—do so because they have to some extent successfully controlled the process of story construction."[28] This chapter is all about the attempt to create and control story. I consider the selection and organization of the interview material to be a creative act, and, as such, the story of *Bedlam* presented here is just one possible way of considering past events. It does not belong to any of the interviewees individually. This story, that you read here, right now, is now mine, and mine alone.

Conclusion

In chapter 2 I wrote about how once I started working as a screenwriter and script editor, I struggled to reconcile my newly acquired skillset and knowledge with the traditional academic work I had done to date. This feeling reminded me of Gérard Genette's rallying cry: "What would theory be worth if it were not also good for *inventing practice*?"[29] It was only after I completed a solid draft of each of the script chapters that I grasped that this book, in and of itself, might be conceptualized as a form of creative practice. But what kind of practice might it be? Craig Batty and Susan Kerrigan make a distinction between "theory-driven practices that use the screen to 'do' research (e.g. research-led practice)" and "systematic reflection upon a production to gain rigorous insights into how a work was made (e.g., practice-led research)."[30] Typically, practice as research (PaR) is focused on a research process that leads to a creative output. It usually includes the artifact (the praxis), documentation of process (notebooks, images, etc.), and a complementary piece of reflective writing (the exegesis). For *Rewriting Television*, we could read the script chapters as praxis and the prose chapters as exegesis (I do also have documentation—every note I have made about this project, dated, scrawled in fading black fountain pen on yellow legal pads—right back to 2017, but I can't imagine anyone would be remotely interested in them.) Can we conceptualize this book, or at least elements of this book, then, as a form of a research-led practice?

Iteration is useful for thinking through the answer. To iterate a process "is to repeat it several times (though probably with some variation) before proceeding." The practitioner must then choose "between the alternative results created by the iteration, focusing on some and leaving others behind (temporarily or permanently." Iteration is cyclical, where "formulations and theorizations" may be "published and/or applied to the generation of future creative works," but also "at every stage in the cycle it is possible to go back to the previous stages."[31] The script chapters are the result of undertaking and transcribing the interviews, reflecting upon this transcription and using the reflection as a basis for organizing the material, then reflecting upon the material and producing supporting chapters that map stories of *Bedlam*'s development and then this book's development. Chapter 11, titled "Glorious," then looks back over this whole process to consider how and why this work might have value. Does this sound so far removed from the process of creative practice? Where is the line drawn between practice and scholarly writing? Do we have to draw a line at all?

Arts-based PaR places "an equally important emphasis" on the interdependence between "the artist-practitioner, the creative product and the critical process" and "the central role that making plays in the creation of knowledge."[32] This erasure of the distinction between creative and critical certainly appeals. Yet at the same time, detractors might suggest that I am missing the point: all academic writing is creative writing. As Kilby and Gilloch acknowledge, "There is the important recognition and caveat that experimenting with the protocols of academic writing is not new: academics have always written with creative flair."[33] We all plot and structure our work, create characters, invoke mood, whether we do it consciously or not. I get it. But it's not as black-and-white as me saying, "Hey team! We can be creative too!" Rather, it's about asking questions as a way of expanding the possibilities for how we might do television studies (or film, or media; let's be honest these questions translate right across mediums). I am trying to free up a mode of working that embraces positionality, subjectivity, and reflexivity, while at the same time generating original research that might be worked through using the same written forms of the industry that we study. It isn't because I think this way of working is the only way or the best way. I simply want to see what happens when we mix the generative potential of form and thought.

CHAPTER 9

"It Is Horrible, It Is Necessary"

CHRIS PARKER: We had read-throughs with the cast.

RICHARD FEE: Those few days before the read-through, are a *massive* few days for the script editor. You've just had a *really intense* few days. In a situation like that, you're working with three different writers on three different scripts—whereas on you know, a Russell [T. Davies] project, you're reading three different scripts but they're all written by Russell so it's one phone call, rather than three. You know. So you're doing all that. While at the same time trying to input it all, and make sure that all the formatting—I know it sounds incredibly boring but—all the production formatting is right. You're making cuts. You're changing names for clearances. There's *loads* going on in those last few days. So that's incredibly stressful! And then, it's a *massive* thing to get the script published for the read-through. It's the big deadline really.

NICOLA SHINDLER: I want the right . . . people [at the read-through] who need to give an opinion before we start filming. And then I want . . . to make sure everything contributes towards making it as peaceful a place as possible.

RICHARD FEE: I've had situations where . . . the read-through is the day before you start shooting. Which is a . . . nightmare. Because then, not only are you having to have [] the creative process of "How are we going to solve these issues?" but you're playing four-dimensional chess. Cos you're trying to solve the issues but also . . . look at your time and "How long have we got before we're shooting that? Oh shit we're shooting the day after tomorrow." Or, "We know we've only got that location for three days next week so all our problems have to be solved by then."

JENNY REEKS: It's an exciting moment because up until then you have just been dealing with pages and words said in your own voice, in your head.

ANNE MENSAH: Oh my god, it is totally exciting.

NICOLA SHINDLER: It is drama. It's not a book. You can read it as many times as you want but until you actually hear it . . .

ANNE MENSAH: It is the first time we get to see the actors inhabit those roles.

DAVID ALLISON: I remember having one-to-one chats with every cast member: "What questions do you have about the character, what do you want to know?" Often there are misunderstandings. They go, "The reason why they're being really quiet here is." "No, that's not the reason they're being quiet. It's because of this." You want to talk through those things.

ANNE MENSAH: Even though they are not acting as such, they are reading, it still brings it to life in a different sort of way.

AMY BARHAM: [The *Bedlam* series 1 read-through] was a great buzzy atmosphere. We all sat down around this big long table in this conference room, with the cast down one side and everyone else round the table. The writers were all down one end of the table, looking really nervous.

RICHARD FEE: You're looking for cues where . . . how are the writers feeling?

ANNE MENSAH: I just feel sorry for the writers because it's way more shattering for them.

RICHARD FEE: It's a *huge* thing for them, to . . . hear their script read, for the first time. By these actors, and visualize these actors as *their* characters, who have been in their head so long.

AMY BARHAM: For the writers, you've had your stuff picked apart for all of the notes process and then you go and hear it out loud and you're like, "oh shit."

RICHARD FEE: I'm not a writer. I could never be a writer. But I imagine . . . it's a vulnerable position to be in.

NICOLA SHINDLER: It is horrible. Well. Some find it horrible. Some find it really useful. It is necessary.

JENNY REEKS: Writing is such an exposing process; you really have to care about [the writers]. You have to protect their feelings otherwise they are not going to be able to deliver the goods.

AMY BARHAM: It was fun to see the cast together and to hear that they had this great chemistry. There were lots of laughs and lots of fun little bits that everyone was already doing and you just thought "Oh, thank god," because not only is this dialogue working but I know these people are going to look cool and sexy on-screen with each other and you believe that they're friends. I just felt so relieved that was working in the way that we wanted it to.

RICHARD FEE: [As a script editor] generally, you're reading the stage directions. Out loud. Which is the worst part. It's just horrible. Ehm. I don't have to do it now, for-tunately, because I'm not really a script editor anymore. I mean, I am, but. We have a script editor. And you're in front of . . . the head of drama . . . and . . . all these actors, and Will Young! And in that situation, stage directions can be quite long. And you don't want everybody in the room sitting there waiting for you to read through half a page of stage directions. So you're trying to condense it. Say it in the briefest way possible. While still conveying the sense of the action. That's all you're concentrating on in that moment. You don't get much chance to *really* listen.

CAROLINE HOLLICK: [As a script executive] you're listening for the most part. For lines that don't sound, that don't leap off the page, sometimes you just need to hear it read. And to make sure everything makes sense. Hearing it read aloud is when you really understand, what makes sense and what doesn't in terms of the plot. So it's a, really crucial stage.

AMY BARHAM: [As an executive producer] you're basically looking for: how's the pacing feeling? Is the dialogue working? The actors doing those roles, are they working? What does that feel like because that's the first time you're—I've seen a few of them on tape working with a casting director, when they put themselves on tape doing some of the dialogue, but not feeding off each other—the chemistry. What is the chemistry going to be like?

NICOLA SHINDLER: You get an absolute indication as to how the actor's going to read the role, even if they have not rehearsed. So, if there are potential issues—you need to listen out for them. Because. You can tackle it at that point. And very infrequently you might have to let go of an actor at that point. We have done it once because we realized we'd miscast someone. They were way too young, for what we wanted. And when you hear it in context you realize.

JENNY REEKS: [As an executive producer] I check the casting is okay and they can do their job. It's a very boring job, mine. I make sure that these people have got it. You can just tell.

NICOLA SHINDLER: [As an executive producer] it is really important for me to listen to it read. To be read, for story, for that is when you find out, "Oh my god, we have not included this" or "we say this five times" or "it doesn't make sense."

NEIL JONES: There will be practical considerations that come out of the table read.

RICHARD FEE: You sit next to the script supervisor. Who will be timing it. When you've finished you'll go "How many minutes over are we?" Then "Oh god we've gotta cut ten pages" or "Shit we're ten pages under." You haven't got much time before you start shooting. After the final read, the fun really starts. You're going from the read-through to the broadcaster meeting.

ANNE MENSAH: I think everybody is emotionally knackered by the time we get to the notes session.

CAROLINE HOLLICK: This is the first time for the most part that the broadcasters have really engaged with the full finalized episodes—so you get their notes.

RICHARD FEE: Sometimes in a read-through it can suddenly [] unlock something for the broadcaster. Or they can suddenly see a problem that they hadn't realized was there.

ANNE MENSAH: There is something amazing about hearing something read out loud that gives you an insight that gets you off the page. You end up feeling it in a different way to reading it. Whereas, when it is on the page, it's not quite as truthful, I guess.

NEIL JONES: It can still be quite radical changes, because it's usually the first time that … the execs have heard it, read, or you've still been doing new drafts really close to the table read.

NICOLA SHINDLER: I do remember going, "That *whole* ghost story didn't make any sense."

CHRIS PARKER: You're really hoping that it's going to be ok with them, otherwise your schedule is thrown out of the window because you should be moving on to the next script.

RICHARD FEE: So you clear the room. All the actors, the heads of production leave. You're left with writer, Nicola, producer, director, script editor, broadcaster. It's nerve-wracking.

ANNE MENSAH: Which is when the commissioners go, "But really, have you thought about this?" [*laughs*]. And they are probably just sitting there thinking, "Could you fuck off."

AMY BARHAM: I can't remember that [meeting] very clearly. [I was pregnant] and I just remember, "I need the loo so badly but I can't leave."

NICOLA SHINDLER: You say some general things that are working, aren't working and then you go through page by page and hope at the end you have a clear plan.

RICHARD FEE: In that meeting, the script editor's taking a load of notes. Not really chipping in too much. Because it's very senior people talking about high-level stuff. You're trying to digest it … in a way that … will be presentable to everyone in note form while also the back of your mind is trying to problem-solve already thinking "shit how do we do that." Whether you're working on a Russell project, a Sally [Wainwright] project, a Danny [Brocklehurst] project, being in those meetings, *understanding* the nub of the argument and being able to … sum it all up in a way that is brief, concise, easily understandable. The big challenge is writing [the notes] up in a way that is coherent. The nature of free-flowing conversation if you write up just literally the notes, it will make no sense. So that's a … *huge* part of the RED script editor's role actually.

NICOLA SHINDLER: What you get mostly from them is what isn't working.

RICHARD FEE: And sometimes it can be *massive*: you know, "We've got a problem here." Sometimes those decisions can get quite *heated*. And sometimes everybody can be on the same page and be "Yeah do you know what that didn't work."

NICOLA SHINDLER: What you have to do is work out how to make it work. Which isn't a bad thing. It isn't their job to come up with solutions. It is our job.

CHRIS PARKER: [RED] have to really keep both sides satisfied. They're very good at thinking of [] practical ways around the notes. Or they may say, "We don't agree with that way of doing it but what about this?" Nicola's obviously very creative about coming up with … ideas and alternatives that are going to work. She's very involved in a lot of this.

NICOLA SHINDLER: Well, that is my job.

RICHARD FEE: In that situation when you've got a problem, it's also pastoral support for the writer. Not in terms of *Bedlam*—speaking generally. Cos you can be left with a writer with their head in the hands thinking "How the hell am I going to do this?"

AMY BARHAM: Those things can be really horrible and really upsetting.

RICHARD FEE: It's in that immediate post-read-through, where *everything*'s been building up to that moment. It's a vulnerable position to be in. That can be the start of a *big* edit process.

NICOLA SHINDLER: There was a lot of that in *Bedlam*. You'd come away and you would go, "There is a big hole in the story" just because they are just such weird, complicated stories. So, there was a lot of story work.

CHRIS PARKER: There was quite a bit of tweaking to do. Changing this and that.

DAVID ALLISON: You can work on the dialogue, the magic, the scare, but you've got that little time, you cannot go "Actually the structure isn't working, we have to take it apart." We probably did have to do that on one or two occasions, it's awful. You feel like "Oh my god nothing works." It's like taking the engine out of a car, hoping you can put it back in again.

NICOLA SHINDLER: But we knew it did work in our head, it was the way that it had been written down. So, there is always a way around it, you just have to pull it back to beat by beat.

CHRIS PARKER: I remember that on some of the scripts we were working—they basically wouldn't let us leave the studio. There were just 101 things had to be tweaked at the last minute.

NICOLA SHINDLER: We will work until very late that night and get all the notes. And then I will leave them to decide how it happens next. Either they'll write up notes or they will start working or they will have another meeting but mostly then I would stay back until . . . sometimes I will get pitched solutions, because they want me to hear before they jump in to do it.

CHRIS PARKER: There was one episode, we had to change an awful lot, we had to start from scratch on an episode we thought we'd. *Finished*. We had to *salvage* this script and to re-brainstorm it, because [a broadcaster] felt a lot of things weren't working so it was "Oh god, we thought we'd finished this" and "We haven't got time to go over this." We had to do a very quick rewrite on it, sit until it was done. We were in the Granada building. I was saying "I won't be able to get home tonight, the last train goes at half-ten," you know, "you'll have to get a taxi" and the three of us were literally in an office on different computers, typing away.

NEIL JONES: It became clear that no one was going home after that so RED booked hotels and yes we were in Manchester all night.

CHRIS PARKER: Obviously we were used to working at home at *our leisure* kind of thing [*laughs*] but it's more of like an American way of working where people are actually in rooms together and bashing stuff out a lot of the time.

CAROLINE HOLLICK: It was the joy of having three of them, we could do it, very quickly, lots of different ideas. So I did really enjoy it. The amount of story you can get out of a team.

NEIL JONES: Often a lot of the most fevered rewriting is going on at that late, late stage just as it gets close to production.

ANNE MENSAH: My job is simple, compared to what it is to really get a show like *Bedlam* on its feet. Oh my gosh. Production is so hard.

NEIL JONES: It's never finished . . . because things change so often during a shoot.

NICOLA SHINDLER: There's a lot of problems that happen when you film. It is problem after problem after problem. Budget problems, locations fall through, actors can't do it suddenly, you have to recast, costumes aren't right. Everything. Every single day.

NEIL JONES: And even after, you know even after the shoot you can be . . . rewriting stuff that didn't work.

RICHARD FEE: And then right through postproduction as well. There may be story issues that come to light in the edit.

CHRIS PARKER: It's not typical of a soap you do get to the point where you do hand it over and that's that.

NEIL JONES: It's never really finished until it goes out.

———◆———

CAROLINE HOLLICK: Series 1 was Living. And, one particular group of execs.

AMY BARHAM: I was due to have my baby in September and so I was going off early August, so for the first couple of weeks of my maternity leave I was looking at the [series 1] rushes from home. Around the same time we all found out that we were being sold to Sky.

DAVID ALLISON: Sky bought Living in the middle of production of the first series.

NICOLA SHINDLER: Yes, that was fun.

AMY BARHAM: It was, "Oh right, okay ehm, I guess we just hand this over to them" ahm and it was so sad because I didn't get to work on it after that.

DAVID ALLISON: So. All Living execs who had been there left. [] Everyone. [] The whole team.

NICOLA SHINDLER: I have had the executives leave before but I have never had a whole channel bought by someone else.

JENNY REEKS: It was gutting.

AMY BARHAM: My email was shut down. It was just gone. Everything was gone. That was it. I did my deal. Done. Gone.

NICOLA SHINDLER: I really liked those women that I was working with, so that was sad.

JENNY REEKS: Well I went on doing my bit on it. I was around for the airing. I don't know why I was still involved in any way. It was like I was doing it for ITV then.

CLAUDIA ROSENCRANTZ: I left at Christmas when the sale went through. Gosh. It was absolutely draining and ghastly.

JENNY REEKS: I severely missed Claud and Amy. I was desperate for them to have a show that would put them on the drama stage—but [Sky] whipped the stage away [from the Living team] before it all happened.

AMY BARHAM: The next thing I know I got invited by Sky to the screening, and the director stood up and gave a speech about how it was such a brave move and I sat there in the audience going, "Okay!" It was my first night out after I'd had my kid and I was like—it was very emotional, to see it and then not to have been a part of it. It was a bizarre night. Just seeing everybody again. And it looked so good, they'd done a great job with it.

JENNY REEKS: It was very disappointing for everyone at Living who had really invested so much of their hopes in—their future hopes.

CLAUDIA ROSENCRANTZ: It was sheer pleasure for me actually to see that you could take something from concept to transmission and for it to just turn out so well.

JENNY REEKS: I didn't bother to work again after that. I thought, "Oh well, tough titty, I am not going to bother now."

AMY BARHAM: And, ahm, the bittersweet feeling of "I wish I'd been able to see it all the way through." Because it was a passion project and my thing that I thought of night and day for months and months and it was really hard to just give it up. I didn't think anyone was going to mess it up, it was just hard to say goodbye to something that had been a big part of your life.

CLAUDIA ROSENCRANTZ: Amy found a great love for scripted through doing this. It probably did, in some ways, change her life.

CHAPTER 10

Voice

When we write about voice and television, what do we mean? Is it my television practitioner's voices? Is it how their voices are transcribed? Or is it how they appear, as characters, on the page? Film and television studies tends to think through voice in terms of the voice of the actor, or the voice-over.[1] Rose Ferrell suggests that in screenwriting studies there is an "absence of a theory of voice in screenwriting," while Levi Dean concludes that "no concrete definition has yet been agreed" on what the writer's voice even is.[2] In contrast, production studies examines voice in terms of method, as in Miranda J. Banks's research on Writers' Guild members. Banks is keen to work through what voice *is*, not only as a mode of oral history but also as a form of data composed of "personal memory and individual representation, not fact."[3] As such, the question of voice in production studies becomes a question of representing voices. This is acknowledged by Vicki Mayer, Banks, and John T. Caldwell in *Production Studies*: "The crisis of representing producers, their locations, industries and products is the burden of representation for production studies."[4] But I've already covered how I represent practitioner voices in earlier chapters, in terms of form and story. So how else might we think about voice?

The multiplicity of voices in chapter 9 reveals a whole stage of preproduction that I hadn't really considered before doing the interviews: the read-through and broadcaster meeting. This is the first time everyone gathers together, in person, and brings *Bedlam* to life. The writers, production company, and channel are (temporarily) united in their goals: listening for coherent story, dialogue that rings true, confirmation of good casting, and chemistry between the actors. This is an act of faith and a working toward a kind of verisimilitude: Does *Bedlam* feel real? Has everyone involved in development successfully created a credible and engaging world that works within the parameters of television storytelling?

It is the performative, real-time dimension of the read-through that interests me the most. The collective, live, in-person experience effectively generates a stage play. The long table in the conference room is the set. The actors *and* the practitioners are the cast, each playing their defined roles. Then, the audience is this same body of people: each takes their turn to perform their role, each then performs as an active audience member, listening in, watching, making sure they understand the story that is unfolding. It is only really the commissioners and development executives who don't have to outwardly "perform"; their job is (initially) not to speak but to listen, and to envisage. The read-through creates a scenario where drama is made, in the moment. Jenny Reeks explains that "it's an exciting moment because up until then you have just been dealing with pages and words said in your own voice, in your head." Reeks conveys here that unlike prose fiction, words alone cannot convey the full impact of writing for stage or screen, and a live setting, populated by living, breathing humans, is needed (and here I paraphrase Mensah) to bring the work to life. In this moment, possibilities are made manifest: "the stage is a space that contains possibilities, not realities: it is a place for imagining."[5]

Developing this further, the read-through can be understood as a "closed-time closed-place" play. In playwriting there are four conventional options for demarcating time and place: open or closed time, and open or closed place. Closed-time closed-space plays "are set in one location and unfold in real time." Stephen Jeffreys suggests that these are "pressure-cooker plays," "hot plays," that "you're stuck in one place" and "they are full of decisions made under pressure."[6] The read-through play is inhabited by different kinds of participants (the actors, the staff of the production company, the broadcaster, and the heads of department for production), who are required to perform their own roles in a pressurized environment, with high stakes. Actors can be sacked. Whole episodes of script can be rewritten. Filming schedules and locations are already locked in, no matter what happens here.

For script editor Fee, these read-throughs are excruciating because he is required to have a voice. He has to perform, when, at every other point in the process, his role is to support and nurture the voices of other creatives, from behind the scenes. As the script editor, Fee has to read out the sluglines and action in front of everyone: "You're in front of . . . the head of drama . . . and . . . all these actors, and Will Young!" He's also very aware of the real-time scenario he is performing in and the need to move forward quickly, to progress to the next moment of actor performance: "You don't want everybody in the room sitting there waiting for you to read through half a page of stage directions. So you're trying to condense it. Say it in the briefest way possible. While still conveying the sense of the action." At the same time, he is also thinking through the larger logistical problems posed by performing this reading. The read-throughs can "take place the day before you start shooting," and when problems inevitably arise, they are, for Fee, a "nightmare" akin to "playing four-dimensional chess."

The closed-time closed-space play is also highly emotional, "in which characters feel hemmed in or are trying to break out," but the physical limitations of space and time prevent escape.[7] In the *Bedlam* reading, the writers all sat together at one end of the table, made more vulnerable than at any other time in the process. Ferrell may have defined voice as the "pervasive authorial presence" of the screenwriter, but in the read-through scenario this does not translate: the writer is, in effect, silenced, the script becomes more than their words as the script editor and actors bring it to life.[8] At the same time, the RED and Sky/Living team are also thinking about what this experience means for the writers, Fee looking for cues as to how they are feeling, explaining that it is a "vulnerable" moment, Reeks wanting to "protect their feelings," Mensah acknowledging that the experience is often "shattering" for writers, while Shindler concludes, "It is horrible. Well. Some find it horrible. Some find it really useful. It is necessary." It is no wonder that Mensah confesses, "Oh my god, it is totally exciting."

The read-through has its own story structure, the reading of the episode from beginning to middle to end. The voices of the actors (and the script editor) are expected to be heard. But, after the read-through, the actors and heads of production leave. The script editor, directors, writers, and production company and broadcast executives remain: the curtain rises on the second act. It is time for the broadcast meeting. The script editor is no longer required to have a voice. Instead, Fee takes notes and keeps his head down, "because it's very senior people talking about high-level stuff." The broadcaster meeting is where the hitherto-silent executives begin to speak. As ever, voice connotes power: who gets to speak, who has to listen, who responds, and how they respond. As Mensah laughs, this is the point when the commissioner goes "But really, have you thought about this?" and she imagines the production company and the writers thinking "Could you fuck off." Barham is as flippant, ruminating on needing to use the bathroom when she should have been concentrating. But from Shindler's perspective, this is serious: the broadcaster explains what does not work for them, while she has to "work out how to make it work." While this is going on, in Fee's words, the writers can be "sat with their head in their hands" (and notably, if you go back to chapter 9, you'll see that the writers have very little to say about either the read-through or the broadcaster meeting).

Throughout this session, the executive-level staff work through good and bad general feedback, then undertake a page-by-page analysis to create a plan of action for revisions. This is a new scene, "a sequence of actions that take place within a continuous time frame."[9] However, unlike the closed-time closed-space format of the read-through, the goal here is not to create drama. Ideally, participants are looking to avoid unnecessary conflict. However, in Fee's words, the conflict in these "scenes" can be "massive" and things can get "heated."

In his book on playwriting, Steve Waters argues that "for a scene to remain a scene rather than a short play, it must yield something partial and unresolved, opening a door onto what follows, as much as closing it on what's transpired."[10] Indeed, in the case of the table read and the broadcaster meeting, what is left partial and unresolved is the script itself.

This is the point that the writers become active again, their voices returned to them. In his work on the "voice of the writer," Ian Macdonald argues that the "struggle" of writers to write is "inextricable" from "their struggle to make sense of, adapt or challenge, the doxa [general received wisdom] of screenwriting, and/or the orthodoxies around which they find themselves working."[11] We see this in *Bedlam* not so much as a "struggle" but as part of an industrial collaborative process. It is less about a specific theory of a "doxa" than being agile in response to the specific requirements of the production company and the broadcaster, and to changing conditions in preproduction and production. The read-through is in fact a process that speaks to, in Eva Novrup Redvall's words, "the actual process of how people develop new products in a specific, highly collaborative context marked by many different types of constraints."[12] The writers may find themselves staying up all night to pitch ideas to Shindler and then revise the scripts. Then, they rewrite again and again and again leading up to and during production, and then, as Neil Jones and Fee note, they may still be writing during postproduction. While the development process of a script—in theory—ends when the project enters preproduction, chapter 9 reveals that this is not the actual practice, evidencing Craig Batty and Stayci Taylor's assertation that script development is "a process that resists both definition and delineation, because elements of the practice—drafts, revisions, feedback and so on—may continue into other erstwhile discrete aspects of production."[13] As Jones concludes, the script is "never really finished" until the episode is actually broadcast.

There are one or two how-to guides aimed at aspiring screenwriters and directors that outline the function of the read-through, but only as one element in a process moving from pitch to production.[14] In academia, there is a paucity of published material of detailed analysis and thinking about this fascinating stage of preproduction. Tom Cantrell and Christopher Hogg include brief references to the read-through as part of actor preparation in *Acting in British Television*, while Richard Hewett has produced an excellent archival study of the BBC's North Acton Television Rehearsal Rooms, but he is more interested in the building as a space of community than in the mechanics of the process.[15] Susan Cake comes the closest when she reflects upon a two-hour read-through she organized for a comedy screenplay and concludes that the table read offers creative possibilities for collaboration.[16]

However, Hogg's recent attempt to create "conceptual texture" in television studies is an ideal—and perhaps the only—reference point for our work. Hogg suggests that "the insights presented" in his interview with actor Julie Hesmondhalgh "stress the value of foregrounding the experiences, perceptions and processes of those working in the production of TV drama." He argues that "the collection and analysis of primary industry interview data aids in avoiding the 'analytical trap' of trying to understand a television drama's complex mechanics of creative agency, meaning and value through the consideration of an endtext and its reception alone."[17] Following this, we can argue that it is only through industry interview data that we uncover the drama of the read-through, where the hidden "experiences, perceptions and processes" of those working on *Bedlam* are brought into light, where their voices are made manifest.

BORED TO TEARS

In *Screen Tastes*, Charlotte Brunsdon reveals that a "formal" preoccupation with voice arose as she collected essays for her collection. She explains that "while it is possible to contextualize and update the arguments of the essays . . . it is more difficult to address the historical variation in the voice in which they were written." She explains that one section of *Screen Tastes* is "teacher's essays" "written in quite a different voice to the early soap opera work" with "much greater self-consciousness of the exclusions of the feminist project, of the particular cultural context of the 'we' of feminism."[18] In touching upon voice, Brunsdon leads us to a bigger question, taken up in the rest of this chapter. What might an academic "voice" look like? Building on this, how might we think through voice in a way that is explicitly responsive to the subject matter at hand—of writers, writing, and creative process?

Few people consider academic writing as having an aesthetic dimension. Certainly, some writers do possess these qualities: in television studies, Sarah Caldwell is a proponent of beautiful, clear writing, as is Rachel Moseley; in literary studies, Catherine Spooner has a similarly compelling, clear-sighted approach to critical evaluation. But many academic authors do not write like Moseley, Caldwell, and Spooner. When I read research in television studies, I often ache to discern some kind of individual voice, some spark, some shine that makes that author's voice clear. Screenwriting studies is just as bad. I don't know why voice is off limits in my chosen discipline(s).

This isn't specific to the fields I study, either. Academic voice in general does not have a good reputation: "Institutional writing discourages voice," creating an "institutional swamp of passive voice, stilted vocabulary, indirect syntax and weak verbs."[19] Part of the problem here is how we handle the narrator. A lot of the time in academia we pretend there isn't a narrator at all; this figure actively made invisible, all "I's" and "my's" scrubbed out, the narratorial guiding hand disappeared, a third-rate conjuring trick. Then, if there is a narrator, there is little to them. In terms of this critique, I demur to Tom Wolfe, who writes on "the voice of the narrator" in nonfiction writing, which—for Wolfe, writing in the 1970s—seems to have much of the same problems as academia. He explains, "Most non-fiction writers, without knowing it, wrote in a century-old British tradition in which it was understood that the narrator shall assume a calm, cultivated, and, in fact, genteel voice. The idea was that the narrator's own voice should be like the off-white or putty-colored walls . . . a 'neutral background' against which bits of color stand out." Wolfe believed that readers were "bored to tears . . . when they came upon that pale beige tone," as it signaled "that a well-known bore was here again . . . the standard non-fiction writer's voice was like a standard announcer's voice . . . a drag, a droning."[20]

We can find much common ground between the academic narrator and Wolfe's nonfiction narrator. As I am sure you have realized by now, in the same way I am tired of practitioner interviews being uncritically folded into academic writing, I am tired of academic writing itself. The passive, lumpen sentences, littered with subordinate clauses, drowning in semicolons. That dutiful revisiting of what someone else has said and where and why they said it wrong, with a discernible lack of interest in keeping the reader engaged. This kind of writing is the very definition of Steven Pinker's "academese," self-conscious writing where the goal is "not so much communication as self-presentation—an overriding defensiveness against any impression that they may be slacker than their peers in hewing to the norms of the guild," manifested through "metadiscourse, professional narcissism, apologizing and hedging."[21] Such "academese" is not just irksome but also really, truly, tedious to read.

So how might we address voice when we write about television? I want to branch out beyond our usual academic disciplines to answer this question. Brunsdon writes that the "dynamic potential" of television studies is "best realized not by policing its boundaries, but in providing a context in which scholars . . . can meet rigorous assessment by colleagues and the benefits of inter-and multidisciplinary approaches," while John Corner suggests that "we need to retain a strong flow of interdisciplinary traffic into (and also out of) work on television" and that "a wide range of humanities and social scientific inquiry is of relevance."[22] I suspect I might be about to go a bit further afield than Brunsdon or Corner envisage, but it is nice to be welcomed on my way.

First, to find useful, working definitions of voice, I suggest we look toward books on the craft of writing, that is, "how-to" manuals. While voice is relatively underserved in screenwriting studies, the same cannot be said for the academic analysis of screenwriting manuals. Steven Maras considers the evolution of the screenplay manual in *Screenwriting: History, Theory and Practice*, Macdonald devotes a chapter to "self-help manuals" in *Screenwriting Poetics and the Screen Idea*, while in *Screenwriting: Creative Labor and Professional Practice*, Bridget Conor offers a critical discourse analysis of screenwriting manuals.[23] However, I am less interested in analyzing these manuals as a body of work and more interested in what the content of these manuals can offer for original academic thinking. This type of literature has been explored by Craig Batty, who notes that "many of these guides often come under suspicion in the academy, viewed by some academics as restrictive, content thin and serving capitalistic models of screen production."[24] Having read many craft books in preparation for working as a script editor and screenwriter and for teaching screenwriting at university level, I do recognize the charges leveled against the material, particularly the "content-thin" note. But I also concur with Batty when he writes, "Critical texts serve a different purpose to those that are craft driven, but for a discipline whose central concern is practice (the screenwriter writes; screenplays are written for production) it feels like we might be missing something by undervaluing work intended to assist writing practice."[25]

The value of these craft books is indeed in their language, their elucidation of specific words that we rarely encounter in the academy, akin to Reeks's use of "editorial" in an earlier chapter. For example, my understanding of voice is built upon multiple how-to-write sources. In his book on writing narrative nonfiction, Jack Hart defines voice as the "signature of a single human being" and "the personality of the writer as it emerges on the page."[26] Then, in *The Calling Card Script*, Paul Ashton describes voice as "a distinctive tone. It is physically unique, individual, unlike any other" part of a writer's "distinctive, individual style."[27] So it is not just about using "I" a bit more than is usual in academia. Voice is the individual person who writes. I very much hope that if you know me, in real life, you can hear me in these pages, and you know that I am the only person who could have written *this* book in *this* way.

Voice also structures story. In *Alternative Scriptwriting*, Ken Dancyger and Jeff Rush consider voice through "the relative foregrounding of the organizing agency in the story."[28] This idea appeals to the self-reflexive element of this project, including the foregrounding of the issues I faced, and the decisions I made, during the writing of this book. Following this, in *Global Scriptwriting*, Dancyger suggests that "each of us has a point of view, a filter through which we see the world. This is no less true for writers and directors who use that filter to translate their world—their screen story—for us." He conceptualizes this in terms of "editorial position."[29] For Dancyger, editorial position nuances the organizing agency principle outlined above. As academics, we each have a similar filter. We make choices about what we study when and why based on (often unconscious at the time) reasons that are unique to each of us (and I am going to address the at-the-time unconscious reason I wrote this book in chapter 11). The distinction between filmmakers and academics here is that while filmmakers are encouraged to bring their voice (at least, in theory) to the project, academic writing actively discourages personality. It is the same as with form, as discussed in chapter 5; too much personality is embarrassing, cringey, the academic equivalent of driving the wrong way down Fifth Avenue. But I love voice. It is a real shame that in most academic books the only place you are allowed to express your personality is in your acknowledgments or, at a push, in your introduction.

FULL OF THEMSELVES

Having set up a working definition of voice through writing manuals, I now want to turn to my second key source for creating voice: essay collections. I don't mean the traditional academic edited book collection. Instead, I'm referring to single-authored essays, often unified by an implicit or explicit theme, collected in a book and published by (usually) a nonacademic publisher. Joan Didion has been a constant companion on the journey of this book, and her nonfiction essay collections—*The White Album* and *Slouching towards Bethlehem* in particular—have had a colossal influence on me. In the same way that I take permission from Brunsdon and Corner to reach beyond our discrete discipline to find answers to my questions, I take permission from Didion to organize my thinking in a way that does not hide my voice. In his introduction to Didion's *Let Me Tell You What I Mean*, Hilton Als writes that "part of the remarkable character of Didion's work has to do with her refusal to pretend that she doesn't exist," and that her narrative nonfiction explores "the idea that the truth is provisional, and the only thing backing it up is who you are at the time you wrote this and that, and that your joys and biases and prejudices are part of the writing."[30] That is, in academic parlance, an essential element of the cultural phenomenological aspect of her writing, as attributed by David Eason, in chapter 5.

Personal essays come with ideological and intellectual baggage though. In "Thick," Tressie McMillan Cottom writes that her writing dances "along the lines of the dreaded 'first-person essay.' Dreaded because the genre has become identified with so many people and things that our culture loves to hate: women, people of color, queer people, young people, and the internet."[31] However, McMillan Cottom argues that her work is not personal essays. She states this because she is "hopelessly tethered to reality, not fiction or even creative nonfiction." Yet, at the same time, she is not "a stodgy sociologist or cut and dried ethnographer" because "my ethnographies have too much structure and my sociology is a bit too loose with voice. A bit slutty it all is, really, jumping between forms and disciplines and audiences."[32] McMillan Cottom inspires me to be joyfully slutty in my own work: to be tethered to reality while at the same time to refuse to write in only the most anodyne, bland way, to draw from multiple approaches to thinking and writing both in and outside academia, all the while accompanied by a joyous refusal to stay in my lane (the "not television studies," to paraphrase Sara Ahmed). The absenting of ourselves in our writing is a ridiculous game we don't have to play. In her essay collection on television, Emily Nussbaum writes, "Criticism isn't memoir, but it's certainly personal."[33] I agree. Academia is not memoir. Academia is not a first-person essay. Yet academia is always personal.

What do we mean by personal though? In "Aesthetics and Audiences," first published in 1990, Brunsdon writes that feminist methodology is an important contribution to feminist television criticism. In particular, she highlights "the use of autobiographical data and the validation of the use of 'I' in academic discourse."[34] Given this note, I now want to unpick how I write with "I" and where this "I" comes from. First, I have attempted to create a strong narratorial voice by composing the prose chapters (to my mind anyway) in a conversational, dialogic form. In essence, I have written you a series of letters. This comes from Maggie Nelson's admission in *Bluets* that "almost everything" she composes she writes "as a letter."[35] This is one of the reasons that I love Nelson's work—it gives a sense of intimacy and proximity to the author and her process (and you can now add her to the list of Woolf, Didion, and Cusk as pivotal to my thinking). Following this, I then take Ottessa Moshfegh's suggestion that when you write, you can think about your ideal reader: you can "write to your mother. Write to your best friend. Write to the love of your life." Or, most intriguingly, "write to your worst enemy."[36] Considering your "enemy" as a reader really punches up your writing. As Moshfegh explains, "You'll discover that the work for the enemy will be of highest quality. It will be the most daring and smart, because if someone is your enemy, she has the power to hurt you, and so you must hold her in very high regard and will take some pleasure in making her fear for her life."[37]

While I have not actually drawn a bull's-eye on the forehead of specific academics in television studies, nor positioned a single television book as a "straw man" to differentiate my work, I am aware you might be disgruntled by what I write or how I write it.[38] But that's okay. Acknowledging this is also rather freeing. Cusk and Moshfegh inspire me to write this book *to* someone, which in turn allows me to write "I" with so much more ease. It creates an intimate, directly implicated relationship between the writer and the reader, the "I" and "you," the dialogical mode beloved of Woolf discussed in chapter 1. Rather than delivering doctrine, I talk, to you, and await your response.

Nonetheless, in the same way that telling stories of real people's lives is potentially problematic, there are equally fraught implications for using I. To better understand what they are, we return to Janet Malcolm. She argues that the "I" employed in journalism is a character "unlike all the journalist's other characters in that he forms the exception to the rule that nothing may be invented: the 'I' character in journalism is almost pure invention."[39] For Malcolm, the journalistic "I" has only the most tenuous connection with the actual nonfiction writer, "the way, say, that Superman is connected to Clark Kent" and this "invented I" is in fact "an over reliable narrator, a functionary to whom crucial tasks of narration and argument and tone have been entrusted, an ad hoc creation, like the chorus of a Greek tragedy."[40]

Given that this book is about method, about what is being studied and how we study it, we do need to dig deeper into this. I must confess that Malcolm is right, once again, and my "I" is the character that I have taken the most liberties with. Partly this is ethics: in terms of self-representation, my quandaries are slight. When it comes to facts, dates, places, and names, I report with accuracy, but other than that, there are no transcripts to approve or redact. I do not have to sign off my narrative with anyone else in advance of publication. In short, the "I" of this book has license to be the most fictitious person in this project.

Why do this though? To what end?

To deploy "I" is to wield storytelling power. Consider the "I" of the prose chapters, seemingly in conversation with you, thinking through key questions, proposing solutions, refining, retracting, relating—I am always trying to get you to see my point of view, to shape and structure your opinions in a way that suits me. Didion has said that writing is "the act of saying I, of imposing oneself on other people, of saying *listen to me, see it my way, change your mind*, it's an aggressive, even hostile act."[41] She explains that it is hostile "in that you're trying to make somebody see something the way you see it, trying to impose your idea, your picture. It's hostile to try and wrench around someone else's mind that way." She clarifies, "You want to tell somebody your dream, your nightmare. Well, nobody wants to hear about someone else's dream, good or bad; nobody wants to walk around with it. The writer is always tricking the reader into listening to the dream."[42] My "I," my voice, is created, as Malcolm notes, to deliver a specific argument, create a tone, and shape the story; at the same time, "I" am insistent, bullish, and argumentative; I demand, as Didion does, for you to *see things my way*. Here I can't help but think of Zadie Smith's assessment of Didion; she suggests that Didion offers "the same essential qualities (or illusions)" as Muriel Spark and Jane Austen, namely "total control (over their form) and no freedom (for the reader) . . . every sentence of Didion's says Obey me! Who runs the world? Girls!"[43]

The potential to aspire one day to total control over form is intoxicating (if, in reality, impossible). It does demonstrate though the power of "I" as a potent tool for rewriting television. But not everyone will like this suggested approach and not everyone will be intoxicated. I will be, for many, *too much*. For some, narcissism will ooze from these pages, repugnant, sticky, abject. In her book on the wives of modernist writers, Kate Zambreno talks about narcissism in relation to the synthesis of personal and analytical writing. She argues that there is an "unconscious bias against women who are full of themselves" that then "bleeds into reactions against their literature." These biased critiques suggest "that it's somehow cheating to draw from one's life, own life," even or especially if it is about "the complex and ambivalent feminine condition." Zambreno reflects "this charge is almost never levelled against male writers."[44]

This distaste, albeit ironically, is worked through in Charlie Fox's *This Young Monster*, a collection of cultural criticism on artists and monsters. He writes that "assembling anything close to an autobiography gives me the creeps, like a third-person dream in which I have to survey my own corpse." He argues for the disappearance of "I," the absence of voice, "at a time when craven self-promotion and mock-confessional bloviating remain, unstoppably, all the rage, there seems to be a certain *unheimlich* power in zoning out, staged disappearance or vampiric imitation."[45] But the knowing game Fox is playing here is one that we all should reckon more often with: the actual impossibility of disguising oneself, even in cultural criticism. When we acknowledge this in academia, maybe we can learn to celebrate our own voices. We can then lean, self-reflexively, into the subjectivity that we currently pretend is not there, that lying denial that our life experience doesn't consciously or unconsciously shape our choice of subjects, our methods, our findings, that is, our reason for doing what we do.

In making the process of constructing voice prominent, in playing with voice on the page, I am attempting to create a body of work that not only illuminates the drama of writing television but also offers a framework for utilizing dramatic techniques in your own criticism. I combine Didion's cultural phenomenological approach with Woolf's dialogical mode to then push this further, to suggest not only that everything in this discipline is a constructed narrative that cannot attain truth, but also that we can have fun with that, that we can *play*; we can be radical and experimental and still produce serious critical thinking. Ultimately, I'm with Zambreno, who concludes that "taking the self out of our essays is a form of repression," that we are "obeying a gag order—pretending an objectivity where there is nothing objective about the experience of confronting and engaging with and swooning over literature."[46] In television studies we have decades of experience writing about fans who love television. Why can't we just admit that we swoon over television too?

MAVERICK AND ICE

It is February 2024, and I'm working, bleary-eyed, on the final pass of this book (seven years in and ten drafts if you are interested), when I finally sit down to properly read Amy Holdsworth's *Living with Television*. Amy and I are the same age, and we first met in 2007 when we were both on the job market, post-PhD. We were introduced in the candidate holding pen at Leeds Metropolitan University, where we were interviewing for a lecturer in television studies post. As you may remember, I was already teaching the television studies modules there, covering Kristyn Gorton's research leave, and I was reasonably hopeful of a shot at the job. But I hadn't banked on Amy, whose brilliance secured her the post the very same day. I was rejected, went and taught the "Television Studies" lecture, and then had a little weep on the train home to Bradford. Nonetheless, Amy and I have excellent taste in people, and so we still became friends and have remained friends ever since. We are different in so many ways (in *Top Gun*, I would be Maverick, and she would be Ice), and yet we are alike, in our very DNA, in so many others (and not just because we both come from West

Yorkshire). Our much-repeated mantra, "best to be the same," can be found in her *Living with Television* acknowledgments, a recognition of our academic lives lived (virtually) in parallel, side by side, even as we carved out our careers in different regions and eventually different countries.

Amy spent eight years working on her book (yep, she beat me again), and I have watched her present many iterations of the chapters over the years. I have worked side by side with her at her sister Jess's dining table in Silsden (just down the road from me), her niece Annie playing LOL Dolls with my daughter Edith, while we wrestled with a particularly recalcitrant chapter of *Living with Television*. In September 2022, I drove up to the University of Glasgow with Beth Johnson to attend the pandemic-delayed *Living With Television* book launch. Amy stood at the podium in the Andrew Stewart Cinema, and read from her book. I sat a few rows back, curled into one of the deep red seats, and listened, starry-eyed. In listening to Amy I understood that I was witnessing the beginnings of a future for television studies as an experimental, interdisciplinary field, as a space in which to do deep critical and creative thinking. But really, if I am honest, all of these engagements with her work were as her friend: proud and supportive but also eager to get a pint in her hand and to hear her unfurl her (in)famous cackle. It wasn't until today, when I read her book cover to cover, as a scholar, that I discovered just how much we were "the same" when it comes to our feelings about voice.

In her opening page, Amy writes that she always reads acknowledgments first, because "they map out the networks and frameworks of support that all authors are indebted to: whom the author works with; where they've traveled; the conversations they've had; the people who have championed them, challenged them, or been a shoulder to cry on; and the ones who have kept them calm, fed, and watered or offered (un)wanted distraction."[47] In other words, this is the place in standard academic writing where we find the person who wrote the book. As such, it is usually the one place where we can locate voice. While this is a standard practice, what Amy and I try to do—I think differently to most—is to carry this narrator throughout our books. She then goes on to tell a story of the moments in her life that were too big and overwhelming and how television was there for her, her balm, her security blanket. She suggests that her story "may not tell us much about the text of television," but "alludes to a set of text-based experiences that are durational . . . and iterative (a pattern of retreat and return that is captured in my own academic comings and goings)."[48]

As you might expect following this statement, Amy makes a case for autobiography as a critical mode in television studies, where "the personal" becomes "a way into specific television texts and experiences."[49] We run, as ever, on parallel tracks. Amy turns inward, to her home for source material, while I look out, keen to inveigle my way into the world of the industry. In *Rewriting Television*, the personal voice is predominantly the lived experiences of the *Bedlam* practitioners, and then how these experiences informed the texts that came to be made. In a more minor key, the personal is also how a series of career decisions led me to the place where I could finally finish this book (revealed in the next and final chapter).

At the same time, other findings can be mirrored in our scholarship. She notes the academic desire for control, order, and sense making in writing about the experiences of on-demand television. She stresses instead the opportunity to take an alternative approach, one that is less a desire for order than an embrace or temporary untangling of what is volatile and messy."[50] I'm almost back into Didion and cultural phenomenology here, with the suggestion that the orderly control and mapping of lived experience is impossible. In addition, how might we take Amy's position to reflect upon what the practitioner voices have revealed? Might we read this book as an embracing of commissioning practice? A (temporary) untangling of the praxis of script development? A revelation about the volatile, messy nature of television drama from pitch to production? However you choose to interpret these words, what is clear is that Amy and I reject linear, closed narratives, that we celebrate narrators, that we embrace "situated knowledge" (for Amy, that might be the "when, where, and with whom of television viewing" and for myself the when, where, and with whom of television production).[51]

We are not alone in making these kinds of decisions about voice. There is a bigger context for our praxis shift that is also taking place across many disciplines. We have a sense of it already in cultural studies, in Jackie Stacey and Janet Wolff's call to "write otherwise," but we can go further afield (and somewhat to my surprise) to organization and management studies to further think this through. The desire for first-person intimacy, for the recognition of the writer as the author, can be found in Alison Pullen's essay, "Writing as Labiaplasty." In this essay she confesses "I would like my writing to speak from me, of me, when I am able to." She views her writing as a political act, for "when we write, we write against a system that affects us in terms of what and how we write. Structural inequalities make writing differently very difficult to achieve", and thus, her writing "writing reclaims a space for me, and possibly others."[52] This kind of writing explores "alternatives to the masculine academic writing styles that not only dominates management and organizational theory, but also haunt those who desire to express themselves through different modes of writing and representation."[53] Or, as Veera Elina Kinnunen, Sandra Sinikka Wallenius-Korkalo, and Pälvi Marjaana Rantala put it, Pullen's scholarship can be understood as "a form of feminist resistance, an attempt to imagine and enact other modes of knowing and being in the world."[54] This understanding of the intimacy and vulnerability of "I" as a political act chimes not just with my feminist principles of voice, of writing my book as "me," but also with my feminist deployment of form, where the scripted chapters reveal the (hitherto-invisible) woman-led commissioning and development of television drama.

Beyond the "I" so beloved of Amy and me, the intentional "messiness" of our sister-books speaks to Pullen and Carl Rhodes's "dirty writing" model, where one "does not seek to clean up the mess in its own analytical authority" but "attests . . . to that mess," defying "the utopian pursuit of conceptual clarity, linear argument and knock-down conclusions."[55] Variations on this model can be seen in a multitude of disciplines, as "anthropologists, ethnographers and historians have established a range of narrative and stylistic innovations while philosophers and historians have always stretched the limits of academic writing through aphorisms, theses, and fragmentary, momentary meditations."[56] Arguably, our mutual decisions to write books filled with voice, reflect our feelings of uncertainty and rupture about television studies, and about academic writing itself.

As she reaches the conclusion of *Living with Television*, Amy reveals that while the ending of her book could be construed as happy, it "still swings, for me, between security and anxiety." She imagines the critiques leveled at autoethnography being applied to her own work: "too solipsistic, too self-indulgent, too parochial, too happy, too sad, too middle class, too neurotic, too subjective, too domestic, too fractured, too partial." She worries about her privilege. She worries about how her book will be received. She worries about the "illegitimacy" of her interdisciplinary approach.[57] (I'm quite relieved to think my only concerns are how annoying I am being; I am grateful to care less than my friend.) Yet, Amy's fears here chime with so much of what I have talked about around voice: McMillan Cottom on the "dreaded" first-person essay, Zambreno on the perceived "narcissism" of women writers, my suggestion that the style of this book will be "too much" for some readers. Nonetheless, I would argue here that Amy's voice *is* the most powerful element of her book. Her "I" and "my" are a rallying call to take situated knowledge seriously; they signal that someone wrote this book, that they experienced life before, during, and at the end of writing it, that this life impacted on what they wrote, when and how they wrote it. This seems almost banal to set out now, in words, but these facts impact every single one of us who write, we are just so rarely allowed to acknowledge them.

Upon finishing Amy's book, I made myself a fresh cup of tea, put the fire on, and ruminated upon how to integrate her ideas into this book. The standard academic practice would be to retrofit them throughout this manuscript, a quote here, a citation there, to weave her in invisibly, as if *Living with Television* had always been there. That's what you would normally do. It made me think of Kilby and Gilloch's point that "academic writing is a set-up, a fiction, of sorts. There is inevitable sleight-of-hand; and a hiding of retrospective logic."[58] But an invisible interweave of Amy would have been a lie to myself and disingenuous to you, the reader. I've concluded that there is more power in honesty, in articulating what it meant to think about Amy's book, when I am so close to finishing my own. I hope that in years to come *Rewriting Television* will be recognized for its kinship with *Living with Television*, for embracing a vulnerable, intimate, and "messy" mode of television scholarship, and for being grounded, so concretely, in the voices of the people who wrote them.

CHAPTER 11

Glorious

When I started the *Rewriting Television* project, I was sure of my intention: to explore creative process and the work of creative people in television drama. But now, seven years later, I understand my original motivation (even if I didn't get it at the time). As I noted earlier, once I started working as a lecturer in playwriting and screenwriting, I despaired of how to bridge the gap between my fiction writing and academic work. I was frustrated with the scholarship I was reading around that period, and was (quite honestly) completely over a lot of the passive and pointless writing I felt duty bound to wade through. Scriptwriting teaches you to ask three questions: Why should we care? Why *this* story at *this* point in time? Why are you the person to tell this story? I would read film and television studies scholarship like a detective, searching for evidence that this research was worth reading, which (to me, at that time) meant it was trying to do something, say something, that I could see that it meant something to the writer as well.

Occasionally I was delighted, as when I read Elana Levine's beautiful introduction to her book on daytime soap operas, *Her Stories*, in which she charts how her life has intersected with her soap opera consumption: "I kept watching, time-shifting every episode throughout high school, college, working years, graduate school, my job as a professor. I moved, attained degrees... lived a life, watched *General Hospital*."[1] Why we should care, why this story now, and why this person, all answered, in a single paragraph. More often than not though, I was disappointed. I read books and essays and just thought "Oh." Or less politely, "What's the point?" My disappointment made me think of Charlotte Brunsdon's reproving note in "Is Television Studies History?": "It is no good to say 'well, no one has ever looked at this program before, and I'm going to show you why it's interesting,' because many people have looked at a great many programs, and have also discussed them within a range of contexts, discourses, and disciplines."[2] I looked ahead and saw, with no little dismay, the prospect of repeating methodologies that I had no heart for, for the three decades remaining of my career.

Then in 2018 I moved to the University of Leeds, where I am now a professor of film studies. When I first moved to Leeds, I still felt conflicted about whether I wanted to continue in academia, and the first few drafts of this book, written between 2018 and 2020, reflected this unresolved antagonism. Reading back over these drafts, I can now see that they were a cry to find a way to exit academia. Janet Malcolm writes that "the characters of nonfiction, no less than those of fiction, derive from the writer's most idiosyncratic desires and deepest anxieties they are what the writer wishes he was and worries that he is."[3] Her wise comment exposes my vulnerability. The screenwriters, script editors, script executives, executive producers, and channel commissioners that you've met in this book all represent my initial desire: to discover *how to do* television storytelling. This desire had a practical purpose. I wanted to meet the people who did this work. I wanted to demystify how to do the work. I wanted to leave academia and do the work myself.

When I completed the third draft of *Rewriting Television*, I needed a break. So I wrote a play under a pseudonym. I submitted the script to RED, who were at the time one of the few British production companies with an open-door submission policy. A few months later, I received a letter through the post, with the square RED logo emblazoned in the top left-hand corner. Freya Boroda, the development editor, had read my script and discussed it with the development department. She concluded that "we enjoyed the sharpness to your dialogue, so we'd be happy to read a full TV script . . . send us a new TV script if you have one." With this single page of A4, RED demonstrated the reality of their open-door policy and made good on their much-discussed commitment to developing new writers.

But Boroda's letter demonstrated the pointlessness of my circuitous attempt to "break in" by researching practice. All I needed to do was write a decent script. Once I realized this, I thought to myself, what is the point in continuing with this book? What on earth was it for? Sara Ahmed suggests that "every research project has a story, which is the story of an arrival."[4] Yet my story is more of a return. In the six years I have now worked at Leeds, I have come back to academia. I don't know whether it is down to the brilliant people in my school or that my own thinking has evolved (hopefully both), but I am no longer desperate to break away. Everything is less binary: academic *or* creative forms of writing are no longer mutually exclusive. By the end of the last draft of this book, in spring 2024, I have realized that what I perceive to be the limitations of academic research *are* an opportunity to create change; that to want to do something outside the norm doesn't mean you have to abandon academia altogether. Perhaps my critical questioning is just what John Caughie describes as the "business of screen theorizing today": that is, "to work through the changing configurations of subject and space; to identify the points at which the institution and its routines break open to other possibilities of meaning and engagement; to find new and appropriate ways of testing ideas and aesthetics, politics and ethics."[5] Perhaps it has just taken me a while to realize what he might mean.

In chapter 1, I argued that it was time for a moment of reckoning about what we were doing in television studies and why. I built foundations for my thinking upon the scholarship of Brunsdon, John Corner, Christine Geraghty and David Lusted, and Christine Gledhill and Linda Williams, with a particular focus on their work in the late 1990s and early 2000s. This was the point when, twenty years in from inception, these eminent scholars were reflecting upon what television, film, and media studies had come to be. Throughout this book, I've attempted to respond to many of the questions raised in these turn-of-the-century essays, including Brunsdon's "sense of *the edge* of the academic—the negotiation of what it is proper to address, and in what terms" and Geraghty and Lusted's not only "*what* is to be studied but also *how.*"[6] I've proposed a synthesis of television studies, screenwriting studies, and production studies as a way to rewrite the field, a gesture toward Gledhill and Williams's proposition to "rethink" film studies through a variety of approaches.[7] However, what I really want to get to grips with in this final chapter is Corner's essay, which I have only touched upon in passing so far in this book.

Corner's essay was first published in *Screen* in 1995, in relation to (British) media studies. He recognizes that "all fields of study" have knowledge problems but suggests that a problem has emerged in media studies as a result of "the history of this field," the "very diverse nature of its object of study," and "the particularly ambitious form of interdisciplinarity to which this diversity tends to lead," which has led to "uncertainties, tensions and regroupings in the area."[8] He suggests that knowledge problems explore "what it is that academic enquiries seek to find out, and the kinds and quality of data and of explanatory relations which particular ideas and methods might be expected to produce." By considering and responding to knowledge problems, Corner argues that "disciplines not only engage more closely and innovatively with questions of conceptualization and technique, but also develop a reflexive, skeptical sense of their own knowledge production and vulnerabilities."[9] His erudite explanation of why there is value in responding to knowledge problems is also an erudite explanation of what I want to do with this book. I want to question how we conceptualize our work, how we do our work, and how we think about what we do.

At the same time, the way he defines media studies speaks to what I am trying to do here in terms of the sources I use and the techniques I bring to bear upon this project. He explains that media studies combines arts and social sciences, essentially "criticism and sociology" to create "modes of academic knowing." For Corner, criticism is "a mode privileging *individual percipience*, in which knowledge is the product of sustained analytic attention and intellection," but sociology, on the other hand, in its classic and defining empirical project, is essentially a mode privileging *method*," with a procedure that produces, "first of all, 'data,' and then an analysis and explanation of this data," where "theories" function as "mostly explanatory propositions."[10] This project utilizes much of the procedural methodology of sociology to create a framework that generates data. I have created a series of scripts though that creatively work through issues of commissioning, developing, and producing television drama. These scripts are then explored through companion chapters privileging individual analytical readings. This approach, then, not only speaks to the past of media studies as Corner envisaged the field in the 1990s, but also charts an intellectual trajectory that can be found in production studies today. We see this theorization in the work of Miranda J. Banks, who writes that "media is not nor has ever been a fixed object," that its practitioners "are not stable subjects," and as such "special care" must be paid when we "theorize these macro-economic, technological and industrial changes through the lens of the lives and experiences of individual media makers."[11] So, in one sense, this whole book—while it positions itself in response to television studies—could be just as fruitfully grounded within media studies, or even offer new ways of thinking for film studies (which has even further to go than television studies in reflexively thinking through its knowledge problems).

However, while Corner offers a useful disciplinary grounding and siting of the approaches in this project, this isn't really why I want to dig into his thinking. Later in his essay, he notes that in the mid-1980s there was a "discernible shift away unifying high theory" and (following cultural studies) a transition into ethnographic inquiry into media meanings in everyday life, a methodological mode with a long-established history in sociology and anthropology. This shift also parallels this project, where I have used qualitative research methods to produce data that reveals something about the everyday meaning making of media practitioners. But—and this is crucial—Corner suggests there are three significant problems with such an approach. I explore each of these, in turn, below.

DESCRIPTIVISM

Corner's first issue is descriptivism, that is, "rendering even thicker accounts of process but being unable to make any clear connection upwards to explanation because of a gravitational commitment to ground-level phenomena."[12] The origin of this concept comes from ethnography. In *The Interpretation of Cultures*, Clifford Geertz explains that ethnography is "an elaborate venture in . . . thick description," a way of writing about culture that offers not only description and context but also interpretation.[13] For Geertz, the interpretation is of "the flow of social discourse," which "consists of trying to rescue the 'said' of such discourse from its perishing occasions and fix it in perusable terms."[14] More practically,

Melissa Freeman describes thick description as "a level of detail: the ability to create a rich, contextualized description of an event to increase verisimilitude and transferability of findings," favored by some researchers due to its "ability to capture the interpretive complexities of social life."[15]

Thick description has long been the method of choice for analyzing media industries. In *Hollywood, the Dream Factory*, published in 1950, Hortense Powdermaker explores Hollywood as a social system and the impact of that social system on the content of its movies. She undertakes participant observation and interviews approximately three hundred people, primarily producers, writers, and directors, including "the very successful, the medium successful and the unsuccessful."[16] Powdermaker utilizes thick description and summarizes her interviewees' opinions in her writing. She also does not cite their real names, offering anonymity, and creating pseudonyms such as "Mr Optimist." Her book is decisively "a factual account of the mores and way they work."[17] In 1983's *Inside Prime Time*, Todd Gitlin writes his story in thick description, conveying anecdotes that reveal "not only how and why I think the networks do what they do, but a sense of the ambiance and the texture of the industry life-as-it-is-lived." Gitlin recounts anecdotes at length, "often in the words of the people telling them," justifying anecdote as "the style of industry speech, dialogue its body, and narrative its structure."[18] But these anecdotes are folded into long, dense passages of description and analysis; the very thickness of his thick description creates an overwhelming density on the page.

In presenting the practitioner interviews as a series of scripts, *Rewriting Television* rejects thick description. And the reason for this rejection is Virginia Woolf. Writing on H. G. Wells's fiction, Woolf suggests that his methods of construction and craftmanship are so solid that "it is difficult for the most exacting of critics to see through what chink or crevice decay can creep in. There is not so much as a draught between the frames of the windows, or a crack in the boards. And yet—if life should refuse to live there?"[19] Thick description provides solidity, that surety of explanation and interpretation, but has the potential to deaden the life of the subject under study. In short, it subdues inner life just as it attempts to take control and bring to order to culture. For Woolf, the fiction in circulation at the time of her writing "more often misses than secures the thing we seek. Whether we call it life or spirit, truth or reality, the essential thing, has moved off, or on, and refuses to be contained any longer in such ill-fitting vestments as we provide."[20] My desire to move away from thick description relates to my desires to break form with interview material. I aim for a clean page filled with white space, where gaps between the words, between the lines of dialogue, allow for an active reader to respond and construct an inner life for the characters. I'm also not entirely systematic with my analysis. In the prose readings that follow the scripts, I tend to home in on the things that interest me most, as is the case with the table read. I leave large sections of interview data unanalyzed.

I often let the voices stand on their merits and allow you to draw your own conclusions from the (carefully selected, edited, and organized) material.

So, while my process may not be "thick," what about a lack of connection "upward," that is, making bigger points about society and culture? This speaks not only to the critique of case study as method but also to Caughie's point in his "Mourning Television" essay for *Screen*, in which he argues that theories that are "only ever fascinated by the perpetual play of difference and endless innovation," or that replace the "analysis of the institution—the institution of text and subject as well as of television—with description of the phenomenon," are "ill-equipped to imagine a different television, one which escapes the 'relentless spectacle of the present.'"[21] This is a potentially damning, if important, critique. I believe this project goes beyond a "fascination with innovation" in two main ways. First, I argue that screenwriting remains a notable "blind spot" in television studies, nearly fifteen years after John R. Cook and Andrew Spicer's special issue of the *Journal of British Cinema and Television*. Production studies has made substantial inroads into the study of writing practitioners, and screenwriting studies has evolved significantly in the past decade. Yet television studies remains remarkably reticent to engage with the screenwriter and the iterative, collaborative process of their work. This book addresses this gap.

Second, this book makes connections "upward" through its grounding in and engagement with feminist television criticism. I didn't particularly flag it at the start of the book, as I felt you had enough to grapple with, but my method, my methodology, and my epistemology are entirely feminist (I'm assuming you picked this up as the book went on). Television, unlike film, has long been considered to be "the medium of the writer, the writer-producer or the showrunner," and in chapters 4 and 7 I decenter the male screenwriter in order to reveal the script contributions of women executives.[22] This can be read as a response to Doris Ruth Eikhof and Stevie Marsden's suggestion that we need to "focus on crucial decision makers—those in powerful positions who decide on individual's opportunities to participate in and advance media work," and that "female, non-white, disabled or working-class workers are still perceived as a deviation from that informal, but powerful blueprint of what a creative media worker does or should look like."[23] As I noted in chapter 7, the fact that these women are in commissioning and development rather than working as writers or directors (at that time) demonstrates an ongoing issue with gender parity in prestigious production roles. But, nonetheless, the women are there.

The focus on the executives working at RED and at Living is also a response to the ongoing erasure of women's voices in male-dominated film and television studies. As Anna Froula reveals, it was not until 2016 that *Cinema Journal* (now *Journal of Cinema and Media Studies*) published an issue where all feature articles were written by women.[24] In 2018, Anthem Press announced a new television studies series in which the series editor and the nine editorial board members were all men, despite women being foundational to not only the formation of the discipline but the ongoing major debates in the field. My book then reflects an attempt to cite beyond television studies, as part of creating a generative, expansive methodology, and a prioritization of the citation of scholars "othered by white heteromasculinism."[25] This is necessary, as Kathryn A. Mariner notes, for "citation necessarily affects visibility for some at the expense of others."[26] When I cite, I am illuminating a voice, and this illumination is a political act, designed to make that person's visibility undeniable. Why is undeniability necessary? In Ahmed's words, when you are a feminist you soon discover that "what you aim to bring to an end some do not recognize as existing."[27] Furthermore, I concur that "to cite narrowly, to only cite white men, to form citation cartels (informal agreements between authors to continually cite one another's work) to boost 'impact' or to only cite established scholars" does a disservice to our discipline(s).[28]

However, this reflection also highlights some of the limitations of this research. In their *Feminist Media Histories* essay, Natalie Wreyford and Shelley Cobb argue that "the need to interrogate one's own bias and subjectivities and to acknowledge the imperfect and partial nature of any research undertaken" is important, and that, in fact, "this interrogation can be one of feminism's greatest contributions to research methodology."[29] Good intent does not always equal good practice, and as Brunsdon notes in *Screen Tastes*, "this 'I' of the feminist discourse is a rather complicated affair in terms of to and for whom it speaks."[30] My desire to focus on the making and telling of television stories has left little space for a more explicitly political engagement with my practitioners. A more reflective, holistic approach to interviewing could have created opportunities for an intersectional critique of who my interviewees were, how they came to inhabit their roles in their workplace, and how their own identities may (or may not) have fed into the production culture that created *Bedlam*. This is about, in Kristen J. Warner's words, "understanding the industrial practices that give rise to those representations and the cultural power that structures the industrial processes in the first place."[31] I didn't do this, even though Geraghty was arguing for a more reflexive mode of thinking in television studies as far back as 1991. She states that "it is not merely a question of arguing for the importance of understanding womanhood as a construction" but also stressing that "it is a construction which is inhabited differently in ways that are to do with race, class, age and experience as well as gender."[32]

So, while there is much to be lauded in bringing to light the stories of the women decision makers, these are still stories of privileged position. As Wreyford and Cobb point out, "In labor markets where there is a gender imbalance, hearing from members of an underrepresented group still only involves the voices and experiences of those who have had some degree of success," and "it does not tell us about the women who are unable to be part of that profession, or the scale or reasons for their exclusion."[33] So, while I believe I avoid Corner's potential charge of descriptivism through the grounding of my research in screenwriting and in feminist thinking, I still recognize that there is much to do here. I acknowledge that "feminists cannot escape all the traps set by the racialized and gendered history of the disciplines, but we can destabilize them, explore their contradictions, and work through them to open up new possibilities."[34]

EMPIRICISM

Corner's second problem is empiricism, whereupon the research "loses sight of its own constructed, authorial character."[35] There are two ways to think through this issue. The first is through the way that I use "I" in writing, as explored in chapter 10. However, here I want to address the second constructed "I," which is the television practitioner's self-presentation. Eikhof and Katharina Chudzikowski argue that "self-presentations can constitute a useful source of information on how individuals or groups want to be perceived by others." They suggest that "the production of self-presentation as linked to workers' identity in cultural industries and as part of individuals labor" is required to secure jobs and progress careers.[36] This tension speaks very much to the bind that media producers find themselves in when representing themselves through personal narratives. As David Hesmondhalgh and Sarah Baker argue, in independent television production "good working relations" play an important role in careers, with the ensuing implications that workers suppress "anger and frustration."[37] Given this, the *Bedlam* transcripts and published script chapters are relatively free of gossip and negative experience. This was not a surprise. I certainly did not expect participants to reveal their potentially "ugly feelings" of envy, irritation, anxiety, or paranoia to a random academic wielding a voice recorder.[38] Yet, in working with me on this project, both the participants' level of engagement *and* their apprehension about the process varied dramatically. The more stable or senior the interviewees' career appeared to be (or had been), the more freely they spoke, and with more humor and self-deprecation. The anxiety around self-presentation was then broadly demarcated across intersections of gender and power, which corresponded to the men working in freelance or more vulnerable roles, and the women in more senior, salaried roles.

For example, the women executives' engagement with the transcripts ranged from light touch to nonexistent. There was very little interest in editing or redacting any of the interview material. This isn't to say the women executives were not self-editing during the interview itself. Several marshalled techniques for side-stepping potentially more problematic or contentious material, usually through recourse to incomplete memory, "I'm not sure about that" or "I can't fully remember." This selective use of memory to bridge potentially difficult gaps is fascinating. As Kristyn Gorton and Joanne Garde-Hansen point out, interviewee "memory" is an intellectual challenge for researchers, which requires us to "shift our theoretical pursuit of verifiable knowledge of television's production and reception . . . toward television as lived cultural memory being remade as personal experience for the purposes of intangible and tangible cultural heritage," a point of view heartily endorsed here.[39]

Arguably, the most open interviewee in the process was Living executive Amy Barham, who left the British television industry and is now a filmmaker in Los Angeles. In short, Barham no longer needs to worry about the presentation of the self in the British television market; she has a whole new series of Hollywood networked relations to participate in instead. The male freelance writer-creators, on the other hand, remained extremely invested in the story being told. They engaged deeply with the written material and returned detailed, marked-up transcripts. The amendments, redactions, and clarifications frequently centered on how the participant's comments could be perceived, that there might be a space for potentially negative readings of statements given in good faith. The first worry was the perception of the rest of the writing team. David Allison, Neil Jones, and Chris Parker all thought carefully about who did what and who wrote what. None of the writers were keen to name specific episodes or arcs that did not work for them: Allison explained that they worked so collaboratively, he could not precisely remember who did what on individual episodes and he did not want to inadvertently offend the others. This careful presentation of one's point of view chimes with David Lee's research on television production, in which he recognizes tension in his interviewees "between the naked individualism engendered by the casualized, precarious labor market on the one hand, and the need to be supportive and co-operative to find work on the other."[40] It also accords with the difficulties of working with friends (or colleagues who become friends) while at the same time all being aware of the capitalist underpinnings of such association, that those friendships can and will create future work opportunities. The "importance of social networks" in the "elite writers' network" of Hollywood has already been documented, but here we witness the importance of networking in British television too.[41]

Consider just a few of the relational networks that brought *Bedlam* into being: Jones and Parker were recruited by Allison based on working together on *Hollyoaks*; *Bedlam* initially came to RED's attention because Allison is married to Hollick; Reeks was employed by Rosencrantz after they worked together at ITV; Barham was put in charge of *Bedlam* after working for Rosencrantz in acquisitions. So, even though I interviewed and transcribed ethically, even though I keep the "script" dialogue in its original context, the "I" in the script pages can only represent, with care, the rendering of words spoken by one person, to another. Really, when you think of it this way, you *could* argue that the "I" when the practitioner speaks is (despite what I said earlier) just as fabricated as the "I" who writes this book.

An Overcorrection of Empiricism

While I think I have made a strong case for avoiding the descriptivism and empiricism of Corner's first two issues, I do fall foul of the third: an "overcorrection of empiricism" whereby "the self-consciousness of researcher is raised to the point at which interest in the researcher-method-subject relationship begins to displace interest in the researched subject itself."[42] Geraghty and Lusted make a similar point in *The Television Studies Book*, that "an excessive reflexivity can mean that more is said about the method (and the researcher) than about what is being studied."[43] Ouch. Yes, I am squirming. I would like to argue though that this is a strength of this book: you might not have had a burning desire to learn about the commissioning and development of *Bedlam*, nor perhaps even cared about the experience of writing horror for British television in the 2000s (admittedly niche), but I do hope that voice is just one way that I have been able to encourage you to continue throughout the book. In so doing, I then hope you have been able to engage with the real heart of this project: how we think about, analyze, and write about television.

I do acknowledge the validity of Corner's "overcorrection" point though. I encounter it a lot in social sciences methodology. I've read journal articles and chapters that spend so long setting up the parameters of their self-reflexive research that the work is almost done by the time the original data are produced (guilty as charged?). However, I can still make an academic case for my "overcorrection" of empiricism, where my achingly reflexive approach does have potential benefits at the level of the discipline. In an essay on production studies methodology, Hesmondhalgh asks the big questions of the subject: "Should analysts prioritize production or consumption? . . . How do we understand the relationship between economics and culture? *To what extent should we conceptualize the social world as an independent reality to which we can gain independent, objective access?*"[44] To rewrite television studies demands that we recognize a lack of consensus about the world we live in; it demands that we focus on individual experience and the way the world is made and remade through these experiences. The multivoiced structure of Woolf's *The Waves*, discussed in chapter 8, inspires my fractured and fragmented, contradictory scripted oral history, which in turn demonstrates the impossibility of establishing a single truth of what happened and when. Then, by following Didion's cultural phenomenological approach to writing, by making myself present, I can focus on "revealing how the interpretation is itself created."[45]

So, to respond to Hesmondhalgh's provocative question, this research has no pretensions to articulating "independent, objective access." Instead, script and prose chapters synthesize to suggest that there is *no* fundamental real life to reveal; what are important, instead, are our interactions, our thoughts, our feelings. This stance parallels Woolf's conclusion in "Modern Fiction," where she argues that art is filled with infinite possibility, and that "no 'method,' no experiment, even of the wildest—is forbidden," only "falsity and pretense" are; and that "the proper stuff of fiction does not exist; *everything is the proper stuff of fiction, every feeling, every thought; every quality of brain and spirit is drawn upon*; no perception comes amiss."[46]

There are risks with such experiment though. As Elizabeth Hardwick has pointed out, there are many criticisms of Woolf's writing (including and especially *The Waves*). For Hardwick, while "some of our emotions are moved, often powerfully," Woolf's novels "aren't interesting. This is the paradox of her work, part of the risk of setting a goal in fiction, of having an idea about it, an abstract idea." Woolf is, in this sense, "all chorus and no plot, that is the danger of her wish, her vision."[47] I'd be intrigued to know if you feel the same way. I hope though that my obsession with form, story, and voice in fact points to a bigger discourse on academic style.

In "The Art of Nonfiction" interview for the *Paris Review*, Didion confirmed that since an early age she has been drawn to issues of style, which mean, for her, the combination of "voice and form."[48] Hart similarly defines style in relation to voice, "if voice is the personality of the writer as it appears on the page, then style is the outermost expression of that personality."[49] For Sontag, style is "the principle of decision in a work of art, the signature of the artist's will."[50] Then, if this is all really about style, we can perhaps consider the distinction between style and stylization, which for Sontag "might be analogous to the difference between will and willfulness." The idea of will and willfulness is something I am always up for debating (see: my hero worship of Ahmed), but I know which side I want this book to land upon. Sontag argues that stylization in art "reflects an ambivalence (affection contradicted by contempt, obsession contradicted by irony) toward the subject-matter. This ambivalence is handled by maintaining, through the rhetorical overlay that is stylization, a special distance from the subject." The problem then is "that either the work of art is excessively narrow and repetitive, or else the different parts seem unhinged, dissociated."[51]

Here we are back to the criticisms leveled at Woolf. As I have rejected the analysis of the television text, and because I have barely analyzed the content of the scripted chapters, is my book all chorus and no plot? Where I see freedom, do you feel boredom? Then, there is a strong stubborn streak in this book, a sense of kicking back against what I am supposed to do, but I do hope by this point in the proceedings that the chapters do hang together, rather than becoming "unhinged." So is my obsession with story, form, and voice innovative? Or has this experiment failed? Does this book offer style or stylization? In his book on essayists, Brian Dillon values style above all else. He says that style is "form and texture rescued from chaos, the precision and extravagance of it, the daring, in the end the distance, such as I think I could never attain. As much in a person, in a body, as in prose: those people who can *keep it together*."[52] When I explore the process of commissioning, writing, and developing a television series, and when I parallel this with the creative process of writing about this work, offering form, story, and voice as a way of trying something else, am I too much? Do you think I have *kept it together*, across the course of this book?

CONCLUSION

At the end of *British Television Drama: A History*, published in 2003, Lez Cooke writes that "the challenge, as British television approaches its seventieth anniversary, is for channel controllers and program directors to encourage experimentation and innovation in television drama, so that a radical and progressive tradition can continue to exist in British television as part of a genuinely diverse and plural culture."[53] While Cooke is pointing to "radical" and "progressive" British television drama, the sort written about in the academy over the past forty years or so, I want to reappropriate his point to a different purpose (of course I do, it's basically the modus operandi of this book). As television studies approaches its fiftieth anniversary, the challenge for its scholars is to encourage and undertake experimentation and innovation in all aspects of their work. *Rewriting Television*, for all its academic baiting, is simply saying it is time to look for change in why and how we do things. As my extensive use of Brunsdon, Corner, and others suggests, this change is not about throwing out the old or established ways of doing things but about using existing ideas in new ways, about contemplating, integrating, and adapting new and existing theories, methods, and forms.

Not everyone will be cool with this. As Ottessa Moshfegh states, "Any significant paradigm shift will incite anxiety," for "there is nothing more upsetting to the status quo than the assumption that such a thing doesn't even exist."[54] Similarly, my choice of case study and how I choose to analyze it mean much of my work lacks a historical foundation, leaving me open to the criticism of being "short-sighted," of being part of the problem in a discipline "that often claims so much for the new without the rigorous investigation of the apparently 'old.'"[55] Nonetheless, I stand firm. This is the time for contestation and evaluation, a new point of reckoning. It is over twenty years since "What Is the 'Television' in Television Studies?"; don't you think it's time we started following up on Brunsdon's recommendations? There is no taken-for-grantedness in the work of Brunsdon, Caughie, Corner, Geraghty and Lusted, Gledhill and Williams, and this is why they are inspiring. I might not apply their ideas in the original way they were intended, but this is part of the policy of rethinking; it is built upon Gledhill and Williams's "reinventing," of "self-fashioning new identities out of old." Such self-fashioning creates ideas. It enables us to ask "what if?" It is an opportunity, as Caughie might put it, to "imagine differently." *Rewriting Television* is an exercise in just how far we can break convention. Through form, story, and voice, this book considers just what this work could look like, and what it could offer the reader.

> Why don't you have a go too?
> It might be,
>> it just could be,
>>> glorious.

Hold on. Wait up.

Do you remember what I talked about in chapter 2, when I first watched *Bedlam* and it raised a whole ton of questions around storytelling? I don't know if you noticed, but I haven't answered them all. We never found out why series 2 had an entirely new cast, nor what on earth was going on with some of the serial storytelling. I've focused on the making of series 1 in this book, but that only tells half of *Bedlam*'s story.

> Don't you want to know what happened next?
> I leave the final words to *Bedlam*'s makers.
> They will tell you how it ends.

Coda

"HOW ARE WE GOING TO GET OUT OF THIS?"

CAROLINE HOLLICK: Series 2 was a *completely* new group of execs.

CLAUDIA ROSENCRANTZ: I had nothing to do with the second series being picked up or not being picked up. It got handed over to [the Sky] drama team, who were probably disparaging of everything we did, as new owners often are.

JENNY REEKS: They are probably very nice people you know, only doing their jobs.

CAROLINE HOLLICK: Ironically, one of them, Anne [Mensah], was the exec who, had developed it at the BBC.

ANNE MENSAH: When I arrived, they had already made series 1.

DAVID ALLISON: We got plenty of press [for series 1], we got a lot of coverage and it did really well, and we were really, really chuffed.

JENNY REEKS: It was a successful show because all the right decisions were taken— by Nicola, RED, Claudia, Amy and me. Directors and editors too. So pats on the back all round.

RICHARD FEE: [Sky had] been *pleased* with [the response to series 1]. I remember them doing a presentation to us and, showing us all the things that worked.

ANNE MENSAH: At the time, it was relatively low budget for a drama. And yet, looked great. Obviously RED can make shows with a big budget brilliantly but they could also, at that time, make shows on a lower budget brilliantly. *Bedlam* is a clever format because it is contained. It maximized the budget because it wasn't running around from location to location.

NEIL JONES: I think what we pitched for series 2 was, a continuation of series 1 with the same characters you know.

RICHARD FEE: We'd written a document we knew where it was going to go.

DAVID ALLISON: We thought that we would get a second series green-lit very quickly and we just didn't.

ANNE MENSAH: I don't remember it taking a while. That is just me not remembering it. Me being new there, everything felt like it was going super-fast, which isn't necessarily how people feel when they are on the outside of it.

DAVID ALLISON: It is one of the stranger things that have happened to me in my career is wondering why that didn't happen quickly.

ANNE MENSAH: Series 1 had done very well, so I don't think there was ever a question about whether the show had done well or not. We didn't have anything else for Living. Gosh, I really can't remember. It could be that there was a question mark about how much money Living had. . . . When I first arrived at Sky, there wasn't as much drama as there is now.

RICHARD FEE: Because of this change in management and the change in the channel, there was a long delay. The channel, understandably, were, trying to establish what the channel would be. Because they wanted [Living] to be something different to what it had been.

CAROLINE HOLLICK: It was challenging moving from one channel and becoming another channel, because we'd just won the trust, and proved ourselves with Living and then we had to do it all over again with Sky which is unusual. A second series is when you can kind of fly a bit, and we had to slightly prove ourselves all over again.

ANNE MENSAH: If there was any holdup, I suspect it was just the evolution of drama on Sky. It was just early days. A lot of the shows we do now, we would recommission before they finish transmitting. But . . . none of that stuff was in place back then.

RICHARD FEE: Until they knew exactly what the channel was going to be, it was hard for them to make a judgment really about what shows they wanted and whether they wanted us.

NICOLA SHINDLER: But the weirdest thing that happened between series was this audience research that Sky do.

ANNE MENSAH: There has been an evolution at Sky, since then.

NICOLA SHINDLER: And that was something which I had *never* experienced before.

CAROLINE HOLLICK: ITV is all about advertising, that's where you need the big raters. The BBC is a mix of all things, they can't just put out bomb after bomb but, they don't have to count ratings, they have to think about serving different audiences. Sky is purely commercial but overnight ratings are not as important as . . . whether or not people like a series enough to maintain their Sky subscription. They want to attract new audiences but a lot of it is about making sure people going "Yes, I like the show, this is one of the shows which means I will pay for my Sky subscription again." They do more audience research than the BBC and ITV.

ANNE MENSAH: We have what we call "passion scores." Essentially, Sky asks lots of people. They ask if they've seen it, how much they would rate it out of ten. And what are their best shows. You would look at, what the press sentiment was, what social sentiment was. It is a more rounded way of judging success because you are not just looking for a show that is popular with numbers. You are looking for shows that are well loved. The thing about Sky that is always worth remembering is that it's television that you pay for. So it is not good enough to be, "If that's on and I'm home then I don't mind watching it." It's got to be, "I actively love watching it." Unless you love it you probably wouldn't pay for it. It's better to get fewer people who love it than a whole bunch of people who are a bit like, "meh" about it.

NICOLA SHINDLER: We had a note about certain characters that were liked and disliked and why they were liked and disliked. But then, when we broke it down, they had only spoken to a hundred people. So, it doesn't feel very valid. But on the other hand, you have got to listen to research so . . . I have never had that again though. Never ever had a research note given to me, so I don't if it was just a phase they were going through.

ANNE MENSAH: Even though we didn't measure stuff like that back then, I bet *Bedlam* would have scored highly because my memory of it was that the audience was really passionate. But, it was way more numbers driven. Back then, it was purely that . . . you were looking for it to hit a certain figure, numbers-wise. Now it is more nuanced.

DAVID ALLISON: If I'm being honest, I think sometimes commissioners don't get stuff themselves and it's not their bag, it's not their baby specifically.

CAROLINE HOLLICK: It's very hard for new broadcasters to keep old projects and we really appreciated the fact that they gave us that second chance.

ANNE MENSAH: When you are commissioning, you are responsible for Sky's money. You are trying to ensure that it is spent responsibly, which Nicola always would do. But also . . . that the show matches your understanding of the channel. And Sky Living is a different channel from Sky Atlantic which is a different channel from Sky One which is definitely different from the BBC. You are trying to be the voice of the channel.

RICHARD FEE: When the research came back on series 1. They were surprised at how old it was skewing. They thought that it was characters in their early twenties and it would probably attract that sort of audience. But it was attracting . . . predominantly women in their forties. So they did want to try and make an effort to skew it younger.

NICOLA SHINDLER: Yeah and that is *really* difficult.

ANNE MENSAH: I don't remember it with that level of specificity. But I can imagine . . . I suspect it skewed even older than thirty-five. Dramas just do skew older than the channel, broadly speaking. Sky is young. If BBC One basically skews fifty-five-plus, Sky skews about thirty-five-plus. So Sky is younger than Channel 4. But I can imagine that at the time . . . that they wanted to keep *Bedlam* in the twentysomething. Now, knowing Sky like I do, I wonder if it would have been ever possible to pull it that young. But I don't know if I would have said that with confidence back then. Seriously, it's a drama thing. It is impossible with twenty-somethings. They do watch loads of drama but there are just not as many of them watching television as there are people who are a bit older. Who might have kids or, you know, aren't going out so much. I am just talking about my own life and the white wine that lives in the fridge.

CAROLINE HOLLICK: It was great to be able to come back and work with Anne again. She came from a very well-established drama background so her understanding of drama was much deeper than . . . probably than the Living execs who—in a very new way—were interested in how to replicate what they were getting from their acquisitions.

ANNE MENSAH: And it is really interesting because we only ever, in the end, apart from *Bedlam*, made one big drama for Living, which was *The Enfield Haunting*, another horror. And actually, it was such a sweet spot for Living, this idea of relationship shows—because actually *The Enfield Haunting* had a lot of that, just the people in it—but that also had the bits of scare around the outside edges. Because I don't think *Bedlam* was pure horror in as much as it wasn't just scare after scare after scare. It was a relationship show as much as it was a horror show.

NICOLA SHINDLER: Because the [series 2 execs] came from a scripted background . . . Suddenly we had a group of proper script—not proper, but people whose experience was in script. They were suddenly much more hands on. I knew [Anne] really well anyway. So that wasn't a problem. *But* what you get is this group of people who have got different tastes. Even though they are respectful to what you have done, they can't help pushing in a different direction. They were more about earthiness and realness and, less about gloss and the glamor.

ANNE MENSAH: [for series 2] with Huw [Kennair-Jones], we would collate the notes together. Or he would have led on it. At the time—there isn't any more—but at the time there was a director of Sky Living. And they would have given notes, they would get a say on key casting and would come to the read-through and get a say on the final cut of the first episode.

NICOLA SHINDLER: You have to take a deep breath and go, "All notes are making it better if I enact them right." But sometimes it is nice when you are feeling that you are left alone. In an ideal world, commissioners really should leave shows alone.

ANNE MENSAH: I'm better now than I used to be at not being in the detail and letting things be what they are. But that has taken me seven years so. . . . Seriously, you would think I would have sorted my life out really. I definitely think that I am better now than I used to be at understanding where you can be useful as a commissioner and where you are not very helpful.

NICOLA SHINDLER: That is a really interesting thing that she said. Yeah, for me, I don't need a commissioner to tell me that the choice of music or a character is wrong, for example. I need a commissioner to tell me "that whole strand is not working" or "that character does not work for what we need on this channel." I need the bigger picture from them because I am into the detail. And that always will make a difference if they get that right.

ANNE MENSAH: Nicola is very patient and has known me a long time.

NICOLA SHINDLER: Anne worries. Or, at least, she worried a lot. I remember that. But I mean, Anne worries in a good way in that she wants everything to be right. But then, because I like her so much, I feel like Anne really was worried, and I really want to help her feel like everything is okay.

———◆———

CHRIS PARKER: So we had this big gap after series 1—after it aired and we had no idea whether we'd come back or not.

DAVID ALLISON: It was long enough for us to have a serious set of problems.

RICHARD FEE: We found ourselves in the weird position of being recommissioned and being really delighted about that, but also not knowing [*laughs*] what the *hell* we were going to do in terms of telling the story.

NEIL JONES: There was a "How are we going to get out of this?" We had this really weird series 1 cliff-hanger to pay off [*laughs*] and we didn't have any of the characters.

CHRIS PARKER: So we lost all our cast. As you probably noticed.

RICHARD FEE: Don't *think* we had formal options on anybody.

CHRIS PARKER: The cast had gone on to do other stuff. Everything had like, moved on.

DAVID ALLISON: Theo James [who played Jed] had been picked up by Hollywood.

CAROLINE HOLLICK: Theo went off to be a massive . . . star.

CHRIS PARKER: We were you know, *desperate* to get him back just for a cameo, just to do a scene and he absolutely, couldn't be made to happen. At all.

CAROLINE HOLLICK: I remember Nicola telling me that he wasn't going to come back and I remember being *really cross* and feeling really let down [*laughs*]. I mean why I thought [*laughs*] he would put aside a Hollywood career for series 2 of *Bedlam*. The other problem we had in terms of casting was Will Young. Who was great, but he's a musician, he wants to make an album. He has a record deal and, he went to make an album.

CHRIS PARKER: I felt it was quite a hard . . . thing to sell second time around. Because the characters that people loved had all gone.

DAVID ALLISON: We just realized that it was falling apart anyway in terms of the original cast so. In a way we knew we had to: we had to reboot.

CAROLINE HOLLICK: We realized that we needed a whole new approach, a reboot.

RICHARD FEE: We had to find a way to press the reset button.

CAROLINE HOLLICK: If we'd just been picking up where we left off, I think we wouldn't have had to make so many radical story decisions.

CHRIS PARKER: We sat in the Granada building and we watched . . . the final episode of series 1. I remember thinking "I'm really apprehensive about this. It might look really shit."

DAVID ALLISON: We did pick over the bones, what worked best, what didn't.

CHRIS PARKER: And you know, there were moments when we sort of groaned.

CAROLINE HOLLICK: We knew that those strong guest characters with, with star parts worked really well.

DAVID ALLISON: The guest characters had to be compelling and have really interesting back stories. They are your lead for that episode.

DAVID ALLISON: There were things you were *really* pleased with and things you were not so pleased with. I might not pick them out. I won't remember who's written what and then I'll end up sounding like a, you know.

CHRIS PARKER: But we all came out of it thinking "Actually this is really exciting because we can take this as a jumping off point."

RICHARD FEE: Even though your first instinct is to hold your head in your hands, when you get into the nitty gritty of it, *that's* the fun bit. Coming up with those big picture things, cracking the big story problems, there's *nothing* more satisfying than that.

DAVID ALLISON: It was less of a problem once we got over it.

CHRIS PARKER: What was great when we got a second series is we were able to sort of tie up those loose ends. Make sense of the mess [*laughs*] we'd left behind at the end of series 1. Because. It wasn't any part of any grand plan or anything.

NEIL JONES: [But] once we realized that [the second series] was going to *happen*, I really loved that, I love sitting down to write things and thinking "How . . . how are we going to do this?" Where it's like a *puzzle* to try and solve for the writer.

RICHARD FEE: That's the best part of being a script editor. Those early discussions. When anything is possible.

CHRIS PARKER: At that stage we didn't know . . . who our lead characters were going to be. So we did have a blank slate really.

CAROLINE HOLLICK: They wanted to skew younger, that's why we ended up building it around [the actor] Lacey Turner, because she was a real everywoman young character that people could invest in. We wanted a woman at the heart of it rather than a man. We needed to have a different vibe from Jed. We wanted . . . to have a kind of ghost-hunting partnership with a sexual tension, because that works better for a younger audience. What was interesting in the second series, we did pick up a younger audience, but we lost a bit of the old audience.

CHRIS PARKER: Having Lacey Turner was brilliant. I had written for Lacey on *Eastenders* so I knew she was very intelligent, she understands . . . how to get the most out of a script about the subtext and everything.

CAROLINE HOLLICK: [Sky also] felt that audiences really liked the serial stuff so they wanted more of the serialized.

DAVID ALLISON: We felt like the arc needed to be point of it. We needed to serve that more.

CHRIS PARKER: I think that's probably the experience of [] having come to that unsatisfying ending of series 1, realizing actually, the series arc is really important, and so giving it more *weight* in series 2. We weren't just trying to think of a series arc for that series, we were trying to justify all the stuff that had gone before.

NEIL JONES: Inevitably we got influenced by whatever else we were watching around that time. That was late 2009/2010 so *The Wire*. It did get under our skin and make us think, well, we had bigger ambitions for the storytelling on this show.

CHRIS PARKER: It seemed harder to get those series stories pinned down in series 2. It just felt like we went back and forth over stuff *loads*. We constantly needed brainstorming, coming up with . . . ideas and then rejecting them. It felt like, ah, a very intense process. We were kind of, more aware of what could go wrong and what *doesn't* work.

DAVID ALLISON: And avoiding things. It's budgetary again. And time.

CHRIS PARKER: And you know, in terms of how much meat the story needs in order to . . . be able to carry through an hour.

DAVID ALLISON: I remember having long conversations about in what order we would tell them so it would help with the serial. I definitely felt like in the first series it was a rush. And we were just scrabbling to make sense of things at times whereas on the second series it felt like we did, we were like, "Okay [*clicks fingers*], we've got this now, right here we go."

RICHARD FEE: Cracking good story. That's what we *try* . . . to do with everything. That's what we're always striving for. Sometimes most successfully than others [*chuckles*] but hopefully more often than not. You know. We pull it off. Which I know sounds a bit glib. But.

NEIL JONES: We worked out the series arc and then. . . .

DAVID ALLISON: We just had to pitch.

NEIL JONES: And we just pitched.

DAVID ALLISON: And boiled them down to the ones we really care about.

NEIL JONES: We pitched half stories sometimes and then developed them together.

CAROLINE HOLLICK: We wanted as much comedy as possible.

RICHARD FEE: I think there are certain things that Nicola is probably drawn to— I wouldn't wanna speak for her—but I think [] interesting characters. Strong women is a fair one. I don't think she'd make something with *weak* female characters in it. But that's not to say that every project that we make has to be banging a feminist drum, either. Humor is . . . really important. She loves writing that makes her laugh. I don't mean five gags a page humor, I just mean how people speak to each other. It's funny but it doesn't feel constructed funny. It feels real funny.

NICOLA SHINDLER: Uhm . . . I don't look . . . I mean, if I like it. If it works for me. If I think it's clever and funny and provocative and interesting and pushing buttons and trying to say something about the world that we live in. All those things.

CAROLINE HOLLICK: We wanted to make sure that there was that kind of lightness in the ... relationship between the main characters, because ghost stories have to be dark and those back stories were really dark.

DAVID ALLISON: They'd released the patient records from [former psychiatric hospital] High Royds [in Leeds]. So we were able to look at the real people's stories.

CAROLINE HOLLICK: Those back stories were really carefully researched, they weren't just pulled out of nowhere ... it was kind of based on High Royds. I mean, whether *now*, whether it would feel maybe, a little disrespectful towards people, with mental health issues, to be turning it into such pure entertainment, with a bit of distance on it? I don't know. Things are changing in the way people are looking at how we *portray* people with mental health issues and, I think, because it was historical, I think we probably avoided ahm ... too many pitfalls.

CHRIS PARKER: I haven't watched it since [the second series] went out [in 2012] so it will be interesting to see how it would play today. Looking at it again as ... as a show that was completely written by men but meant for a female audience. The genre of horror can be problematic, it uses the tropes of violence against women and serial killers, it uses them *again and again* and I think we were aware that there was a *danger* there and we felt like we were justifying it because. We were telling stories of abuse that were based in a sort of real past.

CAROLINE HOLLICK: TV drama has to be careful, there can be a vogue for exploiting—particularly with women, "crazy women"—which we talked a lot about how to avoid.

CHRIS PARKER: I do wonder how it would feel [now]. That wasn't something we ... thought about consciously ... as three men writing it. But, you know, the fact that it did rely so heavily on these things that we've taken from horror. It's a male-dominated genre.

CAROLINE HOLLICK: As a company that has a lot of women in it [] it's important that we put women and strong female storytelling at the heart of everything we do. We always try and make sure that we avoid clichés or crazy women.

NEIL JONES: Then we went off and wrote and did notes on each other's scripts.

RICHARD FEE: There was time pressure. We needed to do it, and we needed to do it quickly.

CAROLINE HOLLICK: We didn't have quite as much time as we would have liked. But then there never is as much time as you'd like.

NEIL JONES: Series 2 was much more Richard Fee with us than series 1 had been.

RICHARD FEE: By series 2, we'd been through *so* much, just the experience of *any* production, does kind of—it'll either tear you apart or bond you together [*laughs*] and we were all really bonded together.

NEIL JONES: Richard became almost the fourth writer on the show. He was such a brilliant person to work with, he is so creative.

RICHARD FEE: When I came to the first series it was an already existing thing, I didn't feel . . . ownership over it. It was very much their show and I was trying to help in any way that I could. Whereas, going through the experience of working on a *whole* series of it, by the end of it, you are *so* invested and you really want to make a success of it. So, for the second series, I felt more ownership. I could be more proactive in coming up with story ideas, that sort of thing. Part of it was confidence, part of it was the relationship that I had with the writers.

CAROLINE HOLLICK: In America you have a showrunner, so I know people who have had the most amazing experience in writers' rooms and really terrible ones because it depends what that showrunner wants from you. Whereas here we all got to feel like we were part of making something new and I enjoyed trying to make something that commercial really, for a channel who knew exactly what they wanted. It's a very different thing from a writer's vision of "this is the thing I feel most passionate about writing in the world." We *loved* being able to write a gang show really.

CAROLINE HOLLICK: I think we consolidated at a million for the opening episode. *Now* that would be a big hit on Sky.

DAVID ALLISON: We thought we would get a third series and we didn't. And the second series did really well. So.

ANNE MENSAH: To be completely honest I can't fully remember why we didn't bring the show back again, so I wouldn't want to be misleading. I am not sure if it was the strategy of the channel or the performance of the show. It is probably best characterized as not quite meeting the needs of the channel at the time.

CAROLINE HOLLICK: We're always really disappointed [when not recommissioned]. I think, Sky, these subscription channels, need to feel fresh and new, all the time and they wanted to free up that space for something different. It just didn't quite do the numbers that made it a no-brainer to return again.

DAVID ALLISON: Sometimes things have their life and they exist in that period of time and often you *don't* get to make things so when you do get to make something you need to just celebrate that you did. This was one of those occasions.

CAROLINE HOLLICK: One of the reasons why I'm really proud of this series is that I did feel like the [writers] just worked *really hard* to make them interesting characters, or any of the ghosts, and not to make anything clichéd. Nicola's— the RED aspect of *Bedlam*—that both Nicola and I feel that we brought to the table is—"does this feel real, does this feel credible?"

NICOLA SHINDLER: Things have to feel real. They can have as many ghosts and horror . . . that isn't what I mean. People have to act in a way that people will act. I have to feel that it's funny and warm. It can be as dark a subject matter as you want but there has to be humor in it and there has to be life in it because that's how people react.

NEIL JONES: And Nicola, she would've have been the first to say, she just treated it as she would a Jimmy McGovern drama. She looked at the characters the same way, she looked at the stories the same way. She approached it the way she would any other script really. Starting with character and psychological realism and story. That's probably how it fitted into RED.

NICOLA SHINDLER: I am really glad that Neil saw that as well because every single thing. . . . Just because something is about ghosts . . . it should feel real. So that is always my job.

CAROLINE HOLLICK: I really miss it and ah . . . [the writers have] all gone in different directions in terms of their focuses, but we keep thinking about other things. I hope one day we can do it again because it was one of my . . . it really was one of my favorite processes.

AMY BARHAM: I like to think [*Bedlam*] did what we wanted it to *do*, like which was to be a big splash and be something that not many of the cable networks were doing at that point. I know now we're commissioning more, and obviously Sky commissions a lot, but at the time they weren't. Nobody was doing it.

ANNE MENSAH: It was a unique show in the British television landscape. The idea of a properly team written show amongst friends is interesting and it was the first drama on a channel that had never had drama on it before. You would still commission it today. It is good that it got made even though it didn't get made at the BBC. And it got two series whereas potentially at the BBC it might not. It is always a good story when a show pops up on the right channel for itself.

DAVID ALLISON: You've got to be pragmatic. Gotta be really pragmatic. You'd go mad otherwise. Yes.

Acknowledgments

Many thanks to David Allison, Amy Barham, Richard Fee, Caroline Hollick, Neil Jones, Anne Mensah, Chris Parker, Jenny Reeks, Claudia Rosencrantz, and Nicola Shindler for giving up their time to be interviewed for this project. Thanks to Lesley-Anne Smith for organizing Nicola's interview. Thanks to Gail Wilsdon and Harriet Mathie for transcribing most of the interviews and to the University of Leeds for funding those transcriptions.

This book has taken time to find its true form. As such, I need to say a special thanks to all the people who have supported me as I have worked through this experiment. Many thanks to Beth Johnson for reading my feral second draft, to Kristyn Gorton for taming my third attempt, to Amy Holdsworth and Karen Lury for their enthusiasm for draft 4, to my manuscript reviewers for Rutgers University Press for advocating for draft 8, and to Lucy Fife Donaldson and Colleen Laird for reading draft 9 and making sure I hadn't lost the plot. I am deeply grateful to you all for your kindness and feedback. This book is made so much better because of your engagement with my work.

A whole team of people ushered *Rewriting Television* through production. Thank you to Cheryl Hirsch and Sherry Gerstein at Westchester, Vincent Nordhaus at Rutgers, Joseph Dahm for copy editing, Valeria Villegas Lindvall for indexing, and last but not least, my editor Nicole Solano who remains ever cheerful, smart and encouraging even when I pitch a curveball of a book to her that appears to have no bearing on my career history to date and yet she still smiles and says yes.

Drafts of sections from chapters 4 and 7 appeared as "The Hidden Work of Women: Commissioning and Development in British Television Drama" in *Feminist Media Studies* 23, no. 4 (2023): 1460–1474. I thank the journal for their permission to reprint.

Notes

CHAPTER 1 — THE ONE-LONG-SLOW-IDEA BOOK

1. John Corner, "Television Studies: Plural Contexts, Singular Ambitions?," *Journal of British Cinema and Television* 1, no. 1 (2004): 7.

2. Charlotte Brunsdon, "Is Television Studies History?," *Cinema Journal* 47, no. 3 (2008): 129.

3. Charlotte Brunsdon, *Screen Tastes: From Soap Opera to Satellite Dishes* (Abingdon: Routledge, 1997), 103–106.

4. Brunsdon, "Is Television Studies History?," 131.

5. Sarah Cardwell, "Television Aesthetics," *Critical Studies in Television* 1, no. 1 (2006): 72–80; Kristyn Gorton, "A Sentimental Journey: Television, Meaning and Emotion," *Journal of British Cinema and Television* 3, no. 1 (2006): 72–81; Amy Holdsworth, "Poetry and / on Television: *Drinking for England* (BBC, 1998)," *Critical Studies in Television* 8, no. 1 (2013): 1–13; Vicky Ball, "The 'Feminization' of British Television and the Re-traditionalization of Gender," *Feminist Media Studies* 12, no. 2 (2012): 248–264; Lucy Fife Donaldson, "Camera and Performer: Energetic Engagement with *The Shield*," in *Television Aesthetics and Style*, ed. Jason Jacobs and Steven Peacock (London: Bloomsbury, 2013), 209–218; Elizabeth Evans, *Transmedia Television: Audiences, New Media and Daily Life* (Abingdon: Routledge, 2011); Catherine Johnson, *Branding Television* (Abingdon: Routledge, 2012).

6. Christine Gledhill and Linda Williams, "Introduction," in *Reinventing Film Studies*, ed. Christine Gledhill and Linda Williams (London: Arnold, 2000), 1, emphasis added.

7. Brunsdon, *Screen Tastes*, 1, emphasis added.

8. Christine Geraghty and David Lusted, "General Introduction," in *The Television Studies Book*, ed. Christine Geraghty and David Lusted (London: Arnold, 1998), 3.

9. John Corner, "Media Studies and the 'Knowledge Problem,'" *Screen* 36, no. 2 (1995): 147.

10. Jonathan Bignell and Faye Woods, *An Introduction to Television Studies*, 4th ed. (Abingdon: Routledge, 2023), Kindle.

11. John Ellis, "Is it Possible to Construct a Canon of Television Programs? Immanent Reading versus Textual-Historicism," in *Re-viewing Television History: Critical Issues in Television Historiography*, ed. Helen Wheatley (London: I.B. Tauris, 2007), 15–16.

12. Jonathan Bignell, "Exemplarity, Pedagogy and Television History," *New Review of Film and Television Studies* 3, no. 1 (2006): 20–21.

13. Glen Creeber, "The Joy of Text? Television and Textual Analysis," *Critical Studies in Television* 1, no. 1 (2006): 81.

14. Sarah Cardwell, "Patterns, Layers and Values: Poliakoff's *The Lost Prince*," *Journal of British Cinema and Television* 3, no. 1 (2008): 134.

15. Joan Didion, *The White Album* (1979; London: 4th Estate, 2017), 162–165.

16. Kristyn Gorton and Joanne Garde-Hansen, *Remembering British Television: Audience, Archive and Industry* (London: Bloomsbury, 2019), 20.

17. Robin Nelson, "Introduction: The What, Where, When and Why of 'Practice as Research,'" in *Practice as Research in the Arts: Principles, Protocols, Pedagogies, Resistances*, ed. Robin Nelson (Basingstoke: Palgrave, 2013), 16–17.

18. Mattias Frey, "Institutions and Agency: Film Studies Special Issue," *Manchester Hive*, April 5, 2016, https://manchesteruniversitypress.co.uk/articles/film-studies-special-issue/.

19. Anna Zoellner and David Lee, "Media Production Research and the Challenge of Normativity," in *Making Media: Production, Practices, and Professions*, ed. Mark Deuze and Mirjam Prenger (Amsterdam: Amsterdam University Press, 2019), 45.

20. John Thornton Caldwell, *Production Culture: Industrial Reflexivity and Critical Practice in Film and Television* (Durham, NC: Duke University Press, 2008); Vicki Mayer, *Below the Line: Producers and Production Studies in the New Television Economy* (Durham, NC: Duke University Press, 2011); Miranda Banks, Bridget Conor, and Vicki Mayer, eds., *Production Studies, the Sequel! Cultural Studies of Global Media Industries* (New York: Routledge, 2016); Jennifer Holt and Alisa Perren, eds., *Media Industries: History, Theory, and Method* (Malden, MA: Wiley-Blackwell, 2009).

21. Melanie Bell, *Movie Workers: The Women Who Made British Cinema* (Champaign: University of Illinois Press, 2021); Francis Galt, *Women's Activism Behind the Screens: Trade Unions and Gender Inequality in the British Film and Television Industries* (Bristol: Bristol University Press, 2020); Susan Liddy, *Women in the Irish Film Industry: Stories and Storytellers* (Cork: Cork University Press, 2019).

22. Gorton and Garde-Hansen, *Remembering British Television*, 23.

23. Erin Hill, *Never Done: A History of Women's Work in Media Production* (New Brunswick, NJ: Rutgers University Press, 2016), 10.

24. Brunsdon, *Screen Tastes*, 117.

25. Vicki Mayer, Miranda J. Banks, and John T. Caldwell, "Introduction. Production Studies: Roots and Routes," in *Production Studies: Cultural Studies of Media Industries*, ed. Vicki Mayer, Miranda J. Banks, and John T. Caldwell (Abingdon: Routledge, 2009), 3; Sarah Ralph and Brett Mills, "'Trying to Ride a Naughty Horse': British Television Comedy Producers," in *Beyond the Bottom Line: The Producer in Film and Television Studies*, ed. Andrew Spicer, Anthony McKenna, and Christopher Meir (London: Bloomsbury, 2014), 161–174.

26. Corner, "Television Studies," 12.

27. Chris Paterson, David Lee, Anamik Saha, and Anna Zoellner, "Production Research: Continuity and Transformation," in *Advancing Media Production Research: Shifting Sites, Methods, Politics*, ed. Chris Paterson, David Lee, Anamik Saha, and Anna Zoellner (Basingstoke: Palgrave, 2016), 3.

28. Andrew Spicer, "The Author as Author: Restoring the Screenwriter to British Film History," in *The New Film History: Sources, Methods, Approaches*, ed. James Chapman, Mark Glancy, and Sue Harper (Basingstoke: Palgrave, 2007), 89–103.

29. John R. Cook and Andrew Spicer, "Introduction," *Journal of British Cinema and Television* 5, no. 2 (2008): 221.

30. Craig Batty, "Introduction," in *Screenwriters and Screenwriting: Putting Practice into Context*, ed. Craig Batty (Basingstoke: Palgrave, 2014), 1.

31. Ian W. Macdonald, *Screenwriting Poetics and the Screen Idea* (Basingstoke: Palgrave, 2013); Eva Novrup Redvall, *Writing and Producing Television Drama in Denmark: From* The Kingdom *to* The Killing (Basingstoke: Palgrave, 2013).

32. Steven Maras, *Screenwriting: History, Theory and Practice* (London: Wallflower Press, 2009), 79.

33. Jill Nelmes, ed., *Analysing the Screenplay* (London: Routledge, 2011); Macdonald, *Screenwriting Poetics*, 161–190; Steven Price, *The Screenplay: Authorship, Theory and Criticism* (Basingstoke: Palgrave, 2010), 43–62.

34. Craig Batty, Radha O'Meara, Stayci Taylor, Hester Joyce, Philippa Burne, Noel Maloney, Mark Poole, and Marilyn Tofler, "Script Development as a 'Wicked Problem,'" *Journal of Screenwriting* 9, no. 2 (2018): 156.

35. Stayci Taylor and Craig Batty, "Script Development and the Hidden Practices of Screenwriting: Perspectives from Industry Professionals," *New Writing* 13, no. 2 (2016): 204–217.

36. Craig Batty, Stayci Taylor, Louise Sawtell, and Bridget Conor, "Script Development: Defining the Field," *Journal of Screenwriting* 8, no. 3 (2017): 225–247; Craig Batty and Stayci Taylor, eds., *Script Development: Critical Approaches, Creative Practices, International Perspectives* (Basingstoke: Palgrave, 2021).

37. Steven Price, "Script Development and Academic Research," *Journal of Screenwriting* 8, no. 3 (2017), 320.

38. Jackie Stacey and Janet Wolff, "Writing Otherwise," in *Writing Otherwise: Experiments in Cultural Criticism*, ed. Jackie Stacey and Janet Wolff (Manchester: Manchester University Press, 2013), 1, emphasis original.

39. Stacey and Wolff, 2–3.

40. Stacey and Wolff, 2–3.

41. Sarah Schulman, *The Gentrification of the Mind: Witness to a Lost Imagination* (Berkeley: University of California Press, 2012), 17.

42. Schulman, 16.

43. Schulman, 17.

44. Jane Goldman, "Virginia Woolf and Modernist Aesthetics," in *The Edinburgh Companion to Virginia Woolf and the Arts*, ed. Maggie Humm (Edinburgh: Edinburgh University Press, 2010), 35.

45. Jane Kilby and Graeme Gilloch, "Sociography: Writing Differently," *Sociological Review* 70, no. 4 (2022): 642.

46. Quoted in Didion, *The White Album*, 164.

47. Didion, 163.

48. Didion, 165–166.

49. Susan Sontag, *Against Interpretation and Other Essays* (1964; London: Penguin, 2009), 7.

CHAPTER 2 — METHODS

1. Keri Facer, Johan Siebers and Bradon Smith, "Introduction: Working with Time as Method," in *Working with Time in Qualitative Research: Case Studies, Theory, and Practice*, ed. Keri Facer, Johan Siebers, and Bradon Smith (Abingdon: Routledge, 2022), vii.

2. Asta Rau and Jan K. Coetzee, "Designing for Narratives and Stories," in *The SAGE Handbook of Qualitative Research Design*, ed. Uwe Flick (London: SAGE, 2016), 701.

3. Bent Flyvbjerg, "Case Study," in *The SAGE Handbook of Qualitative Research*, ed. Norman K. Denzin and Yvonna S. Lincoln (London: SAGE, 2011), 301.

4. Kristyn Gorton, "Re-visiting Melodrama in Contemporary Television Symposium," Screenwriting Research Network JISCMAIL, February 27, 2015, https://www.jiscmail.ac.uk/cgi-bin/wa-jisc.exe?A2=ind1502&L=SCREENWRITING-RESEARCH-NETWORK&O=D&P=15160.

5. Jason Mittell, *Complex TV: The Poetics of Contemporary Television Storytelling* (New York: New York University Press, 2015), 17–18.

6. Trisha Dunleavy, *Complex Serial Drama and Multiplatform Television* (Abingdon: Routledge, 2017), 2.

7. Karen Lury, "Introduction: Situating Television Studies," *Screen* 57, no. 2 (2016): 119–120.

8. Helen Piper, "Broadcast Drama and the Problem of Television Aesthetics: Home, Nation, Universe," *Screen* 57, no. 2 (2016): 164.

9. Deborah L. Jaramillo, "Rescuing Television from the 'Cinematic': The Perils of Dismissing Television Style," in *Television Aesthetics and Style*, ed. Jason Jacobs and Steven Peacock (London: Bloomsbury, 2013), 67–68; Helen Wheatley, *Spectacular Television: Exploring Televisual Pleasure* (London: I.B. Tauris, 2016), 16.

10. Angelo Restivo, Breaking Bad *and Cinematic Television* (Durham, NC: Duke University Press, 2019); Hannah Andrews, "Book Review: Breaking Bad *and Cinematic Television*," *Critical Studies in Television* 16, no. 1 (2021), 69–71.

11. Brett Mills, "Invisible Television: The Programs No-One Talks about Even Thought Lots of People Watch Them," *Critical Studies in Television* 5, no. 1 (2012): 1.

12. Eva Novrup Redvall, *Writing and Producing Television Drama in Denmark: From* The Kingdom *to* The Killing (Basingstoke: Palgrave, 2013), 103.

13. Rosamund Davies, "Nordic Noir with an Icelandic Twist: Establishing a Shared Space for Collaboration within European Co-production," in *Script Development: Critical Approaches, Creative Practices, International Perspectives*, ed. Craig Batty and Stayci Taylor (Basingstoke: Palgrave, 2021), 113–128.

14. Mills, "Invisible Television," 1.

15. Rau and Coetzee, "Designing for Narratives," 703.

16. Jonathan Bignell, "Exemplarity, Pedagogy and Television History," *New Review of Film and Television Studies* 3, no. 1 (2006): 19.

17. Thomas A. Schwandt and Emily F. Gates, "Case Study Methodology," in *The SAGE Handbook of Qualitative Research*, 5th ed., ed. Norman K. Denzin and Yvonna S. Lincoln (London: SAGE, 2018), 601.

18. Flyvbjerg, "Case Study," 302.

19. Flyvbjerg, 311–312.

20. Shulamit Reinharz, *Feminist Methods in Social Research* (Oxford: Oxford University Press, 1992), 18.

21. Mai Skjott Linneberg and Steffen Korsgaard, "Coding Qualitative Data: A Synthesis Guiding the Novice," *Qualitative Research Journal* 19, no. 3 (2019): 268.

22. Mary Jo Maynes, Jennifer L. Pierce, and Barbara Laslett, *Telling Stories: The Use of Personal Narratives in the Social Sciences and History* (Ithaca, NY: Cornell University Press, 2008), 1.

23. Reinharz, *Feminist Methods in Social Research*, 19.

24. Amy Holdsworth, *Television, Memory and Nostalgia* (Basingstoke: Palgrave, 2011); Annette Kuhn, *An Everyday Magic: Cinema and Cultural Memory* (London: I.B. Tauris, 2002); Susannah Radstone, ed., *Memory and Methodology* (London: Routledge, 2020).

25. Durga Chew-Bose, *Too Much and Not the Mood* (New York: Farrar, Straus and Giroux, 2017), 32.

26. Andrea Fontana and Anastasia H. Prokos, *The Interview: From Formal to Postmodern* (Walnut Creek, CA: Left Coast Press, 2007), 46.

27. Kath Browne, "Snowball Sampling: Using Social Networks to Research Non-heterosexual Women," *International Journal of Social Research Methodology* 8, no. 1 (2005): 47.

28. Eleanor McLellan, Kathleen M. Macqueen, and Judith L. Neidig, "Beyond the Qualitative Interview: Data Preparation and Transcription," *Field Methods* 15, no. 1 (2003): 66.

29. Svend Brinkman and Steinar Kvale, *Doing Interviews*, 2nd ed. (London: SAGE, 2018), 34.

30. Irit Mero-Jaffe, "'Is That What I Said?' Interview Transcript Approval by Participants: An Aspect of Ethics in Qualitative Research," *International Journal of Qualitative Methods* 10, no. 3 (2011): 241.

31. Laura Nader, "Up the Anthropologist: Perspectives Gained from Studying Up," in *Reinventing Anthropology*, ed. Dell Hymes (New York: Vintage, 1974), 284, 292.

32. Ulf Hannerz, "Studying Down, Up, Sideways, Through, Backwards, Forwards, Away and at Home: Reflections on the Field Worry of an Expansive Discipline," in *Locating the Field: Space, Place and Context in Anthropology*, ed. Simon Coleman and Peter Collins (Oxford: Berg, 2006), 26.

33. Reinharz, *Feminist Methods in Social Research*, 42; Anna Boucher, "Power in Elite Interviewing: Lessons from Feminist Studies for Political Science," *Women's Studies International Forum* 62 (2017): 100.

34. Boucher, "Power in Elite Interviewing," 99.

35. Kari Lancaster, "Confidentiality, Anonymity and Power Relations in Elite Interviewing: Conducting Qualitative Policy Research in a Politicized Domain," *International Journal of Social Research Methodology* 20, no. 1 (2016): 93.

36. Sherry B. Ortner, "Studying Sideways: Ethnographic Access in Hollywood," in *Production Studies: Cultural Studies of Media Industries*, ed. Vicki Mayer, Miranda J. Banks, and John T. Caldwell (Abingdon: Routledge, 2009), 176.

37. John Tulloch, *Television Drama: Agency, Audience and Myth* (Abingdon: Routledge, 1990), 23.

38. Valerie Raleigh Yow, *Recording Oral History: A Guide for the Humanities and Social Sciences*, 3rd ed. (Lanham, MD: Rowman & Littlefield, 2015), 86.

39. Annukka Vainio, "Beyond Research Ethics: Anonymity as 'Ontology,' 'Analysis' and 'Independence,'" *Qualitative Research* 13, no. 6 (2012): 685–686.

40. Julia Bickford and Jeff Nisker, "Tensions between Anonymity and Thick Description When 'Studying Up' in Genetics Research," *Qualitative Health Research* 25, no. 2 (2014): 276–281.

41. Mero-Jaffe, "Is That What I Said?," 241.

42. Joan Acker, Kate Barry, and Joke Esseveld, "Objectivity and Truth: Problems in Doing Feminist Research," *Women's Studies International Forum* 6, no. 4 (1983): 428–429.

43. Robert K. Yin, *Qualitative Research from Start to Finish*, 2nd ed. (London: Guildford, 2016), 291.

44. Miranda J. Banks, "Oral History and Media Industries: Theorizing the Personal in Production History," *Cultural Studies* 28, no. 4 (2014): 47.

45. Todd Gitlin, *Inside Prime Time*, rev. ed. (Abingdon: Routledge, 1994), 14.

46. Jules Selbo, *Screenplay: Building Story through Character* (Abingdon: Routledge, 2016), ix.

47. James Andrew Miller, *Powerhouse: The Untold History of Hollywood's Creative Artists Agency* (New York: Custom House, 2016), xxix.

48. Quoted in Miranda Banks, *The Writers: A History of American Screenwriters and Their Guild* (New Brunswick, NJ: Rutgers University Press, 2015), 266–267.

49. Fontana and Prokos, *The Interview*, emphasis original.

50. Vicki Mayer, Miranda J. Banks, and John T. Caldwell, "Introduction. Production Studies: Roots and Routes," in Mayer, Banks, and Caldwell, *Production Studies*, 5.

51. bell hooks, *Talking Back: Thinking Feminist, Thinking Black* (Boston: South End Press, 1989), 11.

52. Paul Ashton, *The Calling Card Script: A Writer's Toolbox for Screen, Stage and Radio* (London: A&C Black, 2011), 54.

CAST OF CHARACTERS AND DIALOGUE KEY

1. Brad Birch, *Black Mountain* (London: Bloomsbury, 2017), 2.

2. Alistair McDowall, *X* (London: Methuen Drama, 2016), 2.

CHAPTER 4 — COMMISSIONING

1. Caitriona Noonan, "Commissioning and Producing Public Service Content: British Arts Television," *Media Industries* 5, no. 2 (2018): 2.

2. Laura Mayne, "Creative Commissioning: Examining the Regional Aesthetic in the Work of Channel 4's First Commissioning Editor for Fiction, David Rose," *Journal of British Cinema and Television* 9, no. 1 (2012): 40–57; Hyun Jung Stephany Noh, "Romantic Blockbusters: The Co-commissioning of Korean Network-Developed K-Dramas as 'Netflix Originals,'" *Journal of Japanese and Korean Cinema* 14, no. 2 (2022): 98–113; Florian Krauß, "From 'Redakteursfernsehen' to 'Showrunners': Commissioning Editors and Changing Project Networks in TV Fiction from Germany," *Journal of Popular Television* 8, no. 2 (2020): 177–194.

3. Anna Zoellner, "Commissioning and Independent Television Production: Power, Risk and Creativity," *International Journal of Communication* 16 (2022): 585–603.

4. Ruth McElroy and Caitriona Noonan, *Producing British Television Drama: Local Production in a Global Era* (Basingstoke: Palgrave, 2019), 52.

5. Hanne Bruun, "From Scheduling to Trans-programming," *Media, Culture & Society* 43, no. 4 (2021): 613–628; Mads Møller T. Andersen, "Gatekeeping within the Simplicity Regime: Evaluative Practices in Television Idea Development," *Media, Culture & Society* 42, no. 4 (2020): 571–587.

6. Eva Novrup Redvall, *Writing and Producing Television Drama in Denmark: From* The Kingdom *to* The Killing (Basingstoke: Palgrave, 2013), 6.

7. Novrup Redvall, 20.

8. Ian W. Macdonald, *Screenwriting Poetics and the Screen Idea* (Basingstoke: Palgrave, 2013), 6-7.

9. Bridget Conor, *Screenwriting: Creative Labor and Professional Practice* (New York: Routledge, 2014), 127.

10. Marilyn Tofler, Craig Batty, and Stayci Taylor, "The Comedy Web Series: Reshaping Australian Script Development and Commissioning Practices," *Australasian Journal of Popular Culture* 8, no. 1 (2019): 71–84.

11. Paul Rixon, *American Television Drama on British Screens: A Story of Cultural Interaction* (Basingstoke: Palgrave, 2006), 83.

12. Janet McCabe, "Diagnosing the Alien: Producing Identities, American 'Quality' Drama and British Television Culture in the 1990s," in *Frames and Fictions on Television: The Politics of Identity Within Drama*, ed. Bruce Carson and Margaret Llewellyn-Jones (Exeter: Intellect, 2000), 144.

13. Lez Cooke, *British Television Drama: A History* (London: BFI, 2003), 177.

14. Paul Rixon, "American Programs on British Screens: A Revaluation," *Critical Studies in Television* 2, no. 2 (2007): 98.

15. Faye Woods, "Teen TV Meets T4: Assimilating *The O.C.* into British Youth Television," *Critical Studies in Television* 8, no. 1 (2013): 17.

16. Quoted in Gareth McLean, "The Americans Are Coming," *Guardian*, February 5, 2007, https://www.theguardian.com/media/2007/feb/05/mondaymediasection2.

17. McElroy and Noonan, *Producing British Television Drama*, 29.

18. John Thornton Caldwell, *Production Culture: Industrial Reflexivity and Critical Practice in Film and Television* (Durham, NC: Duke University Press, 2008), 246.

19. Caldwell, 232.

20. Brigid Cherry, "Refusing to Refuse to Look: Female Viewers of the Horror Film," in *Identifying Hollywood Audiences*, ed. Richard Maltby and Melvyn Stokes (London: BFI, 1999), 187–203.

21. Amy J. Vosper, "Film, Fear and the Female: An Empirical Study of the Female Horror Fan," *Offscreen* 18, no. 6-7 (2014), https://offscreen.com/view/film-fear-and-the-female.

22. Julie D'Acci, *Defining Women: Television and the Case of Cagney and Lacey* (Chapel Hill: University of North Carolina Press, 1994), 64.

23. Michael L. Wayne, "Netflix, Amazon, and Branded Television Content in Subscription Video On-Demand Portals," *Media, Culture & Society* 40, no. 5 (2018): 727.

24. Jessica Balanzategui and Andrew Lynch, "'Shudder' and the Aesthetic and Platform Logics of Genre-Specific SVOD Services," *Television & New Media* 24, no. 2 (2022): 156–172.

25. John Corner, "Television Studies: Plural Contexts, Singular Ambitions?," *Journal of British Cinema and Television* 1, no. 1 (2004): 11.

26. Rachel Moseley, Helen Wheatley, and Helen Wood, "Television for Women Dossier Introduction: Why 'Television for Women'?," *Screen* 54, no. 2 (2013): 238–239, their emphasis.

27. Moseley, Wheatley, and Wood, 243, emphasis original.

28. Julia Hallam, "Drama Queens: Making Television Drama for Women 1990–2009," *Screen* 54, no. 2 (2013): 256–257.

29. Charlotte Brunsdon, *Screen Tastes: From Soap Opera to Satellite Dishes* (London: Routledge, 1997), 32, emphasis added.

30. Brunsdon, 32.

31. Miranda Banks, "Production Studies," *Feminist Media Histories* 4, no. 2 (2018): 157, emphasis added.

32. Vicky Ball and Melanie Bell, "Working Women, Women's Work: Production, History, Gender: Introduction," *Journal of British Cinema and Television* 10, no. 3 (2013): 549–550.

33. Alexis Kreager with Stephen Follows, "Gender Inequality and Screenwriters: A Study of the Impact of Gender on Equality of Opportunity for Screenwriters and Key Creatives in the UK Film and Television Industries" (report, Authors' Licensing and Collecting Society/Writers' Guild of Great Britain, 2018), 9; Directors UK, "Who's Calling the Shots: Gender Inequality among Screen Directors Working in UK Television (report, 2018), 2–4.

34. Ruth McElroy, "The Feminization of Contemporary British Television Drama: Sally Wainwright and RED Production," in *Television for Women: New Directions*, ed. Rachel Moseley, Helen Wheatley, and Helen Wood (Abingdon: Routledge, 2016), 34, emphasis added.

35. Beth Johnson, "Leading, Collaborating, Championing: RED's Arresting Women," *Journal of British Cinema and Television* 16, no. 3 (2019): 329.

36. Christopher Meir, "Becoming a Global Producer: Creative and Industrial Change at Post-StudioCanal RED," *Journal of British Cinema and Television* 16, no. 3 (2019): 306.

37. Andrew Spicer and Steve Presence, "Autonomy and Dependency in Two Successful UK Film and Television Companies: An Analysis of RED Production Company and Warp Films," *Film Studies* 14, no. 1 (2016): 6.

38. Spicer and Presence, 26.

39. Beth Johnson, *Paul Abbott* (Manchester: Manchester University Press, 2013); Melanie Williams, Sarah Godfrey, and Martin Fradley, eds., *Shane Meadows: Critical Essays* (Edinburgh: Edinburgh University Press, 2013).

40. McElroy, "Feminization of Contemporary British Television Drama," 39.

41. Quoted in McElroy, 39–42.

42. Natalie Wreyford, *Gender Inequality in Screenwriting Work* (Basingstoke: Palgrave, 2018), 106.

43. McElroy and Noonan, *Producing British Television Drama*, 52.

44. McElroy and Noonan, 53.

45. Caldwell, *Production Culture*, 233.

46. Anne Dunn, "The Genres of Television," in *Narrative and Media*, ed. Helen Fulton (Cambridge: Cambridge University Press, 2005), 132.

47. Craig Batty and Dallas J. Baker, "Screenwriting as a Mode of Research, and the Screenplay as Research Artefact," in *Screen Production Research: Creative Practice as a Mode of*

Enquiry, ed. Craig Batty and Susan Kerrigan (Basingstoke: Palgrave, 2018), 156, emphasis added.

48. Anamik Saha, *Race and the Cultural Industries* (Cambridge: Polity, 2018), 27.

49. Cooke, *British Television Drama*, 3.

50. Caldwell, *Production Culture*, 234.

51. Caldwell, 234, emphasis original.

52. Kobena Mercer, "Black Art and the Burden of Representation," *Third Text* 4, no. 10 (1990): 61–78; Stuart Hall, "The Spectacle of the Other," in *Representation: Cultural Representations and Signifying Practices*, ed. Stuart Hall (London: SAGE, 1997), 223–290.

53. Erin Hill, *Never Done: A History of Women's Work in Media Production* (New Brunswick, NJ: Rutgers University Press, 2016), 6.

54. Susan Sontag, "Against Interpretation," in *Against Interpretation and Other Essays* (1964; London: Penguin, 2009), 8.

CHAPTER 5 — FORM

1. Alexandra Schwartz, "'I Don't Think Character Exists Anymore': A Conversation with Rachel Cusk," *New Yorker*, November 18, 2018, https://www.newyorker.com/culture/the-new-yorker-interview/i-dont-think-character-exists-anymore-a-conversation-with-rachel-cusk.

2. J. P. Kelly, *Time, Technology and Narrative Form in Contemporary US Television Drama: Pause, Rewind, Record* (Basingstoke: Palgrave, 2017); Jason Mittell, *Complex TV: The Poetics of Contemporary Television Storytelling* (New York: New York University Press, 2015).

3. Suzanne Keen, *Narrative Form*, 2nd ed. (Basingstoke: Palgrave, 2015), x.

4. Andrew Lavender, "*Edge of Darkness* (Troy Kennedy Martin)," in *British Television Drama in the 1980s*, ed. George W. Brandt (Cambridge: Cambridge University Press, 1993), 116.

5. Kristyn Gorton, "'A Way to Go': Lisa Holdsworth, Freelance Writer," *Journal of British Cinema and Television* 10, no. 3 (2013): 664–671; Kristyn Gorton, "Sally Wainwright: On Writing 'Heroic Women,'" *Journal of British Cinema and Television* 17, no. 3 (2020): 399–414.

6. Robin Nelson, *TV Drama in Transition: Forms, Values and Cultural Change* (Basingstoke: Palgrave, 1997), 27.

7. Susan Stewart, *On Longing: Narratives of the Miniature, the Gigantic, the Souvenir, the Collection* (Durham, NC: Duke University Press, 1992), 19. Thank you to Joel Burges for introducing me to this writer.

8. Julia Hallam, *Lynda La Plante* (Manchester: Manchester University Press, 2005), 5.

9. Ian Potter, *The Rise and Rise of the Independents: A Television History* (London: Guerilla Books, 2008); Kristyn Gorton and Joanne Garde-Hansen, *Remembering British Television: Audience, Archive and Industry* (London: Bloomsbury, 2019), 20–21.

10. Ian W. Macdonald, *Screenwriting Poetics and the Screen Idea* (Basingstoke: Palgrave, 2013), 3.

11. Irene Shubik, "Television Drama Series: A Producer's View," 45–51, and Madeline MacMurragh-Kavanagh, "Too Secret for Words: Coded Dissent in Female-Authored *Wednesday Plays*," 191–202, both in *British Television Drama: Past, Present and Future*, 2nd ed., ed. Jonathan Bignell and Stephen Lacey (Basingstoke: Palgrave, 2014).

12. John Caughie, "What Do Actors Do When They Act?," in Bignell and Lacey, *British Television Drama*, 143–150.

13. Christopher Meir and Andrew Spicer, "Introduction. The Age of Indies: 20 Years of RED Production," *Journal of British Cinema and Television* 16, no. 3 (2019): 269.

14. Meir and Spicer, 270.

15. Andrew Spicer, "A Regional Company? RED Production and the Cultural Politics of Place," *Journal of British Cinema and Television* 16, no. 3 (2019): 277.

16. Annette Hill, "Push-Pull Dynamics: Producer and Audience Practices for Television Drama Format *The Bridge*," *Television & New Media* 17, no. 8 (2016): 761.

17. David Eason, "The New Journalism and the Image-World: Two Modes of Organizing Experience," *Critical Studies in Media Communication* 1, no. 1 (1984): 52.

18. Eason, 52.

19. Eason, 52–61.

20. Eason, 52–61.

21. Eason, 60, emphasis added.

22. Lizzy Goodman, *Meet Me in the Bathroom: Rebirth and Rock and Roll in New York City, 2001–2011* (London: Faber & Faber, 2017), xvii.

23. Shulamit Reinharz, *Feminist Methods in Social Research* (Oxford: Oxford University Press, 1992), 130.

24. Goodman, *Meet Me in the Bathroom*, 229.

25. Legs McNeil and Gillian McCain, *Please Kill Me: The Uncensored Oral History of Punk* (London: Abacus, 1996).

26. Andrea Fontana and Anastasia H. Prokos, *The Interview: From Formal to Postmodern* (Walnut Creek, CA: Left Coast Press, 2007), 55.

27. Susan Krieger, *The Mirror Dance: Identity in a Women's Community* (Philadelphia: Temple University Press, 1983), xvi.

28. Krieger, xvii.

29. Becky Aikman, *Off the Cliff: How the Making of* Thelma & Louise *Drove Hollywood to the Edge* (New York: Penguin, 2017), 119, emphasis in original.

30. Jonathan Abrams, *All the Pieces Matter: The Inside Story of* The Wire (Harpenden: No Exit Press, 2018), 24.

31. Dallas Baker, "Scriptwriting as Creative Writing Research: A Preface," *TEXT* 19 (2013): 1–2.

32. Levi Dean, "Altering Screenwriting Frameworks through Practice-Based Research: A Methodological Approach," *New Writing* 17, no. 3 (2020): 333.

33. Gorton and Garde-Hansen, *Remembering British Television*, 20.

34. Annette Kuhn, *Family Secrets: Acts of Memory and Imagination* (London: Verso, 2002), 9.

35. Mary Jo Maynes, Jennifer L. Pierce, and Barbara Laslett, *Telling Stories: The Use of Personal Narratives in the Social Sciences and History* (Ithaca, NY: Cornell University Press, 2008), 4.

36. Karen Lury, *Interpreting Television* (London: Hodder Education, 2005), 5.

CHAPTER 7 — DEVELOPMENT

1. Peter Bloore, *The Screenplay Business: Managing Creativity and Script Development in the Film Industry* (Abingdon: Routledge, 2013), 9.

2. Natalie Wreyford, *Gender Inequality in Screenwriting Work* (Basingstoke: Palgrave, 2018), 89.

3. Wreyford, 34.

4. Suzanne Keen, *Narrative Form*, 2nd ed. (Basingstoke: Palgrave, 2015), 21.

5. Trisha Dunleavy, *Complex Serial Drama and Multiplatform Television* (Abingdon: Routledge, 2017), 3.

6. Bob Levy, *Television Development: How Hollywood Creates New TV* (New York: Routledge, 2019), 2; John Yorke, *Into the Woods: A Five Act Journey into Storytelling* (London: Penguin, 2013), 178.

7. Dunleavy, *Complex Serial Drama*, 99.

8. Levy, *Television Development*, 74.

9. Neil Landau, *The Television Showrunner's Roadmap: 21 Navigational Tips for Screenwriters to Create and Sustain a Hit TV Series* (New York: Focal Press, 2013), 169.

10. Janani Subramanian, "The Monstrous Makeover: *American Horror Story*, Femininity and Special Effects," *Critical Studies in Television* 8, no. 3 (2013): 112.

11. Sophie Hannah, *The Orphan Choir* (London: Hammer, 2013), 289.

12. Dunleavy, *Complex Serial Drama*, 48.

13. Stacey Abbott, "'Look Who's Got a Case of Dark Prince Envy': Dracula, Televisuality and the Golden Age(s) of TV Horror," *Horror Studies* 8, no. 2 (2017): 193.

14. Jason Mittell, *Complex TV: The Poetics of Contemporary Television Storytelling* (New York: New York University Press, 2015), 19.

15. Daniel Calvisi, *Story Maps: TV Drama. The Structure of the One-Hour Television Pilot* (Los Angeles: Act Four Screenplays, 2017), 6.

16. Pamela Douglas, *Writing the TV Drama Series: How to Succeed as a Writer in TV*, 3rd ed. (Los Angeles: Michael Wiese, 2011), 36.

17. Catherine Johnson, *Telefantasy* (London: BFI, 2005), 116.

18. Susan Kerrigan and Craig Batty, "Re-conceptualizing Screenwriting for the Academy: The Social, Cultural and Creative Practice of Developing a Screenplay," *New Writing* 13, no. 1 (2016): 132.

19. Sarah Kozloff, "Narrative Theory and Television," in *Channels of Discourse, Reassembled: Television and Contemporary Criticism*, 2nd ed., ed. Robert C. Allen (Abingdon: Routledge, 1992), 91.

20. Robert McKee, *Story: Substance, Structure, Style and the Principles of Screenwriting* (New York: Regan Books, 1997), 80.

21. Maggie Brown, "Living to Air Will Young Thriller," *Guardian*, August 16, 2010, https://www.theguardian.com/media/2010/aug/16/will-young-bedlam-living-tv.

22. Wreyford, *Gender Inequality in Screenwriting Work*, 39.

23. Eva Novrup Redvall, *Writing and Producing Television Drama in Denmark: From* The Kingdom *to* The Killing (Basingstoke: Palgrave, 2013), 189.

24. Stayci Taylor and Craig Batty, "Script Development and the Hidden Practices of Screenwriting: Perspectives from Industry Professionals," *New Writing* 13, no. 2 (2016): 205.

25. Wreyford, *Gender Inequality in Screenwriting Work*; Craig Batty and Stayci Taylor, eds., *Script Development: Critical Approaches, Creative Practices, International Perspectives* (Basingstoke: Palgrave, 2021); Stayci Taylor and Craig Batty, eds., *The Palgrave Handbook of Script Development* (Basingstoke: Palgrave, 2021).

26. Jules Selbo, *Screenplay: Building Story through Character* (Abingdon: Routledge, 2016), 227–228.

27. Craig Batty, Stayci Taylor, Louise Sawtell, and Bridget Conor, "Script Development: Defining the Field," *Journal of Screenwriting* 8, no. 3 (2017): 229.

28. Taylor and Batty, "Script Development," 207–210.

29. Craig Batty and Dallas J. Baker, "Screenwriting as a Mode of Research, and the Screenplay as a Research Artefact," in *Screen Production Research: Creative Practice as a Mode of Enquiry*, ed. Craig Batty and Susan Kerrigan (Basingstoke: Palgrave, 2018), 69.

30. Bridget Conor, *Screenwriting: Creative Labor and Professional Practice* (New York: Routledge, 2014), 71.

31. Steven Price, "Script Development and Academic Research," *Journal of Screenwriting* 8, no. 3 (2017): 323.

32. Steven Maras, *Screenwriting: History, Theory and Practice* (London: Wallflower Press, 2009), 23–24.

33. Personal email correspondence, August 7, 2023.

34. Maryanne Dever, "Archives and New Modes of Feminist Research," *Australian Feminist Studies* 32, no. 91–92 (2017): 2.

35. Dever, 2.

36. Kerrigan and Batty, "Re-conceptualizing Screenwriting for the Academy," 135.

37. Wreyford, *Gender Inequality in Screenwriting Work*, 35.

38. Wreyford, 34–35.

39. Erin Hill, *Never Done: A History of Women's Work in Media Production* (New Brunswick, NJ: Rutgers University Press, 2016), 5.

40. Conor, *Screenwriting*, 71.

41. Ruth McElroy, "The Feminization of Contemporary British Television Drama: Sally Wainwright and RED Production," in *Television for Women: New Directions*, ed. Rachel Moseley, Helen Wheatley, and Helen Wood (Abingdon: Routledge, 2016), 39.

CHAPTER 8 — STORY

1. Horace Newcomb, "Studying Television: Same Questions, Different Contexts," *Cinema Journal* 45, no. 1 (2005): 107.

2. Newcomb, 111.

3. Virginia Woolf, *The Waves* (1931), in *Virginia Woolf: Complete Works* (Cork: Golden Deer Classics, 2016), Kindle.

4. Jackie Stacey and Janet Wolff, "Writing Otherwise," in *Writing Otherwise: Experiments in Cultural Criticism*, ed. Jackie Stacey and Janet Wolff (Manchester: Manchester University Press, 2013), 2–3.

5. Olivia Laing, *The Lonely City: Adventures in the Art of Being Alone* (Edinburgh: Canongate Books, 2016), 252.

6. Virginia Woolf, "Character in Fiction" (1924), in *Virginia Woolf: Complete Works*, Kindle.

7. Elana Levine, "Towards a Paradigm for Media Production Research: Behind the Scenes at *General Hospital*," *Critical Studies in Media Communication* 18, no. 1 (2001): 66–82.

8. Charlotte Brunsdon, *Screen Tastes: From Soap Opera to Satellite Dishes* (Abingdon: Routledge, 1997), 122.

9. Steven Price, "Character in the Screenplay Text," in *Analyzing the Screenplay*, ed. Jill Nelmes (Abingdon: Routledge, 2011), 201.

10. Craig Batty, *Screenplays: How to Write and Sell Them* (Harpenden: Kamera Books, 2012), 145.

11. Lajos Egri, *The Art of Dramatic Writing: Its Basis in the Creative Interpretation of Human Motives* (1942; New York: Simon & Schuster, 1960), 239; Will Dunne, *The Dramatic Writer's Companion* (Chicago: University of Chicago Press, 2009), 177.

12. Janet Malcolm, *The Journalist and the Murderer* (1990; London: Granta, 2018), 155.

13. Stephen Bottoms, "Putting the Document in Documentary: An Unwelcome Corrective?," *TDR: The Drama Review* 50, no. 3 (2006): 58.

14. David Mamet, *On Directing Film* (London: Penguin, 1991), 2.

15. Margot Nash, "Developing the Screenplay: Stepping into the Unknown," in *Screenwriters and Screenwriting: Putting Practice into Context*, ed. Craig Batty (Basingstoke: Palgrave, 2014), 104–105.

16. Linda Seger, *Writing Subtext: What Lies Beneath* (Los Angeles: Michael Wiese, 2011), 2–3.

17. Seger, 2–3.

18. Simon Stephens, *A Working Diary* (London: Methuen Drama, 2016), 171.

19. Seymour Chatman, *Story and Discourse: Narrative Structure in Fiction and Film* (Ithaca, NY: Cornell University Press, 1978), 175.

20. Robert C. Allen, "Audience-Orientated Criticism and Television," in *Channels of Discourse, Reassembled: Television and Contemporary Criticism*, 2nd ed., ed. Robert C. Allen (Abingdon: Routledge, 1992), 113, 102.

21. Horace Newcomb, "Narrative and Genre," in *The SAGE Handbook of Media Studies*, ed. John Downing, Denis McQuail, Philip Schlesinger, and Ellen Wartalla (London: SAGE, 2004), 414, emphasis added.

22. Newcomb, 414.

23. Malcolm, *Journalist and the Murderer*, 152–153.

24. Jane Kilby and Graeme Gilloch, "Sociography: Writing Differently," *Sociological Review* 70, no. 4 (2022): 638.

25. Kim V. L. England, "Getting Personal: Reflexivity, Positionality, and Feminist Research," *Professional Geographer* 46, no. 1 (1994): 35.

26. Sara Ahmed, *Willful Subjects* (Durham, NC: Duke University Press, 2014), 15.

27. Charlotte Brunsdon, "On Being Made History," *Cultural Studies* 29, no. 1 (2015): 89.

28. H. Porter Abbott, *The Cambridge Introduction to Narrative*, 2nd ed. (Cambridge: Cambridge University Press, 2008), 22.

29. Gérard Genette, *Narrative Discourse Revisited*, trans. Jane E. Lewin (Ithaca, NY: Cornell University Press, 1988), 157, emphasis original.

30. Craig Batty and Susan Kerrigan, "Introduction," in *Screen Production Research: Creative Practice as a Mode of Enquiry*, ed. Craig Batty and Susan Kerrigan (Basingstoke: Palgrave, 2018), 1.

31. Hazel Smith and Roger T. Dean, "Introduction: Practice-Led Research, Research-Led Practice—Towards the Iterative Cyclical Web," in *Practice-Led Research, Research-Led Practice in the Creative Arts*, ed. Hazel Smith and Roger T. Dean (Edinburgh: Edinburgh University Press, 2009), 19–21.

32. Graeme Sullivan, "Making Space: The Purpose and Place of Practice-Led Research," in Smith and Dean, *Practice-Led Research, Research-Led Practice*, 47–48.

33. Kilby and Gilloch, "Sociography," 638.

CHAPTER 10 — VOICE

1. Kaja Silverman, *The Acoustic Mirror: The Female Voice in Psychoanalysis and Cinema* (Bloomington: Indiana University Press, 1988); Michel Chion, *The Voice in Cinema*, trans. Claudia Gorbman (New York: Columbia University Press, 1999).

2. Rose Ferrell, "An Introduction to Voice in Screenwriting," *Journal of Screenwriting* 8, no. 2 (2017): 163; Levi Dean, "Scripting Your Voice as a Method for Achieving Originality," *Media Practice and Education* 21, no. 3 (2020): 175.

3. Miranda J. Banks, "Oral History and Media Industries: Theorizing the Personal in Production History," *Cultural Studies* 28, no. 4 (2014): 547.

4. Vicki Mayer, Miranda J. Banks, and John T. Caldwell, "Introduction. Production Studies: Roots and Routes," in *Production Studies: Cultural Studies of Media Industries*, ed. Vicki Mayer, Miranda J. Banks, and John T. Caldwell (Abingdon: Routledge, 2009), 4.

5. Michael Wright, *Playwriting in Process: Thinking and Writing Theatrically*, 2nd ed. (Newbury: Focus, 2009), 2.

6. Stephen Jeffreys, *Playwriting: Structure, Character, How and What to Write* (London: Nick Hern Books, 2019), 33.

7. Jeffreys, 33.

8. Ferrell, "Introduction to Voice," 173.

9. Noel Greig, *Playwriting: A Practical Guide* (London: Routledge, 2004), 179.

10. Steve Waters, *The Secret Life of Plays* (London: Nick Hern, 2010), 19.

11. Ian W. Macdonald, *Screenwriting Poetics and the Screen Idea* (Basingstoke: Palgrave, 2013), 123.

12. Eva Novrup Redvall, *Writing and Producing Television Drama in Denmark: From* The Kingdom *to* The Killing (Basingstoke: Palgrave, 2013), 7.

13. Craig Batty and Stayci Taylor, "Introduction," in *Script Development: Critical Approaches, Creative Practices, International Perspectives*, ed. Craig Batty and Stayci Taylor (Basingstoke: Palgrave, 2019), 1.

14. Farah Abushwesha, *Rocliffe Notes: A Professional Approach for Screenwriters and Writer-Directors* (Harpenden: Kamera Books, 2014).

15. Tom Cantrell and Christopher Hogg, *Acting in British Television* (Basingstoke: Palgrave, 2017); Richard Hewett, "Spaces of Preparation: The 'Acton Hilton' and Changing Patterns of Television Drama Rehearsal," *Historical Journal of Film, Radio and Television* 34, no. 3 (2014): 331–344.

16. Susan Cake, "A Collaborative Reflection between Writer, Director and Actors: Table Read as Scriptwriting 'Intervention,'" in *The Palgrave Handbook of Script Development*, ed. Stayci Taylor and Craig Batty (Basingstoke: Palgrave, 2021), 425–436.

17. Christopher Hogg, "A Class Act: An Interview with Julie Hesmondhalgh on Casting, Representation and Inclusion in British Television Drama," *Critical Studies in Television* 15, no. 3 (2020): 303.

18. Charlotte Brunsdon, *Screen Tastes: From Soap Opera to Satellite Dishes* (Abingdon: Routledge, 1997), 2, 5.

19. Jack Hart, *Storycraft: The Complete Guide to Writing Narrative Nonfiction* (Chicago: University of Chicago Press, 2012), 64–65.

20. Tom Wolfe, *The New Journalism* (London: Picador, 1975), 31.

21. Steven Pinker, "Why Academics Stink at Writing," *Chronicle of Higher Education*, September 26, 2014, https://www.chronicle.com/article/why-academics-writing/148989.

22. Charlotte Brunsdon, "What Is the 'Television' of Television Studies?," in *The Television Studies Book*, ed. Christine Geraghty and David Lusted (London: Arnold, 1998), 110; John Corner, "Television Studies: Plural Contexts, Singular Ambitions?," *Journal of British Cinema and Television* 1, no. 1 (2004): 10.

23. Steven Maras, *Screenwriting: History, Theory and Practice* (London: Wallflower Press, 2009), 154–169; Macdonald, *Screenwriting Poetics*, 36–61; Bridget Conor, *Screenwriting: Creative Labor and Professional Practice* (New York: Routledge, 2014), 81–100.

24. Craig Batty, "Screenwriting Studies, Screenwriting Practice and the Screenwriting Manual," *New Writing* 13, no. 1 (2016): 60.

25. Batty, 60.

26. Hart, *Storycraft*, 63–64.

27. Paul Ashton, *The Calling Card Script: A Writer's Toolbox for Screen, Stage and Radio* (London: A&C Black, 2011), 54.

28. Ken Dancyger and Jeff Rush, *Alternative Scriptwriting: Beyond the Hollywood Formula*, 5th ed. (New York: Focal Press, 2013), 377.

29. Ken Dancyger, *Global Scriptwriting* (Burlington, VT: Focal Press, 2001), 14.

30. Hilton Als, "Foreword," in Joan Didion, *Let Me Tell You What I Mean* (London: 4th Estate, 2021), Kindle.

31. Tressie McMillan Cottom, "Thick," in *Thick and Other Essays* (London: New Press, 2019), 16.

32. McMillan Cottom, 26.

33. Emily Nussbaum, *I Like to Watch: Arguing My Way through the TV Revolution* (New York: Random House, 2019), Kindle.

34. Brunsdon, *Screen Tastes*, 120.

35. Maggie Nelson, *Bluets* (London: Jonathan Cape, 2009), 41.

36. Ottessa Moshfegh, "How to Shit," *Masters Review*, October 19, 2015, https://mastersreview.com/how-to-shit-by-ottessa-moshfegh/.

37. Moshfegh.

38. Jonathan Bignell, "Citing the Classics: Constructing British Television Drama History in Publishing and Pedagogy," in *Re-viewing Television History: Critical Issues in Television Historiography*, ed. Helen Wheatley (London: I.B. Tauris, 2007), 28.

39. Janet Malcolm, *The Journalist and the Murderer* (1990; London: Granta, 2018), 159.

40. Malcolm, 161.

41. Joan Didion, "Why I Write," *New York Times*, December 5, 1976, 270, emphasis original.

42. Linda Kuehl, "Joan Didion: The Art of Fiction No. 71," *Paris Review* 74 (1978), https://www.theparisreview.org/interviews/3439/the-art-of-fiction-no-71-joan-didion.

43. Zadie Smith, *Feel Free* (London: Penguin, 2018), 144.

44. Kate Zambreno, *Heroines* (South Pasadena, CA: Semiotext(e), 2012), 235.

45. Charlie Fox, *This Young Monster* (London: Fitzcarraldo, 2017), 24.

46. Zambreno, *Heroines*, 281.

47. Amy Holdsworth, *Living with Television* (Durham, NC: Duke University Press, 2021), ix.

48. Holdsworth, 4.

49. Holdsworth, 4.

50. Holdsworth, 10.

51. Holdsworth, 5.

52. Alison Pullen, "Writing as Labiaplasty," *Organization* 25, no. 1: 123–124; 128.

53. Katie Beavan, Benedikte Borgström, Jenny Helin, and Carl Rhodes, "Changing Writing / Writing for Change," *Gender, Work & Organization* 28, no. 2 (2021): 449.

54. Veera Elina Kinnunen, Sandra Sinikka Wallenius-Korkalo, and Pälvi Marjaana Rantala, "Transformative Events: Feminist Experiments in Writing Differently," *Gender, Work & Organization* 28, no. 2 (2021): 657.

55. Alison Pullen and Carl Rhodes, "Dirty Writing," *Culture and Organisation* 14, no. 3 (2008): 243–244.

56. Jane Kilby and Graeme Gilloch, "Sociography: Writing Differently," *Sociological Review* 70, no. 4 (2022): 638.

57. Holdsworth, *Living with Television*, 137.

58. Kilby and Gilloch, "Sociography," 637.

CHAPTER 11 — GLORIOUS

1. Elana Levine, *Her Stories: Daytime Soap Opera and US Television History* (Durham, NC: Duke University Press, 2020), 2.

2. Charlotte Brunsdon, "Is Television Studies History?," *Cinema Journal* 47, no. 3 (2008): 132.

3. Janet Malcolm, *The Journalist and the Murderer* (1990; London: Granta, 2018), 149.

4. Sara Ahmed, *On Being Included: Racism and Diversity in Institutional Life* (Durham, NC: Duke University Press, 2012), 2.

5. John Caughie, "Mourning Television," *Screen* 51, no. 4 (2010): 421.

6. Charlotte Brunsdon, "Introduction," in *Screen Tastes: Soap Opera to Satellite Dishes* (London: Routledge, 1997), 1, emphasis added; Christine Geraghty and David Lusted, "General Introduction," in *The Television Studies Book*, ed. Christine Geraghty and David Lusted (London: Arnold, 1998), 3.

7. Christine Gledhill and Linda Williams, "Introduction," in *Reinventing Film Studies*, ed. Christine Gledhill and Linda Williams (London: Arnold, 2000), 1.

8. John Corner, "Media Studies and the 'Knowledge Problem,'" *Screen* 36, no. 2 (1995): 147–148.

9. Corner, 147.

10. Corner, 148–149.

11. Miranda J. Banks, "Oral History and Media Industries: Theorizing the Personal in Production History," *Cultural Studies* 28, no. 4 (2014): 545.

12. Corner, "Media Studies," 152.

13. Clifford Geertz, *The Interpretation of Cultures: Selected Essays* (New York: Basic Books, 1973), 18.

14. Geertz, 20.

15. Melissa Freeman, "The Hermeneutical Aesthetics of Thick Description," *Qualitative Inquiry* 20, no. 6 (2014): 827–828.

16. Hortense Powdermaker, *Hollywood, the Dream Factory: An Anthropologist Looks at the Moviemakers* (London: Secker & Warburg, 1950), 3–4.

17. Powdermaker, 7.

18. Todd Gitlin, *Inside Prime Time*, rev. ed. (Abingdon: Routledge, 1994), 14.

19. Virginia Woolf, "Modern Fiction," in *The Common Reader* (London: Hogarth Press, 1925), 186.

20. Woolf, 188.

21. Caughie, "Mourning Television," 421.

22. Eva Novrup Redvall and John R. Cook, "Television Screenwriting: Continuity and Change," *Journal of Screenwriting* 6, no. 2 (2015): 132.

23. Doris Ruth Eikhof and Stevie Marsden, "Diversity and Opportunity in the Media Industries," in *Making Media: Production, Practices, and Professions*, ed. Mark Deuze and Mirjam Prenger (Amsterdam: Amsterdam University Press, 2019), 252–254.

24. Anna Froula, "Associate Editor's Introduction: Women's Work," *Cinema Journal* 55, no. 4 (2016): 1.

25. Carrie Mott and Daniel Cockayne, "Citation Matters: Mobilizing the Politics of Citation towards a Practice of 'Conscientious Engagement,'" *Gender, Place & Culture* 24, no. 7 (2017): 955.

26. Kathryn A. Mariner, "Citation," *Feminist Anthropology* 3 (2022): 215.

27. Sara Ahmed, *Living a Feminist Life* (Durham, NC: Duke University Press, 2017), 5–6.

28. Mott and Cockayne, "Citation Matters," 955.

29. Natalie Wreyford and Shelley Cobb, "Data and Responsibility: Towards a Feminist Methodology for Producing Historical Data on Women in the Contemporary UK Film Industry," *Feminist Media Histories* 3, no. 3 (2017): 109.

30. Charlotte Brunsdon, "Aesthetics and Audiences," in Brunsdon, *Screen Tastes*, 121, emphasis original.

31. Kristen J. Warner, *The Cultural Politics of Colorblind Casting* (Abingdon: Routledge, 2015), 157.

32. Christine Geraghty, *Women and Soap Opera: A Study of Prime Time Soaps* (Cambridge: Polity, 1991), 97.

33. Wreyford and Cobb, "Data and Responsibility," 108.

34. Barbara Tomlinson, "To Tell the Truth and Not Get Trapped: Desire, Distance, and Intersectionality at the Scene of Argument," *Signs* 38, no. 4 (2013): 1012.

35. Corner, "Media Studies," 152.

36. Doris Ruth Eikhof and Katharina Chudzikowski, "'Creativity Is a Skill Everyone Has': Analyzing Creative Workers' Self Presentations," *Creative Industries Journal* 12, no. 1 (2019): 35.

37. David Hesmondhalgh and Sarah Baker, "Creative Work and Emotional Labor in the Television Industry," *Theory, Culture & Society* 25, no. 7–8 (2008): 112.

38. Sianne Ngai, *Ugly Feelings* (Cambridge, MA: Harvard University Press, 2005).

39. Kristyn Gorton and Joanne Garde-Hansen, *Remembering British Television: Audience, Archive and Industry* (London: Bloomsbury, 2019), 40.

40. David Lee, "Precarious Creativity: Changing Attitudes towards Craft and Creativity in the British Independent Television Sector," *Creative Industries Journal* 4, no. 2 (2012): 162.

41. Patricia F. Phalen, Thomas B. Ksiazek, and Jacob B. Gardner, "Who You Know in Hollywood: A Network Analysis of Television Writers," *Journal of Broadcasting and Electronic Media* 60, no. 1 (2016), 160–161.

42. Corner, "Media Studies," 152.

43. Geraghty and Lusted, "General Introduction," 3.

44. David Hesmondhalgh, "Politics, Theory and Method in Media Industries Research," in *Media Industries: History, Theory, and Method*, ed. Jennifer Holt and Alisa Perren (New York: Wiley-Blackwell, 2009), 245, emphasis added.

45. David Eason, "The New Journalism and the Image-World: Two Modes of Organizing Experience," *Critical Studies in Media Communication* 1, no. 1 (1984): 61.

46. Woolf, "Modern Fiction," 194–195, emphasis added.

47. Elizabeth Hardwick, *Seduction and Betrayal: Women and Literature* (1973; London: Faber & Faber, 2019), 134.

48. Hilton Als, "Joan Didion, The Art of Nonfiction No. 1," in *The Paris Review Interviews*, vol. 1, ed. Philip Gourevitch (New York: Canongate, 2007), 479.

49. Jack Hart, *Storycraft: The Complete Guide to Writing Narrative Nonfiction* (Chicago: University of Chicago Press, 2012), 70.

50. Susan Sontag, "On Style," in *Against Interpretation and Other Essays* (1965; London: Penguin, 2009), 32.

51. Sontag, 34, 20.

52. Brian Dillon, *Essayism* (London: Fitzcarraldo Editions, 2017), 40, emphasis original.

53. Lez Cooke, *British Television Drama: A History* (London: BFI, 2003), 196.

54. Ottessa Moshfegh, "How to Shit," *Masters Review*, October 19, 2015, https://mastersreview.com/how-to-shit-by-ottessa-moshfegh/.

55. Helen Wheatley, "Introduction: Re-viewing Television Histories," in *Re-viewing Television History: Critical Issues in Television Historiography*, ed. Helen Wheatley (London: I.B. Tauris, 2007), 4.

About the Author

Alison Peirse is a professor of film studies at the University of Leeds, United Kingdom. Her research focuses on illuminating women's invisible or overlooked contributions to the production of genre film and television. Her many books include the multi-award-winning *Women Make Horror: Filmmaking, Feminism, Genre* (Rutgers University Press).